St Antony's Series

General Editors: **Jan Zielonka** (2004–), Fellow of St Antony's College, Oxford

Othon Anastasakis, Research Fellow of St Antony's College, Oxford and Director of South East European Studies at Oxford

Recent titles include:

Kerem Öktem, Celia Kerslake and Philip Robins
TURKEY'S ENGAGEMENT WITH MODERNITY
Conflict and Change in the Twentieth Century

Paradorn Rangsimaporn
RUSSIA AS AN ASPIRING GREAT POWER IN EAST ASIA
Perceptions and Policies from Yeltsin to Putin

Motti Golani
THE END OF THE BRITISH MANDATE FOR PALESTINE, 1948
The Diary of Sir Henry Gurney

Demetra Tzanaki
WOMEN AND NATIONALISM IN THE MAKING OF MODERN GREECE
The Founding of the Kingdom to the Greco-Turkish War

Simone Bunse
SMALL STATES AND EU GOVERNANCE
Leadership through the Council Presidency

Judith Marquand
DEVELOPMENT AID IN RUSSIA
Lessons from Siberia

Li-Chen Sim
THE RISE AND FALL OF PRIVATIZATION IN THE RUSSIAN OIL INDUSTRY

Stefania Bernini
FAMILY LIFE AND INDIVIDUAL WELFARE IN POSTWAR EUROPE
Britain and Italy Compared

Tomila V. Lankina, Anneke Hudalla and Helmut Wollman
LOCAL GOVERNANCE IN CENTRAL AND EASTERN EUROPE
Comparing Performance in the Czech Republic, Hungary, Poland and Russia

Cathy Gormley-Heenan
POLITICAL LEADERSHIP AND THE NORTHERN IRELAND PEACE PROCESS
Role, Capacity and Effect

Lori Plotkin Boghardt
KUWAIT AMID WAR, PEACE AND REVOLUTION

Paul Chaisty
LEGISLATIVE POLITICS AND ECONOMIC POWER IN RUSSIA

Valpy FitzGerald, Frances Stewart and Rajesh Venugopal (*editors*)
GLOBALIZATION, VIOLENT CONFLICT AND SELF-DETERMINATION

Miwao Matsumoto
TECHNOLOGY GATEKEEPERS FOR WAR AND PEACE
The British Ship Revolution and Japanese Industrialization

Håkan Thörn
ANTI-APARTHEID AND THE EMERGENCE OF A GLOBAL CIVIL SOCIETY

Lotte Hughes
MOVING THE MAASAI
A Colonial Misadventure

Fiona Macaulay
GENDER POLITICS IN BRAZIL AND CHILE
The Role of Parties in National and Local Policymaking

Stephen Whitefield (editor)
POLITICAL CULTURE AND POST-COMMUNISM

José Esteban Castro
WATER, POWER AND CITIZENSHIP
Social Struggle in the Basin of Mexico

Valpy FitzGerald and Rosemary Thorp (editors)
ECONOMIC DOCTRINES IN LATIN AMERICA
Origins, Embedding and Evolution

Victoria D. Alexander and Marilyn Rueschemeyer
ART AND THE STATE
The Visual Arts in Comparative Perspective

Ailish Johnson
EUROPEAN WELFARE STATES AND SUPRANATIONAL GOVERNANCE OF
    SOCIAL POLICY

Archie Brown (editor)
THE DEMISE OF MARXISM-LENINISM IN RUSSIA

Thomas Boghardt
SPIES OF THE KAISER
German Covert Operations in Great Britain during the First World War Era

Ulf Schmidt
JUSTICE AT NUREMBERG
Leo Alexander and the Nazi Doctors' Trial

Steve Tsang (editor)
PEACE AND SECURITY ACROSS THE TAIWAN STRAIT

James Milner
REFUGEES, THE STATE AND THE POLITICS OF ASYLUM IN AFRICA

Stephen Fortescue (editor)
RUSSIAN POLITICS FROM LENIN TO PUTIN

St Antony's Series
Series Standing Order ISBN 978-0-333-71109-5 (hardback) 978-0-333-80341-7
(paperback)
(outside North America only)

You can receive future titles in this series as they are published by placing a standing order.
Please contact your bookseller or, in case of difficulty, write to us at the address below with
your name and address, the title of the series and the ISBNs quoted above.

Customer Services Department, Macmillan Distribution Ltd, Houndmills, Basingstoke,
Hampshire RG21 6XS, England

Russian Politics from Lenin to Putin

Edited By

Stephen Fortescue
Associate Professor, School of Social Sciences and International Relations, University of New South Wales, Australia

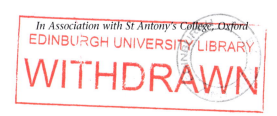

First published 2010 by
PALGRAVE MACMILLAN

Palgrave Macmillan in the UK is an imprint of Macmillan Publishers Limited,
registered in England, company number 785998, of Houndmills, Basingstoke,
Hampshire RG21 6XS.

Palgrave Macmillan in the US is a division of St Martin's Press LLC,
175 Fifth Avenue, New York, NY 10010.

Palgrave Macmillan is the global academic imprint of the above companies
and has companies and representatives throughout the world.

Palgrave® and Macmillan® are registered trademarks in the United States,
the United Kingdom, Europe and other countries

ISBN 978-0-230-57587-5   hardback

This book is printed on paper suitable for recycling and made from fully
managed and sustained forest sources. Logging, pulping and manufacturing
processes are expected to conform to the environmental regulations of the
country of origin.

A catalogue record for this book is available from the British Library.

Library of Congress Cataloging-in-Publication Data
   Russian politics from Lenin to Putin / edited by Stephen Fortescue.
      p. cm. – (St. Anthony's series)
   ISBN 978-0-230-57587-5 (hardback)
      1. Russia (Federation)–Politics and government I. Fortescue, Stephen.
   JN6695.R8675 2010
   947.084–dc22
                                                          2010010801

10   9   8   7   6   5   4   3   2   1
19 18 17 16 15 14 13 12 11 10

Printed and bound in Great Britain by
CPI Antony Rowe, Chippenham and Eastbourne

In honour of T.H. Rigby.
Friend, colleague, teacher, mentor

Contents

List of Tables   viii

List of Contributors   ix

Preface   xii

1 T.H. Rigby on Soviet and Post-Soviet Russian Politics   1
   Stephen Fortescue

2 Institutionalization and Personalism in the Policy-making   21
   Process of the Soviet Union and Post-Soviet Russia
   Stephen Fortescue

3 The Boss and His Team: Stalin and the Inner Circle,   51
   1925–33
   Sheila Fitzpatrick

4 Building the Communist Future: Legitimation and the   76
   Soviet City
   Graeme Gill

5 Legitimation and Legitimacy in Russia Revisited   101
   Leslie Holmes

6 Perestroika as Revolution from Above   127
   Archie Brown

7 How Much Did Popular Disaffection Contribute to the   152
   Collapse of the USSR?
   Peter Reddaway

8 *Pantouflage à la russe*: The Recruitment of Russian Political 185
   and Business Elites
   Eugene Huskey

9 Conclusion   205
   Stephen Fortescue

Index   215

List of Tables

Table 8.1   Earlier State Service of Leading Russian Corporate   192
            Directors and Managers (By Sector of Russian
            Officialdom, post-1991 only)

Table 8.2   Education Backgrounds of the Russian Business   195
            Elite (First Degree of Directors and Senior
            Managers of the Top 20 Russian Companies,
            By Market Capitalization)

List of Contributors

Archie Brown is Emeritus Professor of Politics at Oxford University and Emeritus Fellow of St Antony's College, Oxford. He taught at Glasgow University from 1964 to 1971 and at Oxford from 1971 to 2005. He has been a Fellow of the British Academy since 1991 and was elected a Foreign Honorary Member of the American Academy of Arts and Sciences in 2003. In 2005 Professor Brown was awarded the CMG in the Queen's Birthday Honours List 'for services to UK-Russian relations and to the study of political science and international affairs'. Archie Brown was co-editor with T.H. Rigby and Peter Reddaway of *Authority, Power and Policy in the USSR. Essays dedicated to Leonard Schapiro* (1980 and 1983). His publications include *The Gorbachev Factor* (1996; 1997) which won the W.J.M. Mackenzie Prize of the Political Studies Association of the UK and the Alec Nove Prize of the British Association for Slavonic and East European Studies, *Seven Years that Changed the World: Perestroika in Perspective* (2007), and most recently *The Rise and Fall of Communism* (2009).

Sheila Fitzpatrick is the Bernadotte E. Schmitt Distinguished Service Professor in Modern Russian History at the University of Chicago. A specialist in Soviet social, political, and cultural history, particularly of the Stalin period, she was born in Australia and educated at the University of Melbourne and Oxford. She has worked in the US since the early 1970s, teaching at Columbia University, the University of Texas at Austin, and (since 1990) the University of Chicago. She is a member of the American Academy of Arts and Sciences, a Fellow of the Australian Academy of the Humanities, a Professorial Fellow at the University of Melbourne, and past president of the American Association for Slavic and East European Studies. Her books include *Everyday Stalinism. Ordinary Life in Extraordinary Times: Soviet Russia in the 1930s* (2000) and *Tear off the Masks! Identity and Imposture in Twentieth-Century Russia* (2005), *Against the Grain: Brian Fitzpatrick, Manning Clark and Australian History and Politics* (ed. with Stuart Macintyre, 2007), *Political Tourists: Australian Visitors to the Soviet Union in the 1920s–1940s* (ed. with Carolyn Rasmussen, 2008), and *Beyond Totalitarianism. Stalinism and Nazism Compared* (ed. with Michael Geyer, 2009).

Stephen Fortescue was T.H. Rigby's graduate student, jointly with R.F. Miller, in the Department of Politics, Research School of Social Sciences, Australian National University, from 1973–76. After a period in the private sector, he returned in 1981 to the ANU to carry out post-doctoral research. After another research position in the Centre for Russian and East European Studies at the University of Birmingham, he took up a teaching position in the School of Political Science at the University of New South Wales in 1987. He is now Associate Professor in Politics at UNSW. He has published on Soviet science policy, Soviet and post-Soviet industrial administration, and the Russian mining and metals sector. His most recent monograph is *Russia's Oil Barons and Metal Magnates* (2006).

Graeme Gill is an Australian Research Council Professorial Fellow and Professor of Government and Public Administration at the University of Sydney. He is a Fellow of the Academy of the Social Sciences in Australia. He has written widely on Soviet and post-Soviet affairs, democratization and the state, and is currently working on symbolism, ritual and regime change. His publications include: *The Origins of the Stalinist Political System* (1990 and 2002) and, most recently, *Bourgeoisie, State, and Democracy. Russia, Britain, France, Germany, and the USA* (2008).

Leslie Holmes is Professor of Political Science at the University of Melbourne, and a Fellow of the Academy of the Social Sciences in Australia. He specializes in communist and post-communist politics, including Russian. His most recent sole-authored book is *Rotten States? Corruption, Post-Communism and Neoliberalism* (2006), while his latest edited collection is *Terrorism, Organised Crime and Corruption: Networks and Linkages* (2007). He was President of the International Council on Central and East European Studies (ICCEES) 2000–2005 and of the Australasian Association for Communist and Post-Communist Studies (AACPCS) 2005–2007.

Eugene Huskey is a professor in the Department of Political Science and Director of Russian Studies at Stetson University in Florida. He received his PhD from the London School of Economics and Political Science in 1983 and taught at Bowdoin College and Colgate University before coming to Stetson in 1989. In 1999 he was appointed to the William R. Kenan, Jr. Chair in Political Science. His research and writing focus on politics and legal affairs in the Soviet Union and the post-communist countries of Russia and Kyrgyzstan. His works include *Russian Lawyers and the Soviet State* (1986), *Executive Power and Soviet Politics* (editor, 1992), *Presidential Power in Russia* (1999), and *Russian Bureaucracy and the State. Officialdom from Alexander III to Vladimir Putin* (co-editor with Don Rowney, 2009).

Peter Reddaway is Emeritus Professor of Political Science and International Affairs at the Elliott School of International Affairs of George Washington University. He received his BA and MA degrees from Cambridge University and did graduate work at Harvard and Moscow Universities and the London School of Economics and Political Science. Before joining George Washington University in January 1989, he taught at the London School of Economics and then directed the Kennan Institute for Advanced Russian Studies. He retired from George Washington University in 2004. Peter Reddaway was co-editor with T.H. Rigby and Archie Brown of *Authority, Power and Policy in the USSR. Essays dedicated to Leonard Schapiro* (1980 and 1983). His recent publications include *The Tragedy of Russia's Reforms: Market Bolshevism Against Democracy* (with D. Glinski, 2001), and *The Dynamics of Russian Politics: Putin's Reform of Federal-Regional Relations* (with R. Orttung, vol. 1, 2003, vol. 2, 2004).

Preface

Thomas Henry Richard Rigby (always known as Harry) was born on 13 April 1925, in Coburg, a working-class suburb of Melbourne. His father, after arthritis had ended a career as a golf professional, was forced – in the Great Depression – to take labouring work outside Melbourne, coming home only for the weekends for a substantial part of Harry's childhood. Harry was a clever and conscientious student, and did well enough at school to aspire to the pinnacle of a working class kid's hopes at the time, a career as a school teacher.

That career was cut short before it began by the war. Harry joined up as soon as he was old enough, and the end of the war saw him a Corporal at Advanced Land Headquarters on Morotai (in the then Dutch East Indies, now Indonesia). During his time in the army he had the briefest of flirtations with membership of the Australian Communist Party. Like so many young men returning from war service, Harry found himself with the previously unthinkable opportunity to go to university. He initially enrolled in a pass degree in French and Dutch, but then transferred to an honours degree in French and Russian, ultimately dropping the French for Political Science. He studied Russian with Nina Mikhailovna Christesen, the first Russian he'd ever met. He didn't study Soviet politics per se as an undergraduate, but the topic of his MA thesis was 'The Soviet View of Southeast Asia'. The thesis was supervised by Mac Ball and examined by Lloyd Churchward. He completed it in 1951 just before heading for London on a Melbourne University 'travelling scholarship'.

In London he was invited to work on a PhD at the University of London under the supervision of Professors William Robson and Hugh Seton-Watson. Some details on his early intellectual influences and interests are given in the Introduction to this volume. On completing his PhD in 1954 he returned to Australia to take up a teaching position in Russian studies at the Canberra University College, the predecessor to the teaching faculties of the Australian National University. In 1956 Leonard Schapiro, whom Harry had known in London, came to Canberra and invited him to return to London for a year to assist him on a new research project. Part of the deal was that he would work in the Foreign Office Research Department, and from there he was posted to the British Embassy in Moscow. He finally returned to Canberra in

December 1958 where he resumed his teaching position. In 1963 he transferred to the Department of Political Science of the ANU's Research School of Social Sciences, where he remained until his official retirement in 1990. That was followed by a series of post-retirement appointments and fellowships at the ANU, including the Transition of Communist Systems Project. Harry continued to be active in the discipline until the last few years. Although no longer working in the field, he still likes to hear what others are doing.

Harry Rigby is the mildest of men – although not without a streak of steely resolve, and he is the most modest of men – although not without pride in his own achievements and those of his family and students. This volume is offered as a celebration of the life of a wonderful human being. But it is also offered as a practical commentary on the contribution to Soviet and post-Soviet Russian studies of one of its leading practitioners.

Many years ago the editor of this volume suggested to Harry – was it on his 60th or 65th birthday? I don't rightly remember – that a Festschrift be published. I received a sharp and resolute rebuff. A number of years later his long-term colleague at the ANU, Robert F. Miller, made the same suggestion and received an equally stern rebuff. It was not just a matter of Harry's modesty. He seemed to think that a Festschrift implied that his work as a Russian specialist was over and done with. As wrong as we might have thought that understanding of a Festschrift to be, his wishes were respected. Recently, however, at a meeting between his very old friend, Michael MccGuire, and a young Australian colleague, Roderic Pitty, the idea was revived and taken to Harry's family. They agreed, and since Harry himself now admitted to be no longer working on Russian affairs he could find no reason to object.

The approach adopted was to find contributors, ideally who had had a personal working relationship with Harry, but who above all would write something that would engage with the concepts, ideas and issues that Harry dealt with throughout his working life, essentially the domestic politics of the Soviet Union. That approach meant that some of Harry's closest friends and colleagues over many years are not included in the volume – my apologies to them. Details on the contributors can be found above.

Harry's contribution to the field is set out in the Introduction. It will be seen there that two broad themes most exercised Harry's interest throughout his career: the forms of legitimacy that could be found – and not found – in the Soviet Union and post-Soviet Russia; and the pressure for the institutionalization of its political processes and its interaction with the countervailing force of personalist relations. It is those two themes that feature in this volume. There were a number of possible approaches to ordering the contributions. In the end a rough-and-ready chronological approach was adopted, which allowed some bunching according to theme.

Following the Introduction, in which the editor summarizes Harry's contribution to the field, he then offers as his own contribution a survey of the relationship between institutional structures and personalist politics in the policy-making process from 1917 through to the Medvedev presidency. Sheila Fitzpatrick then deals with essentially the same issue, but with a focus on Stalin's 'team' at the top of the political system in the 1930s. It was a team of individuals bound together by close personal ties, but also with differing and often conflicting institutional interests and functions. Although with an historical setting from the early days of the Soviet regime through to the rule of Khrushchev and Brezhnev, Graeme Gill's contribution shifts to Harry Rigby's other major theme, that of legitimacy. In a novel approach to the issue, Gill assesses the nature of the regime's legitimacy claims through a study of state-sponsored architectural styles and urban planning strategies. With some violence to the chronological principle, Leslie Holmes's chapter follows, in which he subjects Harry's concept of goal-rational legitimacy to close examination and applies it to post-Soviet circumstances. The next two chapters approach perestroika and the collapse of the USSR from two very different angles. Archie Brown talks of a 'revolution from above' and Peter Reddaway of the contribution of popular disaffection. Although the difference between the two might not end up being as great as their approaches promise, they provide a fascinating double view of the late Soviet Union in which issues of legitimacy, institutionalization and personal leadership style all play a role, as well as 'civil society' phenomena, the importance of which Harry himself had come to recognize at the time. In the final chapter before the Conclusion Eugene Huskey takes on an exercise very close indeed to Harry's heart. In the Introduction I suggest that he liked nothing more than to play around with the biographies of members of the Soviet and post-Soviet Russian elites. Huskey does just that for the post-Soviet Russian administrative elite, examining the subsequent career paths of a significant proportion of them into politics and business. In the Conclusion the editor sums up what the contributors have told us about the continuing relevance of Harry Rigby's work to the discipline and, in doing so, the contribution that they have made to issues that still occupy a central place in Soviet and post-Soviet Russian political studies.

I will begin the acknowledgements by offering my personal thanks to Harry Rigby for the exceptional intellectual stimulation and guidance and the close personal friendship that he has offered over many years. My thanks go to Michael MccGuire and Roderic Pitty for finally getting the project off the ground; to Harry's family for their friendship over the years, and to Norma and Richard in particular for their support during the preparation of this volume; to Palgrave and its staff for taking on that most unpopular of publishing projects, the Festschrift, and for getting it through the publication process; of course, to the contributors, but also to those friends and colleagues of Harry, who in many cases are also my friends and colleagues, who are not in the volume but who made their own valuable contributions to Harry's work and to the discipline. My thanks go to all those at my home base in the Faculty of Arts and Social Sciences of the University of New South Wales. Much of my own work on the volume was done while on sabbatical leave, so my thanks to everyone at the Wenner-Gren Center in Stockholm for providing wonderful living accommodation, the Stockholm Institute for Transition Economics for friendship and intellectual stimulation, and to friends and neighbours in Zhazhlevo for providing the perfect environment for writing.

Stephen Fortescue
Kensington, NSW

1

T.H. Rigby on Soviet and Post-Soviet Russian Politics

Stephen Fortescue

In a brief autobiographical sketch in a 1990 volume of collected writings T.H. Rigby described his early intellectual influences.[1] As an undergraduate and Masters student at the University of Melbourne immediately after the end of World War Two he was intellectually most stimulated by Karl Marx and Max Weber – although as he wrote: 'I could never claim to be a real disciple of either'. The influence of Marx was limited even at that early stage by Rigby's inability to accommodate Marx's views on property with what he knew of the social distribution of power and privilege in the USSR. The influence of Weber was far stronger. From the beginning Rigby was excited by the linkages that could be made between Weber's typologies of authority and legitimation and actual social structures, including those of the Soviet Union.

But after completing his studies at the University of Melbourne he put aside his interest in Weber for a decade and a half, while he pursued empirical investigations of Soviet society and its political system. His PhD thesis, at the University of London, was on 'The selection of leading personnel in the Soviet state and Communist Party',[2] and had a strong and pioneering orientation towards the painstaking collection of data on officials. The accumulation of empirical knowledge and expertise continued during subsequent work in the UK Foreign Office Research Department and the British Embassy in Moscow, and then while teaching at the Canberra University College. It was only in 1963, recently arrived at the Australian National University's Research School of Social Sciences, that he found himself part of a working group on Weber and returned to a serious study of the great German. He continued to be interested in Weber and used his concepts for the rest of his career.

1

In the use of theory Rigby was always flexible and pragmatic:

> The search for an adequate conceptual framework for understanding the key elements of the Soviet socio-political order is of the utmost scholarly and practical importance, but we should not let it blunt our sensibility to the rich variety and unpredictability of human behaviour. In seeking to uncover persistent underlying patterns, we must avoid too static an analysis.[3]

That approach to theory meant that there was always a modesty about the way he presented his theoretical ideas to the discipline. There was also a broadmindedness in his approach to theoretical matters. As we will see on various occasions in this chapter, he was not fond of the then mainstream behaviouralist political science. And yet as a theoretical framework for his 1968 classic *Communist Party Membership* he used a heavily modified functionalist approach borrowed from Gabriel Almond.[4]

Although he was far from uninterested in or unknowledgeable of other parts of the world, his comparative interests were as instrumental as his theoretical interests, being totally devoted to the insights they might provide for our understanding of the USSR. If the experiences of the Soviet Union contributed to the verification and development of a theory and to our understanding of the broader world, well and good, but that was not primary.

Rigby's deep empirical knowledge of the Soviet Union told him four key things about it and its political system. Firstly, he knew that in the Soviet Union questions of whether and why people obeyed their rulers were posed more dramatically than in the societies in which he and most of his readers lived. Secondly, he knew that fact led to enormous debate within the discipline of Soviet studies over the nature of political and social control. Thirdly, he knew that the Soviet Union was bureaucratic, in terms both of the powerful bureaucratic institutions that operated within it and how the behaviour of those institutions and those working within them was organized. Fourthly, he also knew that the Soviet Union was a place in which personal links and loyalties were enormously important. These four pieces of knowledge dominated Rigby's research output, both empirical and theoretical.

Legitimacy

One of Weber's greatest influences on Rigby was his concept of legitimacy and authority. Rigby believed that legitimacy was badly neglected in the political science of the 1960s and the following decades, dominated as it was, in his view, by 'an urge to the analytical rigour and quantitative verification proper to certain of the natural sciences.'[5] He was critical of Western scholars who were reluctant to grant communist regimes any legitimacy, 'or if they do, to reduce it to an over-rationalised notion of "ideology".' His own view of the role of ideology was that, 'as far as the Soviet Union is concerned, it would be as misleading to assume a universal cynicism or indifference towards the official legitimating values and world-view as to take avowals of them at face value, but that they probably acquire much of their force by association with other sources of legitimacy.'[6]

Rigby began his search for the sources of Soviet legitimacy in Weber's famous three categories: the traditional, charismatic and legal-rational. (For a description of these categories, see Holmes's contribution to this volume.) As far as the traditional was concerned, particularly in early writings he did not deny the relevance of the Tsarist past for the development of the Soviet system. In a relatively early publication, with the title 'Security and Modernisation in Tsarist Russia and the USSR', he noted the importance of the political culture in which the Bolsheviks operated. Referring to the blind spot they had as to the origins of and correct approach to righting the negative aspects of bureaucracy, he noted:

And here again we see the influence of Russian political experience, which knew no effective method of structuring social action other than through a hierarchy of command, and therefore took it for granted.[7]

However, he was never a strong supporter of political culture views of political and social behaviour, particularly those based on long historical continuities, and over time references to the influence of tradition in his publications became rare. In contrast to the publication just quoted, in 1990 he attributed the early Bolshevik use of the hierarchy of command to combat bureaucracy not to historical continuity but to structural inevitability: 'There is no evidence that Lenin aimed to convert his organized revolutionary vanguard into a bureaucratic machine, but once the traditional and market procedures through which much of the business of society had till then been conducted were largely dismantled as obstacles to the revolution, no mechanism was left to him for keeping things running except chains of naked command, transmitted through hierarchies of full-time officials'.[8] In his last published work Rigby undertook an extensive account of the role of ethnicity and the concept of nationhood through Russia's history, but in doing so made it clear that he had no sympathy for arguments 'that the character of political communities is determined by "national characteristics" persisting virtually unchanged over the centuries, being taken in with one's mother's milk if not encoded in one's genes'.[9]

As we will see in a moment, charismatic authority did appear occasionally and not insignificantly in his writings. Indeed he suggested that it played an important role in the creation of Stalin's particular form of tyranny. But neither it nor the traditional were present in the Soviet Union to nearly the degree needed to explain how the country was ruled.

It was Weber's third category, the rational-legal, which most excited his interest. He quotes Weber for a definition of this form of legitimation – 'resting in the "legality" of patterns of normative rules and the right of those elevated to authority under such rules to issue commands' – and finds it present in the claims of Soviet leaders to a right to exercise power. 'Nor is all this a *mere* façade, since both the character of the institutions and their substantive activities do *partly* correspond with legal forms'.[10] There is also something of Weber's legal-rationality about the bureaucracy which administers the state.

But while there were features of Weber's rational-legal category in the Soviet Union, there were differences so fundamental as to render the concept ultimately inapplicable. There were aspects of the Soviet bureaucracy which made it not a legal-rational one – we will return to that in a moment. But there were also problems with the nature of the leaders' claims to the right to rule. Firstly, the constitution and other normative acts that accompanied it, which purported to set out the law under which the leadership acts, provided a highly misleading guide to the distribution of power. In fact the political leadership was not prepared to limit itself to any laws, including its own. 'There is a rationality here, but it is a substantive rationality rather than the formal rationality essential to rational-legal authority. Action is "rational" in so far as it is appropriate to achieving tasks contributing to some overall goal.'[11] That overall goal was ultimately the achievement of communism. The long road to achieving that ultimate goal produced many tasks, some rigidly fixed, others extremely flexible. The goal-oriented nature of legitimacy in the Soviet Union, derived from the leadership's ultimate lack of respect for the law, was strengthened by the economic structure of the system. For Weber, under capitalism task-oriented functions, as distinct from rule-oriented functions, were left to the market. With the market all but abolished under Soviet rule, Rigby argued that the state's responsibilities for rule-oriented functions were pushed aside by its assumption of task-oriented functions. The tasks were set by the leadership, ultimately in any way it wished within the broad claim that they contributed to the construction of communism. If society worked to carry out those tasks on any basis beyond fear and coercion – which in Rigby's view it generally did – the leadership was ruling with what he called 'goal-rational' legitimacy and authority.

He made one interesting point to which we will return in the context of Gill's contribution to this volume, that particularly when combined with a measure of charismatic authority the logic of goal-rationality was towards a concentration of power that was not so far removed from the sort of power talked about by the proponents of the totalitarian view – 'the requirements of effective task-achievement favour the emergence of a dominant leader who may then exploit the charismatic potentialities in the authority-system to build a position of exceptional personal power.'[12]

For Weber a state which enjoyed legal-rational legitimacy had to have at its disposal a legal-rational bureaucracy. Again, in Rigby's view, there was something of Weber's legal-rationality about the Soviet bureaucracy, in that it 'consists of a hierarchy of offices, each with a prescribed competence, staffed by appointees, salaried, career officials who have no property in their office or the facilities it presides over, and who occupy it at the will of their superiors.'[13] But again, like the leadership's legitimacy, the Soviet bureaucracy did not quite meet the ideal of Weber's ideal type.

There was the fact of patron-client relationships, which meant that competence was far from necessarily the primary qualification for appointment to office. There was also a question mark over officials having 'no property in their office'.[14] But for Rigby the most important difference between Weber's legal-rational bureaucrats and Soviet bureaucrats, and indeed real-life bureaucrats in other political systems, was that they could not be just technical implementers of the law. They had to have a discretionary, decision-making role as well, because their task was not simply to apply rules, but to fulfil tasks. As quoted before, 'action is "rational" in so far as it is appropriate to achieving tasks contributing to some overall goal', and performance is measured not in terms of the application of rules but fulfilment of task-achieving assignments. And despite the image we have of Soviet bureaucrats as blind automata, in fact they were expected, where appropriate, to exercise discretion – including the discretionary neglect of rules – to fulfil tasks and meet goals (and pay the price if they got it wrong).

Rigby's simple but substantial adaptation of Weber's category of legal-rational legitimacy and bureaucracy provided the impetus for valuable further work by those working directly on legitimacy. (See the Gill and Holmes contributions to this volume.) He also made a clear and positive case for the Soviet system and its leadership as having legitimacy, at a time of the dominance of totalitarian theory, which either ignored it or reduced it to a crude concept of 'ideology'.

This author will admit, despite Rigby's gentle urging to overcome the cynicism regarding Soviet belief in and commitment to grand goals induced in him by both totalitarian theory and Western behaviouralism, to have been not quite able to accept the achievement of communism as the goal of the Soviet system and the source for the tasks that were allocated to the population and bureaucracy by the leadership. And yet he will admit that in the memoir literature and his own encounters with Soviet citizens he regularly encountered evidence to support precisely what Rigby was claiming.

Rigby's approach also gave some real content to the relationship between the political leadership and officials. In his view the latter were not, on the one hand, blind automata very efficiently but mindlessly fulfilling the desires of the leadership. Nor, on the other hand, were they totally self-interested free agents. They were people obeying orders, but orders the sense and meaning of which they understood and which to a considerable degree they accepted as legitimate, They had to, since they were required to fulfil them with a degree of flexibility that could be attained only by someone who knew what they were doing and why.

If the author has a problem with Rigby's approach it is that it is too focused on the relationship between the political leadership and the bureaucracy at the expense of the relationship between the leadership and the population. It is an orientation encouraged by Weber and by the nature of the system that Rigby was studying. Nevertheless the implications of the focus on a bureaucratic relationship rather than a civil relationship is something which is raised in Holmes's contribution to this volume and to which we will return in this Introduction.

The nature of political and social control

Rigby's professional life spanned a period of on-going debate, fierce at times, over the nature of political and social control in the Soviet Union. Whether the leadership was legitimated in its activities by a goal orientation towards the achievement of communism – or indeed was legitimated at all – was one controversial issue. Another was the degree of concentration of power in the hands of a single leader or very small group of leaders. At the time Rigby was becoming established in the discipline the dominant approach to understanding the nature of the Soviet system was totalitarianism. Although not someone who could ever be accused of being 'soft on communism', he was never a supporter of the totalitarian view. As the previous section on legitimacy makes clear, he did not believe that the Soviet Union existed and operated purely on the basis of fear and coercion. He was also critical of totalitarian theory on the methodological grounds that as a concept and a word it had so many meanings as to be useless,[15] and even if applicable to the Soviet Union was not sufficiently distinguishing to tell us anything usefully specific about the country.[16] In a rejection of a fundamental feature of totalitarianism, he did not believe that the Soviet Union was an atomized society, not least because it retained remnants of traditional and market forms of social interaction.[17] He also believed that the totalitarian view reduced the potential for comparing the Soviet Union to other systems. In 1973, for example, he wrote:

> The important potential contribution of students of communist and other centralised bureaucratic politics [to the comparative study of bureaucratic politics – SF] was for long stultified by the influence of totalitarian models, and where relevant case material was presented, this tended to be written down (if not written off) as 'Kremlinology'.[18]

Given these attitudes towards totalitarian theory one might have expected Rigby to have been a supporter of the great challenger in the 1960s and 1970s to the totalitarian view, the pluralist or group approach. In fact he could be terse about it. He was suspicious of its origins in mainstream Western political science. As he put it in 1983, and despite his clear hopes for comparative studies just expressed:

> It is ironical that a strong movement has emerged seeking to dissolve the study of Soviet politics more or less completely in this mainstream, at just the time when doubts about its assumptions and achievements have been growing on its home ground. ... In recent years students of US politics have demonstrated the inadequacies of what I have called the 'narrow behaviouralist' approach (or 'pluralist' approach – a misleading label in the present context) to power.[19]

But this is not to say that he rejected the pluralists' claims. Most of his criticisms of them were in fact over priority and incorrect labelling. He would more or less gently point out that there were certain pluralist things that went on in Western societies that did not – and could not – go on in the Soviet Union. As he wrote in a note in response to Jerry Hough's 1976 article on political participation (in which Hough sought to demonstrate that Western democracies did not have a monopoly on political participation):

> Here I feel Hough has thrown out the baby with the bathwater of bourgeois-democratic self-congratulation: the baby's name is 'Opposition'.[20]

He would also gently point out that not everyone before the pluralists had been paid-up members of the totalitarian club. In a 1972 article in which he generally accepted Gordon Skilling's group approach, he cited Rustow's *World Politics* article of 1957 as having made the same points,[21] and noted that Kremlinology had its 'group' aspect, in its linking of leadership factions with 'political forces' in wider society.[22] Even adherents of the totalitarian view had described political conflict.[23]

He was less gentle with those who lumped his own concept of mono-organizational socialism with totalitarianism:

> Such a critical conflating of 'totalitarian', 'bureaucratic' and 'mono-organisational' images of the USSR sometimes rests on the demonstrably erroneous assumption that they all ignore the conflictual pluralistic aspects of Soviet politics and picture the centralised determination of grass-roots behaviour as near perfect.[24]

Clearly, he by no means rejected pluralist views. As already mentioned, he generally accepted Skilling's group approach, even if he referred, somewhat opaquely, to major problems of definition and semantics.[25] He was prepared to accept that his concept of bureaucratic crypto-politics 'may be defined in Jerry Hough's terms as "institutional pluralism", provided it is borne in mind that this form of politics is the *only* form of politics that is allowed to happen'.[26]

In 1964 Rigby published a major article, *Crypto-Politics*, in which he wrote:

> [W]e might reasonably hypothesize that conflicts of interest and aspiration in the Soviet Union, denied a special political sphere of operation, tend to give a political coloration to processes ostensibly

executive and administrative in character, that is, to generate a distinctive *crypto-politics*.[27]

After outlining the achievements and shortcomings of early efforts at describing and analysing Soviet politics, including Kremlinology, he went on to deal rather harshly with 'social forces' theory ('there remains a somewhat noisesome red herring to remove: the notion that the key to policy, institutional and leadership changes is the struggle between various political and social "forces", identified as particular elite segments of society or major divisions of the party and state bureaucracy')[28] and the very early attempts at 'interest group' analysis that followed (specifically Roger Pethybridge's *A Key to Soviet Politics*, published in 1962). But he then outlined how, with an appropriate degree of rigour and awareness of its limitations, such an approach could be usefully applied to at least post-Stalinist Soviet politics.

The crypto-politics Rigby described was very much an intra-bureaucracy phenomenon, and he was adamant always that that was where the Soviet political process was overwhelmingly situated. However, even in 1964 he was prepared to consider the possibility that we have 'sometimes been too ready to dismiss pseudo-democratic institutions and procedures as irrelevant to the Soviet political process'.[29] In 1970 he suggested that there 'is a modest trend, still behind the scenes, to institutionalize a non-bureaucratic level of politics', although his example, the increased activity of the Standing Commissions of the Supreme Soviet, reminds us that he was not talking of Western-style NGOs.[30] Although critical of some aspects of Hough's 1976 article on political participation, overall he supported Hough's line of argument:

> Despite the still subordinate role of the public arena in Soviet politics, its influence on the bureaucratic political process may have grown both in degree and in sophistication since Khrushchev. The notion of a Soviet *obshchestvennost'*, an 'attentive public' as Hough puts it, drawn from the official and scholarly communities and other educated groups, linked by informal bonds of residence, education, friendship, and shared attitudes, has much relevance for the evaluation of political participation patterns.[31]

He had always recognized the remnants of market forms of economic activity,[32] and had never seen Soviet society as atomized. That provided the basis for a recognition of the foundations of a civil society that was to take on greater significance in later times, something to which we will return.

Clearly Rigby was open to the possibility and aware of the limited reality of a variety of forms of political activity in the Soviet Union. However he was also eventually always at pains to keep it all, even the bureaucratic politics, in perspective. There might have been a lot of pursuit of personal and group interests and policy conflict. But in the end the political system was what he described, in probably his most widely known and quoted conceptualization of the Soviet system, as 'mono-organizational socialism'.[33] We have already documented his irritation at the conflation of that concept and totalitarianism. He was at pains to point out that mono- did not mean monolithic.[34]

The features of mono-organizational socialism included the continuing, if subsidiary, role of tradition and exchange (including in personal networks and the shadow economy). It had a politics, 'in the sense of competition to influence decisions and their implementation, [being] mostly structured around the formal and the informal organizations of the official hierarchies'.[35] But the fundamental feature of mono-organizational socialism was the 'leading role of the party'. Once the Bolsheviks came to power 'every field of social activity was soon to become the monopoly of an officially designated organization run by a hierarchy of command that culminated in the party leadership, and the whole complex of organizations to be welded into a single organizational structure by the command hierarchy of the party apparatus.'[36] The party determined the goals, structures and leading personnel of all social organizations; it had a monopoly of public communication and information; and was able to exercise an extraordinarily high level of coercive control.

As far as Rigby was concerned Stalinism was mono-organizational society with the addition of personal tyranny (assisted by the use of charismatic authority referred to above, as well as made possible by technological capacity).[37] Stalin's tyranny was not something historically unique – history is not short of murderous personal tyrannies. However mono-organizational socialism was historically unique.[38] That was one reason why mono-organizational socialism was able to survive the death of Stalin and the end of his style of personal tyranny. Indeed the system reverted to the form it had had before Stalin established his personal dominance, a form of oligarchy. Post-Stalin, 'an oligarchical sharing of supreme power painfully established itself and gradually acquired a fairly settled institutional shape. Those features of "Stalinism" that had flowed from and supported the personal rule of the tyrant were now increasingly found to be inconsistent with oligarchical rule as well as costly to societal performance, while the defence of those features that constituted the mono-organisational system became the common ground on which the oligarchical consensus rested.'[39] While Rigby recognized the personal dominance of Khrushchev and Brezhnev, this was not of the level of Stalin's control. Khrushchev's attempts to go beyond the oligarchical consensus cost him his job. By being very careful in his policy initiatives and very tolerant of his colleagues' personal and professional shortcomings, Brezhnev managed to create for himself within the oligarchical consensus a cult of personality which challenged Stalin's in its scale and surpassed it in its pretensions.

The oligarchical consensus allowed a degree – indeed a considerable degree – of crypto-politics, of intra-bureaucratic competition for resources and policy influence. The oligarchs themselves engaged in political competition ranging from the slightly ludicrous protocol struggles for prominence, through policy debates, to what were now only figuratively life-and-death but nevertheless career-defining struggles for political dominance. But all this went on within the framework of and without challenge to the dominance of the party leadership and its apparatus, regardless of who occupied positions in both at the time.

Hats and chaps

We have already described Rigby's keen interest in Weber's category of rational-legal bureaucracy, and seen the extent to which he emphasized bureaucratic structures and behaviours in his analysis of the Soviet system. But as suggested early in this chapter, if one thing Rigby had learned from his empirical studies of the Soviet Union was that it was bureaucratic, another was that within it personal relationships and loyalties played an enormous role. It was that fact which at least partly rendered Weber's rational-legal category inapplicable to the Soviet Union. It also meant that Rigby's empirical work was divided between substantial research into both the formal bureaucratic structures and procedures of the Soviet system, with their echoes of Weber's legal-rationality, and the complexities of personalist politics.

Rigby liked to refer, in conversation, to the great issue in politics of 'hats' and 'chaps'. In a system of 'hats', the people wearing hats, the hats of office, behaved in accordance with the expectations of their office, of the hat that they were wearing. If they changed their hats, they would accordingly change their behaviour. Things were different in systems of 'chaps'. Chaps wore hats – they occupied formal positions – but they took no notice of them. They were driven in their behaviour by their relationships with other chaps they knew, including chaps who in formal terms were wearing different hats. A system dominated by chaps was not without its institutions. But those institutions could not guarantee the obedience or loyalty of those working within them. That obedience and loyalty would be afforded to a patron who could well be working in another institution.

One of Rigby's great studies of hats was his 1979 book, *Lenin's Government*.[40] It told the story of Lenin's struggle to create some order out of the chaos that was the Bolshevik Revolution and the events immediately following it. The struggle took the form of creating, staffing and establishing procedures for a number of political and administrative institutions, in particular Sovnarkom, the state apparatus body which under Lenin was the centre of Soviet governance, at a time when the party apparatus and its policy-making capacity were rudimentary.

Although it was a story in which Lenin's strivings to bring order out of chaos received a great deal of emphasis, Rigby made it clear that there was more than an individual at work here:

> The casual observer might be forgiven for seeing in the early Sovnarkom little more than the loosely-organised following of a triumphant charismatic leader. ... However this would be a profoundly misleading impression. From the very first weeks of its existence, Sovnarkom displayed an impulse towards articulation of its structures and regularisation and routinisation of its procedures: in other words towards *institutionalisation*.[41]

It was an institutionalization of the Sovnarkom. But it was also the institutionalization of the place in the policy process of the government agencies that were represented in the Sovnarkom. Rigby described the early appearance of the phenomenon of *vedomstvennost'*, the placing of the interests of one's own bureaucratic agency above those of the party, state and nation. It was a problem for Soviet leaders throughout the system's existence and came to receive conceptual recognition in Hough's 'institutional pluralism', which as we have already seen Rigby was not averse to equating with his own mono-organizational socialism.

For Rigby, even at the times of greatest chaos, the most voluntaristic of behaviour on the part of the leaders, and the greatest strains on institutional and personal loyalties, the Soviet system was nevertheless one which displayed not just regularities, but a striving for regularities, for some form of routinized and indeed institutionalized behaviour. But

although he had a strong commitment to the study of the institutionalization of the Soviet bureaucracy, including its formal rules and procedures and the place within it of policy struggles between powerful
bureaucratic agencies, he was also very aware of the major role played by
personalist politics, by chaps. In fact he believed that personalist politics
were more important than institutional politics. He saw strong evidence
even in the Brezhnev period, for 'institutionalists' the time of the greatest
power of bureaucratic agencies, 'that patronage remains a vital element in
Soviet political life despite the expectation of some scholars that it would
wither as the system became "institutionalized"':[42]

> This is not to say, of course, that no important differences and polit-
> ical conflicts exist among the several hierarchies and their dominant
> elites. But conflict between them does not assume the salience in
> Soviet political life that one might expect. Political cleavages tend to
> cut across them, and the informal patronage groupings that strongly
> influence political alignments in the USSR characteristically include
> office-holders in several such hierarchies.[43]

Patronage existed because the structures of supreme power were always
weakly institutionalized, because dictatorships, whether of an individual or an oligarchy, operate without external constraints. With reference specifically to oligarchical dictatorship, this 'means that rules
and conventions about the way this power is structured and exercised
can be enforced only if it suits the interests and inclinations of the
members of the oligarchy itself'. This leaves the system particularly
vulnerable to 'accidents of personality' and changes in the opportunity
costs of members of the oligarchy.[44] Weak institutionalization had
flow-on effects down the system, 'since it is of the essence of dictatorship that formal structures are dissolved in a kaleidoscope of personal
dependence'.[45] Other factors were the Soviet Union's early and under-
developed modernization; unpredictability, insecurity and recurrent
scarcity and dependence; and goal orientation, with success requiring
informal behaviour.[46] Even at times of more-or-less institutionalized
oligarchy, patron-client relations were crucial,[47] because promotion
was still based on performance assessed by one's superior rather than
by abstract rules, and because the frequent need to collude in dubious
acts to get results drove individuals to seek the protection of a patron.[48]

Note, however, that in the Soviet case patron-client relationships
were very job-based, not just in the obvious sense that the networks
were based on placing clients in positions throughout the bureaucracy,

but also in the sense that performance in the job was a requirement of the relationship:

> When one individual dominates, political struggle has been concentrated on competition for office, for the ear and goodwill of the boss, for efficient fulfillment of tasks assigned to the apparatus under one's supervision, for the appointment of adherents to positions where they can enhance one's own programmes and reputation at the expense of one's rivals.[49]

The most common foundation of a patron-client relationship was having worked together, often many years previously, rather than the common birthplaces, schooling, clan or religion more usual in other systems. This was because the patron had to have some confidence in the capacity of the client to do the job. Even given the importance of networks, it was one's position that determined status and rewards. This was because this was a personalist politics operating within a very bureaucratic system. One would indeed try to have loyal clients in a range of important organizational structures (rather than dominate just one structure), although support within the top levels of the most important of them, the party apparatus, was crucial. This view of how things worked was very compatible with Rigby's goal-rational category of legitimacy. While it was very job- and indeed performance-oriented, it was not incompatible with personalist relationships. Indeed in Soviet circumstances it required them.

Given these views, it is not surprising that Rigby was the Kremlinologist par excellence – not in the proverbial and superficial sense of noting the lineup on the Mausoleum, but through the deep knowledge of and fascination with who knew whom, who came from where, who signed an obituary, and, very importantly, who worked and had worked where. His office was full of card files of biographies; he had all the handbooks – the Soviet volumes of biographies of Central Committee members, the CIA handbooks, etc; he had research assistants, including the inestimable Val Ogareff, combing newspapers for personnel details. He loved nothing more than to give a seminar paper and eventually publish an article on the intricacies of the background and career links of some cohort of officials.

This view of the Soviet world was also reflected in Rigby's relative lack of interest – at least as reflected in his published work – in policy issues. Although, as we have seen, he did not reject the institutional pluralist view, he was always a bit suspicious of it, and he did not do the detailed analysis of specific policy issues that were inspired by institutional pluralist conceptualizing and which tended to reveal a more bureaucratic agency-based policy process than Rigby felt entirely comfortable with.

To summarize, Rigby's views of how the Soviet Union worked were based on some early study of Marx and especially Weber, and then a long period of intense empirical study. Once he attempted to conceptualize his empirical knowledge the debt to Weber became ever clearer, although it was always a very flexible use of Weber and indeed of theory in general. His conceptualized vision of the Soviet Union did not change much over the years – he worked to fill in gaps and add to the empirical verification. A two-volume collection of past writings appeared in 1990, and he saw little reason in presenting those volumes to issue mea culpas and retractions. The Soviet Union was not a monolithic system, with the exception of the exceptional years of Stalin's tyranny, and even then it was not totalitarian. However it was always a system entirely dominated by a single organization, the Communist Party of the Soviet Union, and its apparatus. It was also a system which tended towards rule by a small group, and occasionally a single leader. Although the system had a need for and urge towards institutionalization, and the agency-based crypto-politics that went with it, the personal loyalty networks of the top leaders, which were replicated at lower levels, dominated the political process.

The post-Soviet period

Rigby was still an active researcher as the Soviet Union disintegrated and a new Russian state and political system were formed. The main focus of his work in this period was on what had always been his favourite occupation, digging up biographical data about cohorts of officials and systematizing it. This resulted in a series of articles on the governmental, parliamentary, business and provincial elites.[50] He pointed out in these articles that while personal links remained, and indeed were probably talked about even more than in Soviet times, they were not really the same as they had been in the past. The greater market and democratic elements in the post-Soviet system meant that personal networks were much less important in leaders' rise to power, were much less stable, and patrons were much less 'loyal'.[51]

Perhaps unavoidably Rigby also devoted attention to the collapse itself. He saw much in the Gorbachev period that continued to look like bureaucratic 'crypto-politics'. However the forces for change within the

arena of crypto-politics were driven by ideas, not interests, and therefore as far as Rigby was concerned provided no support for 'interest-
group' approaches to understanding the process.[52] He wrote in his last
published article, regarding the primary cause of the collapse of the
Soviet Union

> That cause, in my view, lay in the increasingly manifest inadequacies
> of the socio-economic order and its legitimating ideology, which
> sapped the cohesion and confidence of the ruling elite and thereby
> their will and capacity to maintain effective repression of ethnic,
> social, and intellectual dissent.[53]

As Gorbachev's control of the process weakened, Rigby saw what he
called 'the unleashing of politics', an entirely new experience for the
Soviet system. He was impressed by the increasing strength in the late
Soviet period of 'civil society' elements, above all the pseudo-democracy
which the Soviet regime itself had constantly kept in the public
consciousness through its propaganda, and the 'shadow culture', the
unofficial social zone, which had always been present to some degree
but had developed to a major degree in the last decades of the Soviet
Union's existence.[54]

Rigby had recognized the existence of these 'civil society' phenomena
previously and had noted their possible significance, but had not taken
them any further than that. In terms of his own post-collapse assessment,
his own model was not able to explain the collapse of the Soviet Union.
It could even be argued that his commitment to crypto-politics and
mono-organizational socialism contributed to a failure to predict the collapse. If the Soviet Union collapsed because of the development of 'civil
society' phenomena, the focus on processes within the bureaucracy had
deflected attention from the existence and importance of those phenomena. The same problem is evident in his treatment of legitimacy, which as
we have seen was very focused on the relationship between the leadership and the bureaucracy, less so that between the leadership and society.

In this author's view there was also something about Rigby's attitude towards pluralism that gives us a clue to another problem when it
came to the collapse of the Soviet Union. As we have seen Rigby regularly
declared his support for a range of pluralist approaches. However, there
was always an aversion that constantly reappeared, both in his published
work and in conversation. The aversion was largely based on a nervous-
ness that pluralism would spill over into unjustifiable claims of a process
of democratization, and that even the pluralists not going that far and

limiting themselves to pluralist processes within the bureaucracy were losing sight of the continuing dominance of the party leadership and apparatus. But the author suspects that there was another reason for the lack of enthusiasm for pluralism. This was his purely personal fascination with collecting and analysing personnel data. Pluralist theory pushed the researcher to study not personnel (although that was hardly irrelevant) but to study policy. Rigby was simply less interested in studying policy than personnel. To the extent that pluralist studies revealed cases of successful policy-making through the involvement of a broader range of policy actors, Rigby's lack of interest did no harm, because those cases increasingly were the exception rather than the rule. It was the pluralism-inspired studies that revealed a deep malaise in the policy process that provided more useful information for an understanding of what was to come. The lesson of those studies was not that the Soviet Union was developing a pluralist structure for the more effective making of policy, but rather that it was unable to fit a variety of views, even when strictly limited to the major bureaucratic agencies and a few close academic associates, into the creaky political framework of crypto-politics and mono-organizational socialism.

Rigby was hardly alone in failing to predict the collapse of the Soviet Union. He did not see his job as making such predictions. His job was to understand the way the Soviet Union operated. The knowledge and theories designed to understand how something operates are often not what is required to predict or understand why they will stop operating. Rigby might well be right in his post facto analysis, that it was ideas and values that brought about the collapse of the Soviet system. But to have focused one's attention on those ideas and values for all but the final year or so of the Soviet Union's existence would have produced a very distorted picture of how the Soviet Union worked. Rigby was interested in how it worked, and that is where his contribution remains invaluable. The following contributions will further illustrate that claim.

Notes

1 T.H. Rigby (1990), *The Changing Soviet System: Mono-organisational Socialism from its Origins to Gorbachev's Restructuring* (Aldershot: Edward Elgar), pp.1–3.
2 Two chapters of the thesis are published in T.H. Rigby (1990), *Political Elites in the USSR. Central Leaders and Local Cadres from Lenin to Gorbachev* (Aldershot: Edward Elgar), chapter 5.
3 Rigby, *Political Elites*, pp.9–10.
4 T.H. Rigby (1968), *Communist Party Membership in the USSR, 1917–1967* (Princeton: Princeton University Press), pp.18–28.

5 T.H. Rigby, 'A conceptual approach to authority, power and policy in the Soviet Union', in T.H. Rigby, Archie Brown, Peter Reddaway (eds) (1983), *Authority, Power and Policy in the USSR* (London and Basingstoke: Macmillan), p.10.
6 Rigby, 'Conceptual approach', p.10.
7 T.H. Rigby, 'Security and modernisation in Tsarist Russia and the USSR', in Rigby, *Changing Soviet System*, p.191. Originally published in *Survey* (1967), no.64. Quotations here are taken from the reprint.
8 Rigby, *Political Elites*, pp.2–3.
9 T.H. Rigby (2003), 'Russia's nationhood from its origins to Putin', *Australian Slavonic and East European Studies*, XVII, 1–2, 124.
10 Rigby, 'Conceptual approach', pp.11–12.
11 Ibid., p.19.
12 Ibid., p.22.
13 Ibid., p.12.
14 Rigby's early interest in Marxism made a rare reappearance in a discussion of the bureaucracy as a 'class' (the inverted commas were Rigby's own). In general terms he had doubts about the value of the Marxist concept of class when applied to the Soviet Union, based as it was on property. But he recognized that 'access to administrative resources, by virtue of office in one or other of the command hierarchies through which the whole business of society is conducted', was the main basis of power and privilege, and such office could therefore be regarded as bestowing membership of the 'ruling class'. Weber's rational-legal bureaucrats did not occupy office in order to give themselves access to power and privilege. Rigby, *Political Elites*, p.3.
15 T.H. Rigby, '"Totalitarianism" and change in communist systems', in Rigby, *Changing Soviet System*, p.135. (Originally published in *Comparative Politics* (1972), 4, 3, 433–53.)
16 T.H. Rigby, 'Stalinism and the mono-organisational society,' in Rigby, *Changing Soviet System*, p.108. (Originally published in R.C. Tucker, *Stalinism*, 1977.)
17 T.H. Rigby, 'Gorbachev and the crisis of mono-organisational socialism', in Rigby, *Changing Soviet System*, p.216.
18 T.H. Rigby, 'Bureaucratic politics: An introduction', *Public Administration*, XXXII, 1973, 6.
19 Rigby, 'Conceptual approach', pp.2, 23.
20 T.H. Rigby, 'Hough on political participation in the Soviet Union', *Soviet Studies*, XXVIII, 2, April 1976, 259.
21 Dankwart A. Rustow (1957), 'New horizons for comparative politics', *World Politics*, 9, 4, 530–49.
22 Rigby, '"Totalitarianism" and change', p.135.
23 T.H. Rigby, 'Reconceptualising the Soviet system', in Stephen White, Alex Pravda, Zvi Gitelman (eds) (1992), *Developments in Soviet and Post-Soviet Politics* (Durham: Duke University Press), pp.302–3.
24 Rigby, 'Introduction', in *Changing Soviet System*, p.7.
25 Rigby, '"Totalitarianism" and change', p.135.
26 Rigby, 'Conceptual approach', p.25. The author, as an Honours student at the ANU at the time, remembers the discussion lunch that Rigby organized for academic colleagues and Soviet specialists in Canberra's bureaucracy to discuss

what he immediately recognized as a major event, the 1972 appearance of Jerry Hough's article, 'The Soviet system: Petrification or pluralism', *Problems of Communism*, 2, March–April 1972, 25–45.

27 T.H. Rigby, 'Crypto-Politics', in Frederic J. Fleron (ed.) (1969), *Communist Studies and the Social Sciences: Essays in Methodology and Empirical Theory* (Chicago: Rand McNally), p.117. (Originally published in *Survey*, 50, January 1964, 183–94.)

28 Rigby, 'Crypto-Politics', p.121.

29 Ibid., p.125.

30 T.H. Rigby, 'The Soviet leadership: Towards a self-stabilising oligarchy', *Soviet Studies*, XXII, 2, October 1970, 188. His awareness of the activities of the Standing Commissions would have come from the work at the time of his PhD student, Shugo Minagawa, which was published in 1985 as *Supreme Soviet Organs* (Nagoya: Nagoya University Press).

31 Rigby, 'Hough on political participation', p.259.

32 T.H. Rigby, 'Traditional, market and organizational societies and the USSR', *World Politics*, XVI, 4, 1964, reprinted in *Changing Soviet System*, chapter 3.

33 Originally he wrote of the 'mono-organizational society'. He appears to have changed it to 'mono-organizational socialism', without explanation, for the 1990 volume of collected papers.

34 Rigby, 'Introduction', in *Changing Soviet System*, p.7.

35 Ibid., p.6.

36 T.H. Rigby, 'Mono-organisational socialism in the civil society', in Chandran Kukathas, David W. Lovell, William Maley (eds) (1991), *The Transition from Socialism: State and Civil Society in the USSR* (Melbourne: Longman Cheshire), p.111.

37 Rigby, 'Stalinism and the mono-organisational society', p.95.

38 Ibid., p.92.

39 Ibid., p.108.

40 T.H. Rigby (1979), *Lenin's Government. Sovnarkom, 1917–1922* (Cambridge: Cambridge University Press).

41 Rigby, *Lenin's Government*, p.99.

42 T.H. Rigby, 'Political patronage in the USSR from Lenin to Brezhnev', *Politics*, XVIII, 1, May 1983, 85.

43 Rigby, 'Introduction', in *Political Elites*, p.8.

44 T.H. Rigby, 'The Soviet political executive', in Archie Brown (ed.) (1989), *Political Leadership in the Soviet Union* (Basingstoke and London: Macmillan), p.6.

45 Rigby, *Political Elites*, p.165.

46 Rigby, 'Political patronage', p.88.

47 Rigby, 'Soviet leadership', p.177.

48 Rigby, 'Political patronage', p.88.

49 Rigby, 'Security and modernisation', p.194.

50 T.H. Rigby, 'Russia's clientelism, cliques, connections and "clans": The same old story?', *The Soviet and Post-Soviet Review*, XXV, 2, 1998, 109–23; 'Russia's provincial bosses: A collective career profile', *Journal of Communist Studies and Transition Politics*, XXVII, 4, December 2001, 1–14, 'New top elites for old in Russian politics', *British Journal of Political Science*, XXIX, 2,

April 1999, 323–43; 'Russia's business elite', *Russian and Euro-Asian Bulletin*, VIII, 7, August–September 1999.
51 Rigby, 'Russia's clientelism', p.123.
52 Rigby, 'Reconceptualising', p.310.
53 Rigby, 'Russia's nationhood', p.123.
54 Rigby, 'Reconceptualising', p.312.

2

Institutionalization and Personalism in the Policy-making Process of the Soviet Union and Post-Soviet Russia

Stephen Fortescue

One of the great issues of Soviet studies was, and remains, the relationship between the 'institutionalization', on the one hand, and the 'personalism', on the other, of the structures and procedures of the political process and the behaviour of those operating within it. Some are impressed by the power of Soviet bureaucratic agencies and the complex and all-embracing bureaucratic procedures they used to exercise that power. Others are impressed by the extent to which the system was dominated by the personal power of a very small number – perhaps one – leader, and how personal loyalties which cut across organizational boundaries – usually, although not necessarily, of a hierarchical nature (i.e. patron-client relationships) – took precedence over and indeed subverted institutional structures, procedures and behaviours.

Most analysts of the Soviet Union have been happy to acknowledge that both political forms existed simultaneously throughout the Soviet Union's existence. The majority, one suspects, have nevertheless been of the opinion that the personalist element was dominant. As discussed in the Introduction, T.H. Rigby was in this category, although somewhat tentatively. The same can be said of Graeme Gill, a contributor to this volume:

> The basic power axis within the party, and by extension the system as a whole, was personalistic, ... one in which the tenor of the whole structure was set by the person of the leader, where formal rules were less important than the norms flowing from the exercise of personalized power, and where access to power and privilege was determined by personal relations. This did not mean that there were no institutional norms nor that institutions did not matter. There was throughout the Soviet period a continuing tension between pressures for the

> sort of institutionalization which would consolidate and strengthen the power and position of formal institutions and pressures for the maintenance of a personalised basis of politics. ... Nevertheless as a general principle, the personalist basis of power has been more important for the structuring of Soviet politics than the forces for powerful institutional consolidation.[1]

This author has been, if anything, in the other camp.[2]

As described in the Introduction, the main reason as far as Rigby was concerned that the strong pressure towards institutionalization could not win over personalism was the refusal of the ruling group to allow any external constraints on their rule. This left institutions highly vulnerable to the '"accidents of personality" and changes in opportunity costs' of the members of the ruling group.[3] That is, despite their persistent efforts to create and enforce their own rules of behaviour, without any external referee they were unable to resist – or trust others to resist – the temptation to break the rules. So they fell back to forming patronage networks to ensure their personal political security and to promote the successful fulfilment of the tasks that derive from goal-rationality, something which was necessary for career maintenance and promotion.

Easter, another thoughtful analyst of the institutional-personal relationship who stresses the priority of the personal, has a different explanation. Resort to the personal is a functional reaction to the system's lack of organizational capacity to provide adequate input for interested parties into the policy process and to achieve the implementation of policy decisions. In circumstances of poor communications and inefficient bureaucratic structures, interested parties outside the leadership used personal contacts within the leadership to influence policy. Once a policy was arrived at, the network was used in the opposite direction to achieve implementation.[4]

In this chapter I examine these issues anew, to determine whether, why and in what circumstances (and with what consequences) the personalist might have been more important that the institutional. In doing so, I concentrate on policy-making, which is not to deny the significance of policy implementation. The chapter begins with an outline of the author's views on how the policy process is structured in a complex society. The specific processes that operated under various Soviet leaders are then described, within the terms of the general principles about to be outlined. The chapter concludes by taking the analysis into the post-Soviet period, including an assessment of the prospects of the Russian policy-making process into the future.

The policy-making process in complex societies

A major, perhaps defining, feature of complex societies is the special-ization of function. When I say 'specialization of function' I mean responsibility for taking specified action which is unique to a particular organization. A specialized function goes beyond, but presumes the possession of specialized knowledge. There could well be those in society who have specialized knowledge without having a specialized function – we will see later possible examples of such a phenomenon in the Soviet case. But when combined, function and knowledge give a par-ticular status to the organization combining them. We are dealing with organizations, not individuals, since in complex societies specialized functions are almost invariably carried out by the former.

There are consequences of the specialization of function which while perhaps not totally determined are nevertheless sufficiently widespread as to suggest that they constitute what a Soviet theorist would have called a *zakonomernost'* – I will call it 'the logic of specialization'. Such specialization, which is likely to strengthen as the complexity of the goals and demands placed on social actors increases, produces a need and expectation that those with specialized functions will be involved in those policy processes that are relevant to their area of special-ization. That involvement might, at the minimum, be the provision of information to those who make policy decisions. However, the pro-vision of information, particularly complex, specialized and quite possibly controversial information, is very likely to be followed by explanation, discussion and eventually what could be called consult-ation. By consultation I mean a process through which opinions, rather than simple information, are sought of those with specialized func-tions. The process of consultation becomes particularly complicated, even fraught, when the policy matter at hand touches upon the spe-cializations of a number of organizations, which is likely to be the case more often than not. Different specializations are likely to produce dif-ferent views – whether self-interested or objective – on which policy outcome is desirable. In those circumstances organizations with expec-tations of being consulted are likely to want settled, routinized struc-tures and procedures, quite possibly but not necessarily of a formal nature, to ensure that consultation takes place and in such a way as not to give privileged access to other interested parties. The structure is likely to be a collective decision-making body, with the major organizations with specialized functions represented. At the peak of the political system that body would be something like a cabinet. Once the cabinet is formed demands for procedures that ensure equal participation and consultation for all policy actors are likely to surface. An organization which believed that in a policy process without formalized consultation procedures it would have highly privileged access would not be interested in such procedures. But it is unlikely that across the full range of policy issues in a complex society any single organization could expect consistently to have such privileged access. Therefore a common call for routinized, 'equalising' procedures is likely.[5] The involvement of specialized organizations in policy processes relevant to their areas of specialization, especially when managed by routinized procedures, might go so far as an expectation that each should have a veto over policy outcomes not to their liking.

So far the discussion has been in terms of the expectations of organizations with specialized functions that they be involved in policy processes relevant to their function. This is not a deterministic technocratic view, that by the simple fact of having specialized expertise organizations seize the policy process and indeed rule society. Although it is the nature of complex, specialized societies that it is difficult to ignore the existence and views of specialized organizations – in that sense there is a 'logic' to the process – political leadership nevertheless plays a major role. Indeed political leaders influence if not control how the policy process is structured and how it proceeds, and thereby the degree to which the logic of specialization is recognized. While there are likely to be in most political systems some constitutional, conventional and conjunctural limits on leadership power, the political leader has control over who is represented on collective decision-making bodies, how the meetings of those bodies are conducted, and what sort of consultation takes place in the lead-up to meetings. The leader's general approach could be to limit the representation of organizations with specialized functions to: you provide information, but I do not need commentary, much less discussion. It might be to allow the logic to run further: I will consult with you, but I will not let you enter into debate with other interested organizations; I will allow discussion and debate between interested parties, and will even set up formal structures and procedures for it, but I will take the final decision; except in matters of extreme political sensitivity and importance I will be no more than an honest broker, or referee, in a policy process, the outcome of which will be the result of discussion, negotiation, compromise and consensus among yourselves. At its most extreme: I want the outcomes of the policy process to be fully consensual and will allow all interested parties to exercise a veto.

In making decisions on where along the spectrum to place them-selves political leaders will be aware of the advantages and disadvan-tages of the logic of specialization. If not recognized at all, if decisions are made without any input at all from organizations with specialized functions, the resultant policies are likely to be unimplementable or have lamentable and unintended consequences if implemented. If it is recognized only to the degree of granting specialized organizations membership of a collective decision-making body, it will be discovered only at meetings of the body that disagreements exist, disagreements that are unlikely to be resolved in a meeting. If pre-meeting consulta-tion procedures exist, but do not allow for negotiated outcomes, policy actors will bring all disagreements to the collective decision-making body. As a result agendas and proceedings will be hopelessly clogged.

The disadvantages of the logic of specialization are largely procedural, but with implications for the substance of policy outcomes. Consult-ation takes time, particularly as procedures become more routinized and formalized. Even without a formal right of veto – surely a rare occurrence – consultation procedures can allow in practice an informal veto, as actors manipulate the process so as to delay resolution indefinitely. These are phenomena that lead, at best, to delays in policy-making and at worst the failure to make any policy at all. Somewhere between the best and the worst, outcomes might be so negotiated and compromised down to the lowest common denominator as to be little better than no outcome at all or, as the public choice literature has copiously described, policy results that is more recognisant of special interests than of the public good.

Despite the fact that the public choice critique is largely based on the experience of democracies,[6] democracies do have mechanisms for con-trolling the logic of specialization, which allow a balanced recognition of the rights of representation of organizations with specialized functions. It is highly unlikely that the democratic process would allow a political leader not to recognize the logic of specialization at all. The danger is more likely to be in the other direction, with excessive consultation being allowed to compromise the policy process. Ruling politicians might be prepared to let issues drift or allow them to be resolved in a lowest com-mon denominator manner for a variety of reasons: lack of political nous, indebtedness to a particular interest, an unwillingness to take sides in a matter of particular political sensitivity, or simply the exhaustion of leaders who have been in power too long. But the expectations of the electorate, particularly as articulated by the opposition, force political leaders to exercise control over the policy process. It is the task of the opposition, with relentless persistence and often pettiness and hypocrisy, to attack a government which fails to do so. A democratically elected government which gives the opposition too many opportunities for such attacks will suffer by earning in the eyes of the electorate an image of weakness, even before the policy consequences of such weakness become clear. NGOs and other associational groups also pressure the government for policy action in their particular areas of interest.

The existence of an opposition allows democracies to cope with the logic of specialization reasonably well. Political leaders in non-democratic systems do not have oppositions. The only mechanism they have available to them is to introduce a strongly personalist element into the policy process, that is, they themselves have to take full responsibility. They can do so in two ways.

The first is the use by a political leader of his or her personal strength of personality to dominate the policy process. That strength of personality might be applied directly to the participants in the policy process, to gain their loyalty and obedience. Or it might be applied to the general population, using populism as a weapon against recalcitrant participants in the policy process. Tyrants rule by totally imposing their personality. A foolish tyrant might be tempted to refuse to entertain the logic of specialization at all, or to cut it off at an inappropriately early stage – tyrants by definition have the capacity to do so. Such a ruler is likely to pay the price in the form of poor policy and ultimately a failed state. A non-democratic leader with less than tyrannical power who attempts to ignore the logic of specialization is even more likely to pay the price, and sooner rather than later. However an outstanding non-democratic leader, with natural policy skills and cunning supplemented by experience, might be able to rule complex societies reasonably effectively even while cutting off the logic early.

One would, nevertheless, expect non-democratic leaders, even tyrants, to give some recognition to the logic of specialization. However, their consultation processes, based on their personal power, are likely not to involve formal representation at organizational level, and so are likely to be highly private, non-collective and disrespectful of formal hierarchies. The danger of the use of something similar to Weber's charismatic authority to control the logic of specialization is that it leaves the system open to cults of personality and populist politics, the leader vulnerable to sudden and catastrophic losses of personal popularity, and the system vulnerable to the loss by the leader of the physical and mental capacity to exercise the required degree of leadership.

The second form of personalist politics is the use of patronage networks to increase the leader's control over the policy process.[7] Leaders place in key policy-relevant organizations people with personal loyalty to them, and expect them to work to support their policy preferences, including within routinized consultation procedures. There are three dangers in this form of politics, the first being that the leader's placemen are so loyal and perhaps so incompetent as to render the consultation process meaningless. The reverse danger is that the leader's placemen become 'captured' by the organizations in which they are placed, and come to represent their interests as enthusiastically as if they had been born into them. Responding to this problem by the rapid circulation of personnel is likely ultimately to threaten the position of any leader with less than tyrannical power. The third problem with the patronage approach is that it leads to a highly factionalized politics. In a less than tyrannical system rival groups form, competing for access to privilege and resources and quite possibly basing their claims on policy differences. The political leader has either to become the patron simultaneously of a number of rival groups, or tolerate influential figures the level below having their own client groups. Either way the political leader has to play the rival groups off against each other, quite possibly through manipulation of the policy process. Factionalized politics is dangerous both for the leader and for policy.

The logic of specialization in the Soviet Union

The Soviet Union was clearly not a democracy, and so did not have available to it an opposition as a control mechanism for the logic of specialization. That means that in the survey of Soviet history that follows, we will be looking at how political leaders in a non-democratic regime calculated the degree to which they should recognize the logic of specialization and how personalist methods could be used to handle it.

Lenin

Although not without his tyrannical tendencies and certainly with a powerful capacity to manage the policy process as he liked, Lenin nevertheless also displayed a strong interest in creating a policy process appropriate for a modern, complex society. As Stefan Breuer puts it, Lenin was enough of a realist to know that the abolition of state and administration, as called for in *State and Revolution*, was a distant goal:

> For the present, he contented himself with the destruction of the old patrimonial apparatus and its replacement by a new one modelled on

rational organizations such as the German postal system or the major banks, which in Lenin's mind were nearly perfect embodiments of efficiency.[8]

In the first month after the Bolzhevik seizure of power the highly flexible and 'revolutionary' Military Revolutionary Council (MRC) operated in the same policy space as the more traditionally structured Council of People's Commissars (Sovet narodnykh komissarov), Sovnarkom. Although the appellation *narodnyi komissar* was revolutionary enough, it was really just another name for minister, meaning that we are talking simply of a Council of Ministers. The MRC created chaos and was abolished in December 1917. That left Sovnarkom. T.H. Rigby has described in absorbing detail Lenin's efforts to turn it, if not into the German postal service, then at least into an effective policy-making body.[9] It had the form that the logic of specialization suggests. Firstly, each major area of policy responsibility was represented by a member, with it being seen as increasingly important that people's commissars had expertise in the commissariat's area of responsibility.[10] Secondly, there were formal consultation procedures, which became particularly important after the commissars moved their personal offices out of the Smolny (the Bolshevik headquarters immediately after the seizure of power) into their commissariats, that is, when they no longer worked in close physical proximity to each other.[11] Lenin ensured that standing orders existed and that they included the requirement that policy proposals be circulated and signed off in advance. He tried, persistently but somewhat in vain, to have standing orders enforced.[12] There was also ever increasing use of ad hoc inter-agency meetings (*soveshchaniia*) to iron out policy differences in advance of the formal meetings of Sovnarkom.[13]

Despite the creation of these structures and Lenin's efforts to enforce consultation procedures, Sovnarkom nevertheless struggled to operate as an effective policy-making body, as its meetings were taken over by so-called 'vermicelli', minor matters of dispute between organizations. This suggests that bureaucratic agencies were not prepared to use consultation procedures to deal with issues outside the cabinet room. Given that according to the logic of specialization as set out at the beginning of the chapter organizations with specialized functions should be demanding the right to use consultation procedures, why in this case were they refusing to use the procedures that were offered to them? It might simply have been because they were too disorganized. The structures were new, their functions not always clear, they were swamped with work, a lot of the staff were far from dedicated in their attitudes to the Bolsheviks, initially they were led by people without technical expertise, and there was rapid staff turnover at the top. They were simply not well enough organized to take advantage of a consultation process, and it was organizationally easier for them to take their problems directly to Sovnarkom and rely on Lenin to sort them out for them. As far as they were concerned recognizing the logic of specialization only to the extent of granting them membership of a collective decision-making body was sufficient.

As Sovnarkom, because of its inability to enforce an effective consultation procedure, became less effective as a policy-making body increasing use was made of the Politburo as a court of appeal. Representatives of bureaucratic agencies looking for a quick decision, or simply recognizing that a higher authority existed from which they might get what they wanted, looked to the higher body.[14] This suggested an element of 'cheating', as some agencies hoped to get preferential treatment by going to the higher authority, rather than submit to the collective rules of the consultation process. Lenin did not want party bodies to be sucked into an operational policy role, but it was apparent that he was fighting a losing battle. During the Civil War the party apparatus had become bigger, more organized, and more involved in operational administrative matters. The drift of the party, the Politburo included, into operational policy-making could not be kept at bay.

Stalin

With Lenin's death economic policy became highly politicized, as debates over industrialization strategies became part of an ideologically charged struggle between individuals for political supremacy. In these circumstances party bodies became ever more the domain for economic debate and decision making.[15] The post-Lenin power struggle ran to special rules. Because policy issues were heavily politicized they were not subject to the logic of specialization. Albeit with the considerable involvement of expert opinion and intellectual argument, the industrialization debates were ultimately not about the representation of the possessors of specialized functions, but a political fight between politicians with a mixture of specialized and ideological knowledge. The outcomes of those debates were decided not by bargaining and consultation between the possessors of specialized functions, but by politicians' decisions, with the outcome based to a considerable degree on who had the numbers in political bodies (with control of political appointments crucial in getting the numbers).

Sovnarkom remained in existence throughout the Soviet period (being renamed the Council of Ministers in 1946). It retained a role in economic policy-making, with the phenomena of the logic of specialization remaining present in its procedures. But party bodies, especially the Politburo and Central Committee Secretariat, became increasingly important economic policy-making bodies. (Fitzpatrick describes this shift in her chapter in this volume.) Did they also struggle to arrive at an appropriate form of consultation within the policy process, as Sovnarkom had under Lenin?

Initially membership of the Politburo had not been related to the administrative position of its members. It was based purely on their party status and prestige. But its increasing involvement in economic administration came to be reflected in its membership. Once it started making decisions affecting the various economic policy actors, those policy actors had to be included in its membership. Initially it took the form of party leaders with party prestige and status taking on economic administrative roles, rather than economic administrators being granted membership of party bodies.

Were the party backgrounds of these Politburo members reflected in their behaviour? Not if the complaints of Stalin can be believed. We find in Stalin in the early 1930s a now dominant political leader frustrated in his efforts to arrive at an appropriate and effective form of representation of specialized functions within the policy process. His general policy line had won a decisive victory and within the boundaries of that line policy was for the moment no longer a matter of political and physical survival. There were still fierce policy debates, but the issues, being less politically fraught, came to be seen as being in the domain of the possessors of specialized functions. The possessors of specialized function were now represented in party bodies by senior party leaders. Stalin found that his most loyal lieutenants, when placed in policy-relevant organizations, came quickly to represent the interests – at times, in his view, the all too obviously narrow and self-serving interests – of those organizations in persistent bureaucratic infighting. In the terminology of T.H. Rigby, as described in the Introduction, they behaved as the true wearers of hats, to the extent that when they changed hats, that is, moved to another organization, they changed their behaviour.[16] To quote Politburo member and senior Bolshevik Lazar Kaganovich:

> When we [Kaganovich and Molotov] worked together in the [Politburo], we worked in a friendly manner, but when he became prime minister and I minister of transport we argued.[17]

Khlevniuk claims in his archive-based examination of the workings of the Politburo in the 1930s that most conflicts in that body were based on conflicts between bureaucratic agencies.[18] According to Belova and Gregory the most notable conflicts were between Politburo members representing industrial ministries, on the one hand, and Gosplan and the Council of Ministers on the other.[19]

Stalin professed to be highly frustrated by these developments. Belova and Gregory quote him as saying: 'Bolsheviks cannot take this path if they wish to avoid turning our Bolshevik party into a conglomerate of branch groups.'[20] However, although Stalin regularly complained about the *vedomstvennost'* (the placing of institutional over national interests) and bureaucratization of his Politburo colleagues, Khlevniuk suggests that it was an arrangement that was well suited to his own purposes, of playing the referee between the warring sides and thereby having the last word.[21] Fitzpatrick, in her contribution to this volume, also suggests that Stalin was relaxed about the behaviour of members of his team, and took it as the natural order of things.

While strongly representing agency interests, there was still something in the behaviour of these politicians-bureaucrats that was similar to that of the members of Sovnarkom under Lenin. In the early 1930s they appeared reluctant to use consultation structures and procedures and rather preferred to bring their inter-agency differences to the Politburo for decision. The Politburo's agenda became as clogged with 'vermicelli' as Sovnarkom's had been earlier. A 1932 decision to limit a single meeting's agenda to 15 items did not work.[22] It appears probable that the agencies were still insufficiently organized to participate in a full consultation process. Possibly they also did not fully trust each other and so preferred to have their differences aired and decided 'in the open', at a full meeting of the Politburo. They were wise not to trust each other, since they were all indeed 'cheating', by trying to get Stalin on their side through direct, informal approaches before the formal meeting.[23]

By the mid-1930s there is evidence that the situation was changing. The bureaucratic agencies were becoming more settled and self-confident and the levels of bureaucratic in-fighting peaked, particularly over economic policy at the beginning of the Second Five-Year Plan.[24] It was at this time that Politburo commissions, with the task of negotiating away differences between the agencies, came to be widely used. As a result more and more Politburo decisions were taken without debate on the basis of pre-agreed documentation and draft decisions.[25] These developments are often taken as evidence of Stalin taking ever more direct and personal control of the policy process. It would be a foolish commentator who denied Stalin's dominant role. Nevertheless it is possible to interpret the evidence as an indication that the logic of specialization was coming into operation, that specialized agencies were more confident about shifting the policy process out of the main collective body into smaller consultative bodies where they could negotiate and bargain among themselves.[26]

Stalin responded to the new self-confidence of the bureaucratic agencies by adopting a tyrannical response to the logic of specialization. He all but destroyed the agencies and their leaderships, he effectively closed down the main collective decision-making body (as the number of Politburo meetings declined),[27] and now indeed took personal control of the policy process. Bureaucratic agencies were denied the right to be involved and the policy process became a closed shop among a very small group of insiders.

This is not to say that Stalin did away with the logic of specialization altogether. It appears that he carefully collected information from various possessors of specialized knowledge before making a policy decision.[28] He did so through personal conversation with informed individuals.[29] Although there is no reason to believe that he did not expect those individuals to represent organizational views, he did not respect organizational hierarchies in his choice of interviewee. Indeed the interviewees were chosen as the possessors of specialized knowledge, not function. It appears that he did not limit these conversations to a simple transfer of information; discussion was permitted. However the conversations did not provide the structure or procedures for interviewees to argue an organizational position in the context of the positions of other interested parties. There was certainly no opportunity for interested parties to bargain and negotiate between themselves. The assessment of different positions was made by Stalin himself, perhaps with the help of his closest lieutenants.

This was a system that greatly reduced the barriers to expeditious policy-making that arise from the logic of specialization. But it placed a huge amount of responsibility on the leader to make an informed and balanced decision. Most observers would consider Stalin's record to be mixed in that regard, mixed enough to suggest that a talented leader with experience can shortcircuit the logic of specialization, but the risk of making bad decisions is considerable. With time Stalin's interest in and sheer physical capacity to push policy change declined, and in the final years of his rule policy stagnation set in. Some writers have suggested that as Stalin withdrew from the policy process his loyal lieutenants took over and engaged in the building of patronage networks, engaging in fierce factional fights which focused on a few key policy areas.[30] For others it was a prime example of what happens when the physical powers of a tyrant decline. Nobody was prepared to be the first to issue a challenge, particularly when there was a sense that change would inevitably come sooner rather than later. As a result nothing got done. Either way the experience shows well the dangers of using a personalist approach focused on the leader to control the logic of specialization. Even if the leader has the talent and experience to manage a highly personalized policy process, the individual's capacities inevitably decline with age and the policy process suffers as a consequence.

No evidence has been presented here of Stalin using patron-client networks to control the policy process, that is, placing people loyal to him in a range of organizations in order to push his preferred position through the policy structures and procedures. When in the early 1930s he tried something like this, placing his loyal lieutenants at the head of bureaucratic agencies, they were rapidly 'captured' by those agencies. Once he adopted the tyrannical approach, he had no need of client networks.[31]

Khrushchev

After the death of Stalin the status and prestige of the major collective decision-making bodies, including and particularly the Politburo, were quickly re-established and largely maintained.[32] The bodies met as and when they were supposed to, not just because there was a general desire among the leadership to show the world that order and 'socialist legality' were being re-established, but because they themselves needed a forum in which their respective claims to leadership could be presented and ultimately ruled upon. Even once Khrushchev had established his dominance the minimal degree of recognition of the desirability of a collective decision-making process was maintained, and a regularized consultation process operated for many policy processes. Bezborodov, for example, cites archival material in describing the process of preparing a Central Committee-Council of Ministers decree on the coordination of scientific research. In the second half of 1959 the Central Committee secretariat prepared a draft (presumably with previous informal consultation with interested parties). The draft was then sent in January 1960 to the Academy of Sciences, the civilian and defence departments of the Central Committee, and other relevant bodies for formal signing-off (note that the industrial ministries did not exist at this time). It was then approved at a meeting of the Central Committee secretariat and sent on to the Politburo (then known as the Presidium of the Central Committee).[33]

However, Khrushchev's whole persona is of a leader who had little patience with the logic of specialization. His was a highly personal approach to policy-making – he knew what he wanted and was not inclined to allow consultation to get in the way. He had a habit of interrupting and interfering, especially when he believed a matter not worth considering or already decided.[34] The public record indicates the extent to which Khrushchev interrupted speakers at meetings, his interjections and on-the-spot decision making bringing to naught any preliminary consultation that might have taken place. He also allowed individuals to violate the principles of consultation. Bezborodov describes a meeting of a working group on the 1961 CPSU Programme, at which members of the group wanted to remove a particular contribution. The author of that contribution produced his copy with a note from Khrushchev saying 'Include'.[35] This member of the group had 'cheated' by going in advance of and outside the consultation process to get the approval of the political leader. Structurally Khrushchev was no respecter of the very existence of specialized bureaucratic agencies, abolishing and reorganizing them wantonly.

While Khrushchev had little respect for the logic of specialization in its routinized, bureaucratic form, he, in a sense like Stalin, allowed consultation outside the regular bureaucratic hierarchies. In his case it took a semi-public form which produced one of the great debates in Western Sovietology. Western analysts began to note a degree of 'public' involvement in policy debate, with individuals with specialized knowledge presenting policy positions in openly available publications. Such publications had long been used as part of intra-elite debates – Kremlinology relied on it for its very existence. But what was new here – or what had not been seen at least since the industrialization debates of the 1920s – was the apparent involvement of expert opinion outside and independent of the institutionalized elite, that is, of those with specialized knowledge rather than those with specialized function. It was a phenomenon given conceptual development by Gordon Skilling and the some who preceded him and the many who followed.[36] This early application of interest group politics to the Soviet Union strongly stressed the lack of organizational authority of those who participated. They used semi-formal channels – the press, conferences, etc – to get their views across, rather than formal agency-based consultation procedures within the policy process.[37]

Even if one were prepared to recognize these types of public discussions as serious contributions to the policy process – and not all do – it was a particular form of recognition of the logic of specialization, a form one would expect of a dominant party leader who wanted to assert personal authority over the policy process. Khrushchev almost certainly used appeals to extra-institutional expert opinion to help get his way against the agencies with specialized functions.[38] Opinions were presented in public and so unlike in Stalin's case differing views could be compared. Nevertheless, these were not discussions in which policy actors could bargain and negotiate. Like Stalin calling individual experts to his office for a briefing, so here individuals with specialized knowledge presented their points of view and it was left to the leader to collate the information received and make a decision.

Khrushchev's shortcircuiting of the logic of specialization was effective in the sense that policy issues were identified and decisions made quickly – strikingly so, compared to the policy stagnation of the final years of Stalin's rule. But he suffered the consequences of a lack of consultation, in terms of the appropriateness and legitimacy of the policies that were decided and implemented, to a degree that in the end cost him his job. Khrushchev had neither the cunning, experience nor ruthlessness of Stalin, and so his attempts to control the logic of specialization directly through the force of his personality failed dismally.

Brezhnev

Somewhat paradoxically, given the greyness of his character and capabilities, it is in the characterizations by commentators of Brezhnev's eighteen years as General Secretary that we see the greatest divergence. On the one hand, there are those who see such a degree of institutionalized involvement in policy-making of organizations with specialized functions that terms such as Hough's well-known 'institutional pluralism' – and even corporatism – are used to describe it.[39] On the other hand, there is the view of Brezhnev as the personalist politician *par excellence*, the efficient promoter of clients into key positions and the perpetrator of a cult of personality which if anything was more extreme, and pathetic, than Stalin's.

The evidence is that in the early years of his General Secretaryship Brezhnev ran a collegial Politburo. While materials would be circulated in advance, there would be genuine discussion at meetings. According to Roi Medvedev, Brezhnev would remain silent until the end of the discussion and usually then support the side of the argument which seemed to have majority support.[40] But as Brezhnev became less interested in a wide range of policy areas, including the economy, and increasingly incapable physically and mentally of playing a leadership role, the Politburo degenerated as a forum for collective decision making. While it continued to meet regularly and the procedural niceties were observed, increasingly there was little discussion as items went through on the nod.[41] This was, however, after an extensive process of consultation and signing-off, directly between Politburo members as well as officials. There was also increasing use made of ad hoc and eventually standing commissions of the Politburo to iron out differences of opinion.[42] Some claim that these phenomena of the logic of specialization were taken to the degree of an effective veto power among Politburo members. Leon Onikov claims:

> Under Brezhnev a 'right of veto' (the principle of consensus and unanimity) in practice arose in decision making in the Politburo and Central Committee Secretariat. ... Collegiality came to be understood by the Central Committee secretaries as a courtly gallantry, exaggerated courtesy and deference (*svetskaia kurtuaznost', galantnaia vzaimovezhlivost' i ustupchivost'*) in their relations with each other. If a matter was being considered, it was enough for one member of the Politburo or a single secretary of the CC to oppose the matter, for it to be put off (with the rare exception of when 'Number One' insisted).[43]

The consultation process would usually prevent controversial issues getting to the Politburo before differences had been ironed out, but not always. Cherniaev, in reporting a December 1978 Politburo discussion, provides a classic example of an issue which cut across institutional interests, military service. Kosygin, representing the civilian economy, wanted to keep young men who had received skilled training out of the army for as long as possible; Ustinov, the Minister of Defence, wanted them all immediately and without exception. Ustinov brought a proposal to the Politburo. It is not clear what form of sign-off it had gone through, but once it became clear at the meeting that there was an unresolved difference of opinion between the two, the matter was sent back to the Council of Ministers for further work.[44]

More often than not policy proposals that went through this process, if they made it to the decision stage at all, did so in a severely watered-down form. Cherniaev, in describing the very long consultation process involved in arriving at a draft new Constitution, notes – before the process was even nearly completed – that 'looking at it overall, anything new has already been thrown out of the draft'.[45] He also describes how Brezhnev's very frank description of the state of the economy in the draft of his December 1979 Central Committee plenum report that was presented to the Politburo was eventually delivered in greatly watered-down form.[46]

There were efforts to cheat, although as reported by Cherniaev these were usually made by staffers, with at best the very reluctant support of their political superiors, who would try to remain committed to the rules of behaviour described above by Onikov. They usually took the form of trying to shortcircuit the sign-off process by getting Brezhnev's intervention. This required getting through his gatekeepers, either to get him to express an opinion before a document was circulated or to present an alternative view to the Politburo when the signed-off proposal was presented.[47]

It was the unchallenged capacity of Brezhnev to get any policy outcome he wanted, right to the very end of his time in power, that led Cherniaev to claim that he had introduced into the Soviet system a degree of personal power that had not existed earlier.[48] But it was a personal power that he was increasingly unable or unwilling to apply. So while on the one hand he had the total power to shortcircuit the logic of specialization, he rarely chose to do so. In those circumstances the logic ran riot and the resulting stagnation in policy-making arguably led to the collapse of the Soviet system.[49]

This is a picture which fits the logic of specialization well. Beyond issues directly related to his political security or a particular personal interest in foreign policy, the political leader, despite the vast personal power that he had, was disinclined to use it to control the logic of specialization. This was partly for personality reasons. His many detractors write of a lazy individual with limited intellectual capacity, who was more interested in the trappings of power than its substantive use. It was probably also a conscious and 'rational' reaction to reduce the personal element in policy-making after the excesses of Khrushchev. Ultimately physical and mental incapacity played a major role. The result, in a system which had no strong checks on the logic of specialization other than the personalist element, was consultation taken to the dysfunctional extreme.

Gorbachev

Anyone who was in the Soviet Union in the first half of the 1980s, or who has read diaries and memoirs from the time, felt the palpable sense of impatient expectation as the Brezhnev generation faded away. Some time before he came to power in March 1985 the focus of those expectations was Mikhail Gorbachev. Foreign leaders flocked to meet him, insiders with hopes for the future were enthralled by the contrast he offered to those around him, many party officials regarded him with fatalistic apprehension.

In the circumstances it is hardly surprising that Gorbachev was a leader with little time for the logic of specialization. For him it meant the endless circulation of paper and the opportunity for unreconstructed bureaucrats to frustrate change. From very early on it was clear he was going to do things differently. That was enough to make him an attractive figure to many insiders and outsiders. It is fascinating to read Cherniaev's admiration for Gorbachev's approach to meeting procedures as Central Committee secretary and heir apparent, when we know that it was precisely that approach which was going to irritate and disillusion his supporters, including Cherniaev, once the going got tough. Cherniaev writes with clear delight in 1984 of Gorbachev's performance as Central Committee secretary at a Politburo meeting on agricultural policy:

> The smallest imprecision, or sign of incompetence, the smallest attempt to be tricky (*slukavit'*) – there's an immediate response from him, and the speaker is left looking very stupid. It's particularly hard for them because he can't stand ... when they read from prepared notes. ... He immediately begins asking questions, trying to get to the heart of the matter.[50]

With time those very forms of behaviour, which rather remind one of Khrushchev, came to be seen as a sign of his rudeness and disloyalty to colleagues and his excessive opinion of his own capabilities.[51]

He relied on small, informal groups of advisors and like-minded intellectuals, at the expense of the institutionalized organizations of specialized function. Boldin, who worked as a Gorbachev advisor, complains that Gorbachev spent so much time travelling, receiving visitors and giving speeches, that the very long-standing process of signing-off the texts of speeches by Politburo members in advance broke down, meaning that Politburo members were increasingly likely to find out about Gorbachev's new policy initiatives after the event from broadcasts and the press.[52] The genuine discussions at Politburo meetings that had so excited Cherniaev early on became interminable discussions in which agreement could not be reached. In 1989 Cherniaev referred to the Politburo as 'a place where Mikhail Sergeevich can speak frankly and at great length'.[53] In Boldin's frustrated words, 'If the question was prepared in advance, then it should be adopted, if not then it should be sent for further work', that is, controversial matters should be negotiated through the consultation process, not argued about in meetings.[54] Gorbachev's reaction to the problem was to more and more often cancel scheduled meetings, declare new policy without

Politburo approval,[55] and eventually set up new policy structures which bypassed the Politburo as the centre of decision-making power but which never gained any true authority of their own.

One could argue that Gorbachev respected the logic of specialization even less than either Stalin or Khrushchev. Stalin had been careful to consult privately with individuals with specialized knowledge, in order to get a sense of views within organizations but without giving those organizations direct representation; Khrushchev allowed the similar presentation of views in the public arena. No one can accuse Gorbachev of not allowing the public debate of major policy issues, or of failing to respond to public pressure on these issues. But this was not the sort of engagement with the logic of specialization that was needed for effective policy-making. At the bureaucratic level he relied entirely on his own personal approach, a personal approach which proved incapable of dealing with the policy challenges of perestroika. The inadequate recognition of the logic of specialization produced chaotic and no less voluntaristic policy-making than Khrushchev's.[56] And while he certainly unleashed the forces of public opinion, there was no solid structure for feeding that public opinion into the policy process in a way that different views could be negotiated and bargained to an effective but consensual outcome.

The author will leave it to others to debate whether Gorbachev was responsible for the collapse of the Soviet Union, or whether the die was already cast and his valiant efforts to save it were never likely to succeed. It should be clear from all that has gone before in this chapter that the author believes that along with all its other inadequacies the Soviet system, well before Gorbachev, had fundamental flaws in its policy process, in its incapacity to deal adequately with the logic of specialization. Lenin tried in vain to implement a routinized process of consultation. Although the structures were created for the representation of specialized functions, they were unable to foster an efficient policy process. As soon as specialized agencies showed any sign, in the mid-1930s, of realizing the potentialities of the consultation process, Stalin brutally established his personal domination of the policy process, relying on direct and informal briefings with informed individuals. Khrushchev continued the highly personal approach, albeit with the addition of a small degree of public debate, also involving informed individuals. Both Stalin and Khrushchev demonstrated the risks of the leader's personal dominance of the policy process at the expense of routinized consultation in the form of voluntaristic 'hare-brained' schemes and policy stagnation following the physical and mental decline of the leader. Brezhnev can be interpreted in contrasting ways, but it is the author's view that his rule shows what happens in a non-democratic system when the political leader fails to exercise personal control. In many key policy areas Brezhnev failed to do so – through lack of inclination and intellectual and ultimately physical capacity – and as a result the logic of specialization ran riot. Gorbachev reverted to a radical personal approach, and again demonstrated how difficult it is to arrive at a balanced policy process within that framework.

It will be noted that no evidence has been presented here of political leaders using the second form of the personalist approach to controlling the logic of specialization, the use of patron-client networks. Did leaders use loyal clients situated across the range of specialized agencies to bring about a policy position that suited them as it progressed through the bureaucratic process, that is, did they in a sense use clients to replace consultation? This is a matter which requires further investigation, but the author has not found much evidence of patron-client networks being used by political leaders to further the policy-making process. Certainly they would place client figures at the head of major agencies. Once major bureaucratic agencies had routine representation in the Politburo they had to, in order to ensure that for reasons of their political security they had a majority in that body. But when Stalin put loyalists at the head of bureaucratic agencies in the early 1930s, he was disappointed at the rapidity with which they were captured by those agencies. This did not mean that those clients were fundamentally disloyal, in the sense that they would not provide Stalin with unconditional political support. It did not even necessarily mean that they would not work to implement policy once it was decided. But Stalin felt that he could not be confident that those clients would not frustrate efforts to adopt policies that he thought appropriate. We know the tragic outcome of that lack of confidence.

During the same period, as described by Easter, regional leaders were using, or trying to use, personalist links with their patrons in Moscow to influence agricultural policy-making.[57] Not only was this a bottom-up rather than top-down use of the network to influence policy-making, but it was also something which one suspects they resorted to because they lacked institutional representation. Easter claims that they were keen to routinize their access to rule-making power and to be formally included in the agricultural decision-making process.[58] They certainly would have used institutional representation if they had had it.

The author is open to the idea that evidence of the patron-client form of personalist management of the policy-making process is there to be found. But so far, to the extent of the author's knowledge, patron-client networks were used primarily to facilitate a leader's rise to power and to maintain his dominant position, as well as to assist in the policy implementation process, that is, to help, and thereby protect, members of the network as they went about the business of running their little piece of the Soviet Union.

Yeltsin

I will leave it to others to decide whether the capacity of post-Soviet Russia to deal with the logic of specialization was path-dependent – essentially, doomed from the beginning because of historical precedent – or whether it developed sui generis. Certainly it can be argued that Yeltsin was very similar to Gorbachev in his approach to policy matters. He used teams of like-minded reformers from outside the established policy-making structures, working in the government dachas on the outskirts of Moscow to write the major shock therapy documents.[59] Beyond the major programmatic documents, the most important determinant of policy influence was access to Yeltsin. Being part of a consultation process was a poor second. While it appears that Yeltsin imposed his own views on the policy process far less than Gorbachev, nevertheless it was a highly personalist approach, with little respect for the logic of specialization. It could be argued that it was a highly effective process, in that radical, indeed revolutionary, policy change was rapidly conceived, formulated, accepted by the political leader, and implemented. Nevertheless, it was never likely to be a sustainable process,[60] even if the system had not suffered the inevitable fate of a personalist regime, the physical and mental deterioration of the leader.

Despite Yeltsin's highly personalist approach, the logic of specialization began to assert itself during his presidency. Previously autonomous reformers moved into institutional positions, and so gained an incentive to take institutionalized consultation procedures more seriously. The president's decrees, although having the force of law, were usually enforceable only with enabling normative acts, often legislative, that required a formalized deliberative process. Parliament, having a constitutional right to be involved in policy-making as well as an oppositional role, developed quite an effective committee and parliamentary hearing system.[61] Particularly as Yeltsin's personal popularity and physical and mental capacities declined, these structures, which by their nature were more recognisant of the logic of specialization, played an ever greater role. In doing so they presented both an opportunity and a challenge to the new president, Vladimir Putin.

Putin

Putin's presidency presents a mixed picture. Some policy issues were dealt with quickly, even briskly; others dragged on for years. There are also two characterizations of Putin's policy-making persona: the common one of a strong leader imposing his personality on the policy process, and one revealed through a closer examination of a range of policy issues of Putin either maintaining his distance or being ineffective when he intervened in a heavily bureaucratized process. The strong personality and brisk policy-making were most likely to occur when Putin's personal power was directly affected – personnel appointments, constitutional arrangements, etc. It was in the actual running of society, including the economy, where the mixed, and perhaps negative, picture became stronger.

Putin came to power stressing stability after the chaos of Yeltsin, as had Brezhnev when he replaced Khrushchev. Part of that stability was a regularized and therefore depersonalized policy process. We see, for example, that as president Putin virtually ceased using his right to issue decrees, something that Yeltsin had done on a grand and controversial scale.[62] Up until at least 2003, he was probably not in a position to fully assert himself. He had to recognize the role of institutionalized agencies, and even some that existed outside the government apparatus. Big business had a major influence on the policy process, and in a more institutionalized way than had been the case under Yeltsin, when personal access was the primary instrument. Having famously 'equidistanced' himself from the oligarchs, Putin was nevertheless prepared to meet them in an official way, and looked on as they used other institutional policy channels to advance their causes, particularly the Duma and its committees. Big business was effective at driving a vigorous policy process in areas that interested it, particularly taxation. At times, for example his major tax reforms of 2001, business involvement met with Putin's approval. On other occasions he was far from approving, the notorious 'Yukos amendment' on oil export duties, that was pushed through the Duma by Vladimir Dubov, a Yukos shareholder and chair of the taxation subcommittee of the Duma's Budget Committee, being the prime example.[63]

Within the government itself the policy process included a strict process of consultation. A clear example of its negative effect on the policy process comes from early in the very drawn out process of rewriting the Law on Subsurface Resources. In 2003 the Ministry of Economic Development and Trade was the lead agency in the process, but was unable to get the Ministry of Natural Resources to sign off on its drafts of a new law. In those circumstances prime minister Kasianov was unwilling to allow the matter to come to cabinet.[64]

Putin dealt with the pretensions of business in spectacular fashion, with the imprisonment of Mikhail Khodorkovsky and many of his subordinates and the bankrupting of his company Yukos in 2003. But Putin still recognized the status of business as an organization with a specialized function and its right to be involved in a routinized way in business-related policy-making, including taxation. The reform of tax administration procedures after Yukos showed that business could be heavily involved in such a sensitive area of policy, along with specialized governmental, presidential and parliamentary agencies. Following a full array of consultative procedures a negotiated outcome that satisfied all participants was arrived at reasonably expeditiously.[65]

But other policy matters, including the subsurface resources legislation already mentioned, completely bogged down in the consultation process within the government apparatus, despite the regular intervention of Putin with demands of a quick resolution.[66] Interestingly this was a case in which business did not play a major role, seemingly because of a lack of consensus within the business community as to what would be a desirable outcome. It could be suggested that it was the absence of business from the debate that made it harder to push to an expeditious outcome.

Further consideration of why some policy issues were dealt with effectively and others not is required. As already mentioned, those directly related to Putin's personal power, for example the appointment of governors and electoral procedures, clearly fell in the category of those dealt with very expeditiously. Regarding those with less direct political implications for Putin personally, the evidence from the two mentioned here, tax administration and the Law on Subsurface Resources, suggests that the explanation lies in the nature of the issues and the attitudes to them of the specialized agencies – essentially how easy it was for them to come to agreement – rather than the role of the political leadership. In both these cases Putin intervened along the way. In one case the debate was resolved quickly; in the other it was not.[67]

As suggested at the beginning of this chapter, non-democratic leaders have no recourse to other than personalist involvement to control the logic of specialization. We have seen that Putin has been reluctant to impose his own personality strongly on the policy process. It has already been suggested that his reluctance was based on a need to present himself as an 'orderly' contrast to Yeltsin. He could well also have been driven by knowledge of the failures of the personalist approach in the Soviet period. It is also probable that he was reluctant to take sides in too committed a way in what had become a highly factionalized policy arena.[68] Policy arenas become factionalized when there is a weakening of institutionalized structures through the personalization of the regime. Factionalized politics can be dealt with in a tyrannical way, as Stalin did. Putin is unable or unwilling to adopt that approach, and the only other approaches are to play the factions off against each other by never taking too conclusively one side over the other. Maintaining an institutionalized core to the policy process also helps him maintain an aloofness from factionally sensitive policy disputes by allowing the matter to be fought out in a routinized way.

There have been negative consequences in terms of policy-making of the restraint in Putin's use of the personal element. But what of the second form of personalist politics, the use of patron-client networks to control policy-making? Putin has been a dedicated creator of a huge network of clients. Much of his effort has been clearly devoted to creating political security for himself, by ensuring that he has loyalists in those positions that are sensitive for the maintenance of his position in a whole range of possible circumstances. Others are rather too obviously a case of being 'loyal' to his clients, often no more than old friends, by giving them access to the perks of position. But has he placed clients in positions within organizations with specialized functions specifically to influence the policy process? There is no strong evidence of that in the policy cases with which the author is most familiar. However in two policy areas Putin does seem to have invested considerable hopes in loyalist appointments: the use of Dmitrii Kozak to deal with regional policy, including a stint dealing specifically with the problems of the Caucasus, and the placing of Serdiukov in the Ministry of Defence to pursue military reform. It could not be said at this stage that those have been examples of great policy success, but it requires further examination to determine how policy outcomes have been affected by Putin's use of loyalist appointments.

Certainly Putin has not fully relied on the patron-client approach to controlling the logic of specialization. Indeed he has devoted serious attention to the structural and procedural elements of the institution-alized policy process. By becoming prime minister he hoped to be in the institutional position to assert himself more directly and 'opera-tionally' in the cabinet room and government apparatus. He has also weakened formal sign-off procedures. Changes made in late 2008 allow those drafting normative acts to proceed to the registration of those acts as legally valid and enforceable if other parties involved in the sign-off process have not responded within a month.[69] The change was made explicitly to counter the deliberate misuse of sign-off procedures to obstruct the policy process. The procedures nevertheless leave the principle of sign-off fully intact and there is plenty of room for specialized agencies to use the logic of specialization to their advantage. Agencies still have the option of attaching a negative opinion within the month, and extensive and time-consuming appeal mechanisms remain.

The indications are that neither Putin – nor Medvedev, whether in a tandemocracy or not – are prepared to be strongly personalistic in their approach to policy-making. The tyranny option is probably not realistic. But Putin is also clearly not prepared to allow a genuine opposition, even if one were potentially capable of materializing. In those circumstances he – and any successor he might have – will continue to struggle, as his Soviet predecessors did, with the logic of specialization and therefore suffer from a less than effective policy process.

Conclusions

The historical survey has confirmed reasonably well the outline of the logic of specialization outlined at the beginning of this chapter. As non-democratic systems the Soviet Union and post-Soviet Russia have struggled to establish structures and procedures appropriate to the logic of specialization.[70] When serious deference was paid to the consultation processes that arise out of the logic of specialization – by Lenin, Brezhnev and to some extent Putin – the policy process has suffered from inefficiency and *vedomstvennost'*. That has encouraged a considerable reliance on personalist politics, above all the direct personal involvement of the leader. When mixed with a judicious use of informal consultation procedures, it has allowed for a reasonably assured policy process. However generally the personal approach has been a failure, resulting in Khrushchevian 'hare-brained schemes' and policy vacuums created by the physical and mental deterioration of the leader.

There has been less evidence of the use of patron-client networks for policy-making than might have been expected. Although it is a matter which requires further review of the historical evidence, patron-client relations seem to have been used more to ensure the leader's political security and for policy implementation than for policy-making.

Another finding not quite in keeping with the initial outline is the unexpected reluctance of specialized agencies to use consultation processes. Having gained representation in the collective decision-making body, they were often content to conduct their bargaining and negotiation there, at the expense of the policy effectiveness and even viability of the committee. There is some evidence that this was a feature primarily of the early period of Soviet history, so might be explained by organizational immaturity at the time.

The analysis has indicated the very strong role of the personalist element in Soviet and post-Soviet politics. It has also, however, confirmed the view of those, such as T.H. Rigby, who while acknowledging the persistence of the personalist element, have also noted the extremely powerful drive within the system for institutionalization. Rigby, characteristically given his relative lack of interest in policy issues, saw the source of that drive in the desire of political leaders to regulate their political relationships. He therefore focused heavily on patron-client relationships. The author of this chapter, with his greater focus on policy, sees the pressure for institutionalization as deriving from the demands of effective policy-making. That in turn has lead in this chapter to a greater focus on the personal role of the leader than patron-client networks. But albeit by different routes we arrive at the same conclusion. Ultimately the personal element derived from a lack of democratic control over the political process. As stated in the Introduction, Rigby regularly noted the implications for institutionalization of the lack of external constraints on leadership behaviour, and in a late publication suggested that the dilemma thereby contained could be solved only by democratization.[71] The analysis in this chapter also suggests that without a democratic opposition the policy process is unlikely to cope with the logic of specialization.

Notes

1 Graeme Gill (1992), 'From the USSR to the CIS: Plus ça change ...?', *Australian Slavonic and East European Studies*, VI, 2, 97–8.
2 See my response to the Gill article just quoted in Stephen Fortescue (1993), 'Institutions vs. personalities in the USSR and Russia: a response to Graeme Gill', *Australian Slavonic and East European Studies*, VII, 1, 1–12.
3 T.H. Rigby, 'The Soviet political executive, 1917–1986', in Archie Brown (ed.) (1989), *Political Leadership in the Soviet Union* (Basingstoke and London: Macmillan), p.6.
4 Gerald M. Easter (2000), *Reconstructing the State. Personal Networks and Elite Identity in Soviet Russia* (Cambridge: Cambridge University Press).
5 The process is not unlike Weingast's classic statement of the emergence of the rule of law, which 'is based on uncertain constellations of actors' resources and their intention to avoid the risk of a zero-sum game'. B. Weingast (1997), 'The political foundations of democracy and the rule of law', *American Political Science Review*, XCI, 2, 252–3.

6   As applied to the Soviet Union, see G.M. Anderson and P.J. Boettke (1997), 'Soviet venality. A rent-seeking model of the Soviet state', *Public Choice*, XCIII, 37–53.

7   Political leaders also use patronage networks, perhaps in their eyes more importantly than for control of the policy process, to ensure their own political security.

8   Stefan Breuer (1992), 'Soviet communism and Weberian sociology', *Journal of Historical Sociology*, V, 3, 282. Not everyone sees Lenin as a bureaucratic rationalizer. Easter, for example, has the opposite view. *Reconstructing the State*, pp.68–73. See also Graeme Gill, *The Origins of the Stalinist Political System* (Cambridge: Cambridge University Press), p.108.

9   T.H. Rigby (1979), *Lenin's Government. Sovnarkom 1917–1922* (Cambridge: Cambridge University Press).

10 Rigby, *Lenin's Government*, p.141.

11 Ibid., pp.34–5.

12 Ibid., pp.34–5, 69, 197.

13 Ibid., p.100.

14 As Rigby describes it, top leaders stopped attending Sovnarkom meetings and, if their proxies were unable to obtain the decision they wanted, they would appeal the matter to the Central Committee and Politburo. Rigby, 'Soviet political executive', p.13.

15 T.H. Rigby, 'The government in the Soviet political system', in Eugene Huskey (ed.) (1992), *Executive Power and Soviet Politics: The Rise and Decline of the Soviet State* (Armonk: Sharpe), pp.19–20.

16 O.V. Khlevniuk (1996), *Politbiuro. Mekhanizmy politicheskoi vlasti v 1930-e gody* (Moscow: ROSSPEN), p.79; Eugienia Belova and Paul Gregory (2002), 'Dictator, loyal, and opportunistic agents: the Soviet archives on creating the Soviet economic system', *Public Choice*, CCIII, 273.

17 F. Chuev (1992), *Tak govoril Kaganovich* (Moscow), p.61. Quoted in Belova and Gregory, 'Dictator', p.269.

18 Khlevniuk, *Politbiuro*, p.8.

19 Belova and Gregory see Gosplan and the Council of Ministers as playing the role of the 'loyal agents' of Stalin. Since they did not have direct responsibility for operational management of the economy, they were considered less likely to be driven by narrow departmental interests. Stalin did not, however, always take their side. '[Stalin's] puzzling siding with [economic managers] against [his] loyal agents is explained by the fact that [economic managers] could play effective games against loyal agents. They could cite conflicting rules; they could use their personal influence; and they could employ delaying tactics.' Belova and Gregory, 'Dictator', p.276. The first and third of those weapons are classic 'logic of specialization' phenomena.

20 Belova and Gregory, 'Dictator', pp.268–9.

21 Khlevniuk, *Politbiuro*, pp.95–6.

22 O.V. Khlevniuk, A.V. Kvashonkin, L.P. Koshelova and L.A. Rogovaia (eds) (1995), *Stalinskoe Politbiuro v 30-e gody* (Moscow: AIRO-XX), document 7.

23 Khlevniuk, *Politbiuro*, p.97.

24 Ibid., p.263; Belova and Gregory, 'Dictator', p.280.

25 Khlevniuk, *Politbiuro*, pp.118, 136. For an example of such a commission, see Paul R. Gregory, 'The dictator's orders', in Paul R. Gregory (ed.) (2001),

Behind the Façade of Stalin's Command Economy: Evidence from the Soviet State and Party Archives (Stanford: Hoover Institution Press), p.23.

26 As a non-policy indication of the strength of the bureaucratic agencies at the time, in spring 1934 the prosecutor's office guaranteed economic managers immunity from prosecution without permission of their agencies. O.V. Khlevniuk (1993), *Stalin i Ordzhonikidze. Konflikty v Politbiuro v 30-e gody* (Moscow: Izdatel'skii tsentr Rossiia molodaia), p.36.

27 E.A. Rees, 'Leaders and their institutions', in Gregory, *Behind the Façade*, p.43.

28 Joseph S. Berliner, 'The contribution of the Soviet archives', in Gregory, *Behind the Façade*, p.8.

29 Rees, 'Leaders', p.47; Gill, *Origins*, p.305.

30 William O. McCagg (1978), *Stalin Embattled, 1943–1948* (Detroit: Wayne State University); Werner G. Hahn (1982), *Postwar Soviet Politics: The Fall of Zhdanov and the Defeat of Moderation, 1946–53* (Ithaca and London: Cornell University Press).

31 T.H. Rigby, 'Stalinism and the mono-organisational society', in T.H. Rigby (1990), *The Changing Soviet System: Mono-organisational Socialism from its Origins to Gorbachev* (Aldershot: Edward Elgar), p.193.

32 Rigby, 'Government', pp.31–2.

33 A.B. Bezborodov (1997), *Vlast' i nauchno-tekhnicheskaia politika v SSSR serediny 50-kh – serediny 70-kh godov* (Moscow: Mosgorarkhiv), pp.47–8.

34 Bezborodov, *Vlast'*, pp.24–5.

35 Ibid., pp.46–7.

36 H. Gordon Skilling, 'Interest groups and communist politics', *World Politics*, XVIII, 3, 435–51.

37 Theodore H. Friedgut (1976), 'Interests and groups in Soviet policy-making: The MTS reforms', *Soviet Studies*, XXVIII, 4, 524–47.

38 Richard M. Mills (1970), 'The formation of the virgin lands policy', *Slavic Review*, XXIX, 1, 66–7.

39 Jerry F. Hough (1972), 'The Soviet system: Petrification or pluralism', *Problems of Communism*, XXI, 2, 25–45; Jerry F. Hough (1976), 'The Brezhnev era: The man and the system', *Problems of Communism*, XXV, 1–17; Valerie Bunce and John M. Echols III, 'Soviet politics in the Brezhnev era: "Pluralism" or "corporatism"', in Donald R. Kelley (ed.) (1980), *Soviet Politics in the Brezhnev Era* (New York: Praeger), pp.1–26.

40 Roi Medvedev (1991), *Lichnost' i epokha. Politicheskii portret L.I. Brezhneva* (Moscow: Novosti), vol.1, pp.311–12.

41 V.I. Boldin (1995), *Krushenie p'edestala. Shtrikhi k portretu M.S. Gorbacheva* (Moscow: Respublika), p.66; Bezborodov, *Vlast'*, p.64; Medvedev, *Lichnost' i epokha*, pp.282–3.

42 For some examples, see A. Cherniaev (2008), *Sovmestnyi iskhod. Dnevnik dvukh epokh, 1972–1991 goda* (Moscow: ROSSPEN), pp.352, 388–9, 417, 418, 494.

43 Leon Onikov (1996). *KPSS: anatomiia raspada* (Moscow: Respublika), pp.77–8.

44 Cherniaev, *Sovmestnyi iskhod*, p.348. For other examples of things going to the Politburo, apparently without prior circulation, see pp.347, 487–8. The decision to invade Afghanistan appears to have been made without Politburo discussion at all. p.386.

45 Cherniaev, *Sovmestnyi iskhod*, p.275.

46 Ibid., p.382. See also the fate of Brezhnev's report to the 26th Party Congress, as Politburo members 'smoothed it out, removed its sharpness, frankness, etc'. Cherniaev, *Sovmestnyi iskhod*, p.436. It should be noted that the initial frankness and sharpness in these documents were put there by Brezhnev's personal staff and their academic advisors.

47 Twice Cherniaev used the influential academic, Georgii Arbatov, to get a 'message' to Brezhnev. Cherniaev, *Sovmestnyi iskhod*, pp.12, 496. In the latter case Cherniaev's boss, Boris Ponomarev, was very unhappy about his assistant's 'policy activism'. See Arbatov's account on his role in Georgii Arbatov (2002), *Chelovek sistemy* (Moscow: Vagrius), p.138.

48 Cherniaev, *Sovmestnyi iskhod*, p.549.

49 For a small example of the effect on the policy process of the political leader in a system of personal power not using that power, see Chernaiev's frustration when Chernenko, as General Secretary, circulated a Cherniaev policy proposal without comment. Because Chernenko had not indicated support, Gromyko felt entirely at ease removing all of Cherniaev's initiatives. The implication is that if Chernenko had indicated, in even the smallest way, approval, Gromyko also would have approved. Cherniaev, *Sovmestnyi iskhod*, p.545.

50 Cherniaev, *Sovmestnyi iskhod*, p.571.

51 Ibid., pp.778, 813, 865.

52 Boldin, *Krushenie*, pp.145, 218.

53 Cherniaev, *Sovmestnyi iskhod*, p.803.

54 Boldin, *Krushenie*, p.213. See Cherniaev's characterization of a hapless meeting of Gorbachev's short-lived Security Council in 1991, at which the search for new foreign credits was discussed: 'The approach to discussing things at the SC is like the Politburo a year or so ago. Instead of having prepared calculations and proposals at hand and moving directly to making decisions, over six hours', the discussion dragged on fruitlessly. Cherniaev, *Sovmestnyi iskhod*, p.933.

55 Boldin, *Krushenie*, p.444.

56 A couple of direct comparisons of Gorbachev to Khrushchev appear in Cherniaev, *Sovmestnyi iskhod*, pp.798, 811.

57 Easter, *Reconstructing the State*, esp. pp.90, 132.

58 Ibid., pp.17, 132.

59 Writing teams settling down to work in these dachas was an old tradition, but Yeltin's teams were more isolated from institutionalized structures than the Soviet-era dacha teams. Indeed it could be argued that in the Soviet period the dachas were part of the consultation process; in the Yeltsin period they were an alternative. On the use of isolated 'change teams' working to bring about radical policy change, see John Waterbury, 'The heart of the matter? Public enterprise and the adjustment process', in Stephan Haggard and Robert R. Kaufman (eds) (1992), *The Politics of Economic Adjustment. International Constraints, Distributive Conflicts, and the State* (Princeton: Princeton University Press), p.191.

60 See Peter Evans on the need for autonomous policy reformers – 'change teams', and the like – once they have achieved the initial policy change, to consolidate it through the 'development of impersonal institutional roles and organisational goals'. Peter Evans, 'The state as problem and solution: predation, embedded autonomy, and structural change', in Haggard and Kaufman, *Politics of Economic Adjustment*, chapter 4.

61 Stephen Fortescue (1997), *Policy-Making for Russian Industry* (Basingstoke and London: Macmillan), p.123.
62 Haspel, Moshe, Thomas F. Remington, and Steven S. Smith (2006), 'Law-making and decree making in the Russian Federation: Time, space, and rules in Russian national policymaking', *Post-Soviet Affairs*, XXII, 3, 264–7.
63 Stephen Fortescue (2006), *Russia's Oil Barons and Metal Magnates. Oligarchs and the State in Transition* (Basingstoke: Palgrave), pp.119, 140.
64 Stephen Fortescue (2009), 'The Russian law on subsurface resources: A policy marathon', *Post-Soviet Affairs*, XXV, 2, 163.
65 Stephen Fortescue (2006), 'Business-state negotiations and the reform of tax procedures in post-Yukos Russia', *Law in Context*, XXIV, 2, 36–59. See the positive comments regarding the process from Aleksandr Shokhin, president of the big business association RSPP. 'Ot dobra dobra ne ishchut', *Vedomosti*, 17 August 2006, http://www.vedomosti.ru/newspaper/print.shtml? 2006/08/17/111154.
66 Fortescue, 'The Russian law'.
67 Although undoubtedly it was Putin's eventual support for the siloviki in the Law on Subsurface Resources debate and the subsequent involvement of his presidential administration that brought about a resolution of sorts.
68 S.P. Peregudov (2008), 'Konvergentsiia po-rossiiski: "zolotaia seredina" ili ostanovka na poluputi', *Polis*, 1, 98.
69 'Izmeneniia, kotorye vnosiatsia v Pravila podgotovki normativnykh pavovykh aktov federal'nykh organov ispolnitel'noi vlasti i ikh gosudarstvennoi registratsii, utverzhdennykh postanovleniem Pravitel'stva', 29 December 2008, No.1048.
70 A fair assessment of the democratic nature or otherwise of post-Soviet Russia at various stages of its development would require a far more nuanced statement than this. Opinions vary enormously, but it could be argued that particularly in Yeltsin's second term, as his relationship with parliament became more settled, the latter played a role something like that of an opposition in a democratic system. Putin's efforts to create a quasi-opposition role for the Duma and the United Russia party have been far from convincing.
71 Rigby, 'Soviet political executive', p.45.

3

The Boss and His Team: Stalin and the Inner Circle, 1925–33

Sheila Fitzpatrick

For many years, study of the Soviet political leadership usually took the form of Stalin biographies.[1] This was natural, both in view of the comparative paucity of sources and Stalin's unchallenged authority within the leadership from the end of the 1920s. It meant, however, that as far as the historiography was concerned, the Leader seemed to exist in a vacuum. There was a political 'system', usually described in mechanistic terms (the 'totalitarian model') with little reference to contingency or individual actors; and at the top of the system stood Stalin – a more or less human figure (thanks to the biographies) alone in an otherwise mechanical landscape. One of the many new ideas that T.H. Rigby introduced into the study of Soviet politics was that Stalin did not exist in a vacuum. He was a 'boss' with 'lieutenants', a gang leader, the most powerful of all political patrons, operating in a system in which, as Rigby disclosed, patronage was a key element and whose clients were themselves powerful men.[2]

This insight of Rigby's is the starting-point for my chapter, which focuses on Stalin and his team and the way they operated in the crucial transition period of the late 1920s and early 1930s. In the second half of the 1920s, Stalin's 'team' was in process of consolidation and primarily preoccupied with the struggle with the factions, especially the Right. In the early 1930s, the tasks changed radically. Having taken on an immensely ambitious transformational agenda, Stalin and his team had to develop structures to implement it and, at the same time, find out how to run a government.

Like Rigby and others, I use the term 'boss' as an equivalent of *khoziain*, the word Stalin's closest associates often used when speaking of Stalin to each other. It is not fully adequate to my argument, as I see Stalin functioning at this period not only as the team boss but also as

51

its *khoziain* in an economic sense: the man responsible for the running of a working household or an enterprise. However, no better word seems to exist in English. I use the term 'team'[3] for Stalin and his closest political associates – rather than possible alternatives like 'faction',[4] 'gang'[5] and 'inner circle'[6] – to emphasize that the group, like teams in competitive sports (or, in a more recent usage, corporate management), had its own esprit de corps and a shared agenda that its members worked together to implement. I see 'team' as, in most contexts, a better term for this group than 'gang' because the basic common purpose was not to engage in criminal activity (as with a gang) but to win political power and, having won it, to use it: that is, to implement a political programme and run a government.[7] I examine how the team was formed and the nature of the relationships between the members, including the degree of familiarity with each other; how Stalin maintained discipline within the team; and how it ran the country.

The main source base for this essay are the personal archives (*lichnye fondy*) of Stalin and a number of his associates that became available to scholars in the latter part of the 1990s, especially the correspondence files, parts of which have been published.[8] Two sets of correspondence are particularly valuable: the letters between Stalin and Molotov (the major source on the faction fights of the 1920s) and those between Stalin and Kaganovich (a key source for the first half of the 1930s).[9] The great bulk of these are business letters – but not without their personal touches[10] – written when Stalin was on vacation in the south, and Molotov and/or Kaganovich were running the shop for him in Moscow.

The making of the team

The Bolsheviks in the 1920s used the pejorative term *fraktsiia* (faction) for political groups within their party,[11] except for those groups that were currently dominant. In the 1923–4 struggle with Trotsky, Trotsky's opponents – Stalin prominent among them – called his group a *fraktsiia* and their own 'the Central Committee majority'. But that 'Central Committee majority' did not yet constitute a team, for it was a disparate group that included various blocs, alliances, potential leaders, and people who were simply independent or uncommitted. One starts to sense the emergence of a Stalin team a few years later, with Stalin and Molotov at its core and others like Klim Voroshilov and 'Sergo' Ordzhonikidze fairly closely allied, politically and personally. At this point, however, the team membership was still fairly fluid. It included future Rightists such as Nikolai Bukharin and (less definitely) Aleksei Rykov, the chairman of Sovnarkom,[12] and no strong party whip was imposed. 'Relatively free of constraints', Gorlizki and Khlevniuk write, 'members of the Politburo were allowed to migrate from one ad hoc alignment to another, depending on the issue on hand'.[13]

In this milieu of Old Bolsheviks, linked by long ties and the common fight against 'factions', we see a comradely, often friendly, atmosphere whose members – including Stalin – often addressed each other in the familiar form (*na ty*) even in official correspondence. This had not been the custom when Lenin lived, or rather, nobody appears to have addressed Lenin as *ty* in business correspondence, nor he them.[14] But in the 1920s Stalin was not a Lenin to most of his circle. Many of them wrote to him, as they did to each other, *na ty*, and continued to do so well into the 1930s. The notable exception was Lazar Kaganovich – a relatively junior member of the circle at first – who could not bring himself to use anything but *vy*, though Stalin asked him to. ('Did you ever call Lenin "thou"?' he protested).[15]

There were, of course, degrees of intimacy within the team: the familiar form was not obligatory. 'Sergo' (Ordzhonikidze) was one who seemed to attract intimacy. Almost everyone called him *ty*, and he often got an extra '*dorogoi*' or '*rodnoi*' in salutation from particularly close friends such as Kaganovich and Anastas Mikoian. Nikolai Bukharin was another with whom it was easy to be intimate. He himself continued to use *ty* when writing to Stalin even after the tone of Stalin's replies might have discouraged this.[16] At the other end of the spectrum of temperaments were Viacheslav Molotov and Valerian Kuibyshev, both of whom usually signed off with their full first names (if not their last name alone, which was one of the options within the group) and were relatively sparing in their use of the intimate form.

Molotov was *na ty* with Stalin and, like Voroshilov, he often addressed him as 'Dear Koba', using his conspiratorial pseudonym from the old days in the revolutionary underground in the Caucasus.[17] Mikoian and Enukidze, also *na ty* with Stalin, wrote to him as 'Dear Soso'.[18] In writing to Molotov, Stalin's usual forms of salutation was 'Dear Viacheslav', 'Hello, Viacheslav', or simply 'Molotov' or 'comrade Molotov', but there were jocular exceptions – 'Molotovich!' is how he started a letter in September 1926, and in December 1929, 'Molotshtein, greetings!'[19] Less, inclined to jokes, Molotov nevertheless once started a letter to Stalin with an affectionate greeting 'to big man (*kurbashkomu*) Koba'.[20]

The origins of the political alliance between Molotov and Stalin, and the reasons for its strength, are not altogether clear. In the inner-party struggles after Lenin's death, Molotov 'unambiguously and unwaveringly took Stalin's side' and 'for much of the 1920s remained his only unconditional supporter in the Politburo'.[21] However, as Montefiore puts it, 'Molotov admired Koba but did not worship him'.[22] For all his public solidarity – which led Trotsky to mock him as a mere bearer of Stalin's instructions in 1926[23] – Molotov was quite capable of disagreeing with Stalin in private, though he did it less often as time went on. They had two angry private exchanges on a theoretical question, the dictatorship of the proletariat, in 1924[24] and 1927.[25] In the latter exchange, Stalin accused Molotov of 'bombarding' him via third parties, a ploy that Stalin 'could not consider acceptable in the circle of intimates *(blizkikh liudei)*', though he added the conciliatory 'Was I mistaken in my suppositions? It's possible that I was mistaken'. (Crossed out in the handwritten draft is another sentence underlining his distress: 'I'll say more: I hope to God *[dai bog]* that I made a mistake').[26] Ignoring the olive branch, Molotov sent a short reply saying essentially that Stalin was being silly. But the storm blew over, and in a few months they were back on the old 'Dear Koba'/'Dear Viacheslav' terms.[27]

In addition to Molotov, Ordzhonikidze and Voroshilov must be counted as core members of the Stalin team in the late 1920s. Nevertheless, both of those two could disagree with Stalin in the Politburo without any suggestion, in Stalin and Molotov's private correspondence, that by doing so they were forming a 'bloc' (that is, an incipient faction) or were in any danger of being dropped from team membership. There were several internal Politburo disagreements on China policy in the summer of 1927. First, as Molotov reported to Stalin (on vacation in the south) there was a 'sharp argument' in the Politburo between Ordzhonikidze and Voroshilov, on the one side, arguing that the Politburo was making too many concessions to the Left, and Bukharin and Molotov on the other.[28] Stalin took this relatively well, commenting simply that Ordzhonikidze was 'a good lad' but 'a lousy *(lipovyi)* politician', while Voroshilov 'must have been simply "in a bad mood" *(ne v dukhe)*'. As for Rykov, who seemed inclined to support the Ordzhonikidze-Voroshilov position, he was 'playing politics *(kombiniruet)*', a comment that suggests that Stalin already had doubts about his reliability as a team member.[29]

A month later, Voroshilov, with Ian Rudzutak and Rykov supporting him, was still sharply critical of the party's China policy. Stalin's old friend and ally went so far as to make 'unfounded attacks' (as Molotov reported to Stalin) on 'your [evidently Stalin's] leadership for the past two years'.[30] This appeared to have no particular untoward consequences with regard to his team membership or relationship with Stalin. On a different but equally important issue around the same time, the question of expelling Trotsky from the party, much the same group voted against the proposal,[31] with Kalinin 'this time support[ing] us' (two weeks earlier, he had been opposed) and the proposal squeaking through by one vote.[32]

To be sure, Molotov was concerned about all these disagreements within the team, and suggested that Stalin might consider coming back early from vacation to get the troops back in line.[33] Stalin agreed to this, though saying he wasn't worried, for reasons he would explain in person on his return.[34] Perhaps Stalin had simply decided to play it cool, a not-uncharacteristic response when he sensed danger. Certainly he had been less cool a few weeks earlier, when he felt that on the same issue of Trotsky's expulsion Ordzhonikidze had let him down, when (either through his presence or absence) he had allowed Trotsky-Zinoviev supporters to turn a meeting of the Central Control Commission into an attack session, aimed particularly at Stalin, 'who [Stalin refers to himself in the third person] is not in Moscow and on whom, for that reason, everything can be blamed'. 'Where is Sergo?' Stalin asked indignantly. 'Where and why has he hidden himself? It's disgraceful'.[35]

Stalin could be tough on his team. Ordzhonikidze, the most wilful and independent, was a frequent target, though Molotov and Stalin often reminded each other to tread carefully because of his volatile temperament and easily injured vanity.[36] Mikoian also came in for repeated criticism from Stalin. He was a mere 'duckling in politics', according to Stalin in a private letter to Molotov in 1926.[37] Later, at the beginning of the 1930s, he had the misfortune to be in charge of supply at a time of chronic food shortages, thus incurring frequent criticism. One particularly vicious attack in 1931 deeply offended Mikoian, though Stalin later apologized, as he quite often had to do after losing patience with one of the team.[38] Stalin said worse things, of course, to and about political opponents, but for those he never apologized. Members of the team were in a special category.

The team ('our leading group') was 'consolidated historically in the struggle with all kinds of opportunism', Stalin wrote to Kaganovich in 1931.[39] The struggle with the Right in 1929–30 was particularly important in this respect. The 'Rightist' leaders – Rykov, Bukharin, and Mikhail Tomsky – had had much closer personal and political relations with Stalin's group than the Leftist leaders ever had. They had been effectively team members, and it is quite possible to imagine a situation in which some of them (with the exception, perhaps, of Rykov) stayed on the team while some others – perhaps Kalinin or Rudzutak – were dropped. There were quite a few 'friends inclined to panic', as Molotov wrote to Stalin in the late summer of 1928. The tone of Molotov's letter implies an expectation that some at least of these 'political weathervanes' (*maiatniki ot politiki*) would have to be dropped.[40]

The process of dropping the Rightists – or rather, those who failed to overcome their reservations about Stalin's go-for-broke policies – was an extended one. Stalin's famous *dozirovka* principle was involved: one cautious step at a time, until the victim found himself not only isolated but also complicit in the waves of criticism directed against him. In the private correspondence between Stalin and Molotov, it is evident that the two felt caution and secrecy were essential. ('Rykov and his gang must be driven out', Stalin wrote to Molotov in the autumn of 1929. '*But for the time being this is just between ourselves.*')[41] Whether their fear was primarily of protests within the party or of reactions in the country as a whole and of foreign observers is unclear. Surely, however, one of the reasons for caution was the likely reaction of the rest of the team, especially those who were personal friends of those under attack.

Disciplining the team

The team was important to Stalin. Although he was capable of dressing down its members and playing them off against each other, he nevertheless valued the team and did not want to see its team spirit eroded. When Ordzhonikidze had a particularly passionate disagreement in the Politburo with Molotov and Kuibyshev, Stalin strongly condemned his behaviour: it 'leads objectively to the erosion (*podtachivanie*) of our leading group... – creates the danger of destroying it. Does he really not understand that <u>on that path</u> he will get <u>no</u> support from our side. What stupidity!'[42]

At the same time, Stalin was a suspicious man – suspicious even of his own team (though particularly of those who were not at a given moment at the core of the inner circle). He kept tabs on them (via the police and the encouragement of informing, including within the inner circle), liked to keep them off balance, and sometimes set traps for them. He could practise 'conspiracy' – a concept and set of practices dear to the Bolsheviks[43] – not only with respect to the broader world but even with respect to the team. It was 'in the interest of conspiracy (*v vidakh konspiratsii*)' that, in 1930, he instructed his secretary Poskrebyshev to tell people he would not be back from vacation until the end of October, although in fact it was his intention to return several weeks earlier. This caused problems with his wife Nadezhda, who, on the basis of information from

Enukidze, thought she was the one who had been misled. Stalin had to write reassuringly to her explaining his conspiratorial strategy. 'I put about the rumor through Poskrebyshev. ... Avel [Enukidze] evidently fell victim to [it].' Some of the inner circle, however, had been trusted: 'Tatka [Stalin's pet name for Nadezhda], Molotov and, I think, Sergo know the date of my return.'[44]

As of the early 1930s some of Stalin's more devious and conspiratorial methods of disciplining the team (like arresting their wives, family members, and secretaries) still lay in the future. But it appears that he already sometimes blackmailed them – for example, in the case of Kalinin and Rudzutak, waverers at the time of the struggle with the 'Right'. It was perhaps because Stalin had documents from the Tsarist police archives showing that they had betrayed fellow revolutionaries that these two potential Rightists jumped back into line and stayed on the Stalin team.[45]

A more subtle technique for compromising leading political figures was to have them named as sympathizers or pawns in the interrogations of persons under arrest for counter-revolutionary crimes. In the period 1927–30, large numbers of non-Communist specialists, mainly engineers and economists, were arrested and some of them later appeared as defendants in well-publicized 'show trials' on apparently trumped-up charges of industrial sabotage. The Shakhty trial of 1928, in which Stalin evidently had some personal interest,[46] constituted an opening salvo against the Right, though as yet without the naming of names.[47] More interrogations were conducted in the first half of 1930, and from them the OGPU extracted a fascinating account of the specialists' old-boy networks, manipulation of their Communist bosses, and doubts about the radicalism of Stalin's new course, all of which Ordzhonikidze (then head of the Central Control Commission) used to good effect in his attack on Vesenkha at the 16th Party Congress in June–July 1930.[48] The interrogations may already have contained politically compromising material on leading political figures – as against simply reflecting on their competence in their jobs – but if so, Ordzhonikidze and the OGPU did not circulate it.[49]

Immediately after the 16th Party Congress, the significance of interrogation material changed: it became simultaneously a weapon for *politically* compromising and intimidating Communist leaders and a medium for sending a warning political message abroad. This seems to have been a direct result of Stalin's initiative. At some time in 1930 (unfortunately not precisely dated), after reading through some of the interrogation transcripts, he sent Menzhinsky of the OGPU a letter that can be read either as an encouraging response to a new line in interrogation or an instruction to Menzhinsky to pursue such a line. The important thing, he told Menzhinsky, was to get more information from the arrested specialists on the imperialist powers' plans for military intervention. 'Make the question of the intervention and the date of the intervention one of the most important key points of new (future) testimony', he instructed.[50]

In August, Stalin was instructing Molotov to circulate a number of particularly important 'confessions' (i.e. interrogation transcripts) 'to all members of the Central Committee and Central Control Commission, and also to the most active of our industrialists (*khoziaistvenniki*)'.[51] 'I don't doubt that a *direct* link will be uncovered (through Sokolnikov and Teodorovich) between these gentlemen and the Rightists (Bukharin, Rykov, Tomsky)'.[52]

Molotov correctly understood that the interrogations were to be used to smear the Right. But, wrongly assuming that the only intended targets were people already tarred as Rightists, he commented that the transcripts would need a bit of editing to protect those still on the team. He noted, for example, that one confession 'dirties ... the name of Kalina [i.e. Politburo member Mikhail Kalinin]', showing him among their candidates in a 'coalition government with Rightists Sokolnikov, Rykov etc.'[53] But Stalin quickly set him right: '*All* confessions without exception should be sent out to members of the Central Committee... That Kalinin has sinned (*greshen*) cannot be doubted. Everything that is said of Kalinin in the confessions is the naked truth. The Central Committee absolutely must be informed about all this...'[54]

The point of all this was evidently not to drop Kalinin from the team – like Kuibyshev, he stayed on it, although in a relatively marginalized position – but to intimidate him or, as Stalin put it, make sure 'that in future Kalinin won't get mixed up with scoundrels'. [55] That was a message not only to Kalinin, but to the team as a whole. It was perhaps also a message to Molotov, who had taken the notion of team loyalty a step too far. Staying on the team was not a given. Compromising material could always be found or, if necessary, manufactured.

Running the country

To enable the team to run the country effectively required first some careful allocation of team members to various posts, particularly to head Sovnarkom and Vesenkha. Until his death in 1924, Lenin was both the de facto leader of the Politburo (that is, the party) and the head of the Soviet government (that is, chairman of Sovnarkom). As

Rigby convincingly argued, Lenin thought the Sovnarkom side of the political equation mattered, assuming in effect that the state apparatus should be the main mechanism for governing the country.[56] Stalin saw things differently – or perhaps it was simply the logic of his political power base in the party that led him to the conclusion that the Politburo should be the key governing body. Even more than Lenin, he distrusted the non-party specialists in the state bureaucracy. He complained in 1925 that the Politburo was 'cut off from economic affairs... transformed from a leading organ to an appeals organ, something like a "council of elders"'. It was bad enough to have a state institution (Gosplan, the economic planning agency, in this case) making important decisions about economic policy. Still worse was the fact that it was probably not Gosplan's Communist leaders but its non-party specialists who in practice were making these decisions.[57]

The heads of Gosplan and Vesenkha, in effect the industrial ministry, were members of and answerable to Sovnarkom, which after Lenin's death was headed by Rykov. The position was much less important during Rykov's tenure than it had been under Lenin, but all the same Sovnarkom was a possible competitor for supreme authority with the Politburo. That knowledge was a factor in Stalin's dealings with Rykov. By the autumn of 1929, Stalin was angry at Rykov's failure to recant his 'Rightism' and seemed ready (in private, not yet in public) to write him off as a team member. A particular cause of annoyance was that, in Stalin's absence, Rykov, as Sovnarkom chairman, was still chairing Politburo meetings. 'Why do you allow this comedy?' Stalin wrote angrily to Molotov.[58]

Stalin's own handling of the Rykov affair had comic elements, as he allowed him to remain Sovnarkom chairman for another year, all the while eroding his authority and marginalizing him. But by autumn 1930 Stalin was ready for the decisive move of dislodging Rykov from Sovnarkom. 'Our top Soviet leadership in the centre (STO, Sovnarkom, the meeting of Sovnarkom's deputy chairmen) is sick with a fatal illness', he wrote to Molotov. 'STO has changed from being a businesslike and militant organ into an empty parliament. Sovnarkom is paralyzed by Rykov's insipid and essentially antiparty speeches'. The meeting of Sovnarkom deputy chairmen – a key body in the implementation of economic policy at the time – was becoming a kind of rightist factional headquarters '*opposing* itself to the Central Committee'. 'It's clear that this cannot go on ...'.[59]

If Rykov was to go, however, who should head Sovnarkom? To some members – probably a majority – of the Stalin team, it seemed obvious that Stalin should take over. 'What is needed at the present time is firm, unwavering leadership', Mikoian wrote to Stalin. 'A single (*edinoe*) leadership, the kind there was under Il'ich [Lenin]. That's why the best way out of the position is your candidacy for chairman'.[60] Voroshilov felt the same. 'It would be good to put you in Sovnarkom and take over – as you know how to do – the leadership of the whole building [of socialism]'. That's what Lenin did in the civil war; and even though the situation now is different, 'all the same Lenin would have sat in Sovnarkom and directed the party and the Comintern under present conditions, too'. And in any case, 'the leadership is in your hands anyway' – it's just that without coordination of command in Sovnarkom and the Politburo, everything is harder to organize.[61]

Stalin, rather surprisingly, had a different take on the matter. In his opinion, the man to take over Sovnarkom was Molotov. He broke the news to Molotov by letter from the south, saying that Molotov's appointment was 'necessary' so as to avoid 'a split between the soviet [i.e. Sovnarkom] and party leadership. With that combination [Molotov in Sovnarkom and Stalin in the Politburo] we will be able to have complete unity of soviet and party leaderships (*verkhushki*), which undoubtedly doubles our strength'.[62] This was certainly a strong statement of Stalin's trust in Molotov, but Molotov seemed a little nonplussed. He expressed uncertainty in his own ability to be anything but a 'weak, unprepared, non-authoritative' chairman 'in the eyes of the leading comrades' – in other words, he was not sure that he had the support of the team. Yet he did not firmly close the door. In the final analysis, 'it's the party, the Politburo, that rules Sovnarkom'.[63]

For Ordzhonikidze, the answer was obvious: 'Of course Molotov should be put in Rykov's place', he wrote to Stalin. As for the team not accepting him in the position, that's 'rubbish (*chepukha*). We will all support him...'.[64] It was, in fact, a good choice, not only because Molotov was an excellent organizer, a hard worker, and a details man, but because Stalin was impatient with administrative detail. The duumvirate lasted more than ten years, a very long time in politics. It is interesting, nevertheless, to reflect on the implications of Stalin's choice. Evidently he was not, at this point and with regard to this particular question, interested in assuming Lenin's mantle – or at least not sufficiently interested to overcome his disinclination to take the Sovnarkom job. As Molotov later recalled, Stalin thought a Russian should head the government;[65] he also seems to have felt that 'a *complete* fusion of party and soviet leadership' would send the wrong ('Revolution is over'?) message to the outside world.[66] These considerations, however, were not so powerful as to prevent him finally taking the Sovnarkom job in 1941, following a cooling of relations with Molotov.[67] The arrangement set up in 1930 both expressed Stalin's confidence in Molotov and allowed him to run the government the way he thought it ought to be run, that is, from the Politburo.

If Molotov's appointment to Sovnarkom was one of the keystones of the new political structure emerging at the beginning of the 1930s, Ordzhonikidze's appointment as head of Vesenkha in November 1930 was almost equally important.[68] Although Vesenkha was formally subordinate to Sovnarkom, in practice there could be no question of Ordzhonikidze, a top member of the team, being responsible to any body but the Politburo. Moreover, Vesenkha was the executive bureaucracy in charge of industry, at a time when crash industrialization was the top priority of Stalin and his government. One of the predictable consequences of the two appointments was that Molotov and Ordzhonikidze had many squabbles in the Politburo in the years that followed. More significantly, Ordzhonikidze's appointment, and the vigour with which he subsequently represented the interests of heavy industry in the Politburo, helped to turn the Politburo into a forum for competing institutional interests, each represented by a member of the Stalin team, with Stalin adjudicating the competition.

The political process changed radically with the defeat of the Right. In the 1920s, the real dynamics of Politburo politics was struggle between factions, despite the fact that factions in the party were formally outlawed. Issues were argued to a considerable extent on factional lines. If your faction lost, you were sooner or later kicked out of the Politburo. With the last of the factions gone, the Politburo needed a new modus operandi, and found one – once again, without anyone acknowledging what was happening – in the adjudicated competition of institutional interests.[69]

Within the Politburo, issues were now argued to a large extent in terms of institutional interest (the military, industry, agriculture, and so on). The big difference from the past was that, unlike disagreement based on factional alliances, disagreement based on institutional interest was seen as natural and tolerable, if not exactly fully legitimate.[70] If you lost an argument, so much the worse for the institution you headed – but it didn't mean being kicked out of the Politburo or dropped from the team.

A prerequisite for this way of functioning was that chief branches of government – industry, agriculture, railroads, the military, Moscow and Leningrad city governments – had to be headed by Politburo members,[71] and, conversely, that the majority of Politburo members should hold such positions. In the Politburo of the first half of the 1930s, Ordzhonikidze represented heavy industry (Vesenkha, later reorganized as Narkomtiazhprom), Mikoian food supply (Narkomsnab), Kuibyshev Gosplan, Rudzutak and then Andreev railroads (NKPS), Voroshilov the military, Kosior the Ukraine, and Kirov Leningrad. Kaganovich cycled through a series of key executive positions: heading the Ukraine, straightening out the railroads, running Moscow.[72] All of these – along with Iakov Iakovlev, head of agriculture (Narkomzem), who was not formally a Politburo member but regularly attended its meetings[73] – were core members of the Stalin team.

As head of Sovnarkom, itself a coordinating body, Molotov was to some extent outside this institutional representation pattern, although he defended his institution's prerogatives when they were usurped by a people's commissariat. Kalinin, as head of the Central Executive Committee (TsIK), the body that later became the Supreme Soviet of the USSR, was in a similar position to Molotov, but without the clout (either personal or institutional). The other Politburo member with no special interest to represent – except that of the Politburo, when its prerogatives were encroached upon by another institution! – was Stalin.

Being above the institutional interests, adjudicating their conflicts, and taking the broader view were central elements of Stalin's leadership in the Politburo. He was the team's *khoziain* – and in the early 1930s, this was a term to take literally, not only in its meaning as boss but as head of a working household or economic enterprise. If one reads Stalin's correspondence with Kaganovich and Molotov in this period, putting aside everything one knows about his political persona before 1930 (the virtuoso faction fighter) or after 1935 (the Great Purger), an unexpected image emerges. Stalin is above all the *khoziain*, with a tight hand on the purse strings and a sharp eye on team members who, because of their institutional affiliations, lack the big picture and just want to get more money and resources for the government agencies they head.

It was part of Stalin's special role not just to set the priorities but also to make sure that other team members remembered them. In the late 1920s and beginning of the 1930s, the top priority (judging by his letters to Molotov and Kaganovich) was exporting grain to pay for industrialization – and that meant that grain procurements must be pushed to the utmost. 'If we win with grain, we win in everything, both in the domestic arena and the arena of external politics';[74] 'We have to force the export of grain in every way. That's now the key. If we export grain, credits will follow';[75] 'If we don't export 130–150 million puds of grain in [the next] one and a half months, our valiuta position may then become simply desperate...'.[76] Particular government agencies, looking at the problem through their narrow institutional lens, were naturally going to get it wrong. For example, the foreign trade authority (Narkomtorg) wanted to wait for better international market conditions to export the grain, but this was missing part of the big picture: 'In order to wait, you have to have foreign currency reserves. And we don't have them. In order to wait, you need to have a secure position on the international grain market. And for a long time we have had no position there – we are only in the process of winning one... In a word, we must force the export of grain like crazy (*besheno*).'[77]

The other side of the foreign currency question was that imports should be kept down to the lowest possible level, despite the natural tendency of every enterprise and branch of industry to think it *must* have what it wanted, or the whole industrialization drive would fail. Trying to inculcate in Kaganovich (deputizing for him in Moscow) his own habit of keeping the big picture in mind and resisting pressure from special interests, he wrote: 'You have to remember that our foreign currency position is desperate. One mustn't forget that things are going to be still harder for us in the next two years as a result of the intensifying reduction of our export to Italy, Germany, England, America... Are you taking that perspective into account?'[78]

Stalin took it for granted that bureaucracies have institutional interests which their Politburo representatives will seek to further. But it was his job to stop them, as we can see from the stream of instructions to this effect that came up from the south in the early 1930s: 'You gave too much foreign currency to Vesenkha... If you behave like this, the greed of Vesenkha will have no end.'[79] 'You gave too much money to Narkomtiazh [People's Commissariat for Heavy Industry] for capital construction' – it just encourages them not to make proper use of their existing plants.[80] 'You gave too much money to Narkomtiazh for the 3rd quarter. You should have given them less. They are rolling (*zakhlebyvaetsia*) in money.'[81] Nor was it only industry that felt Stalin's razor. He wrote to Kaganovich to keep down the military budget for 1933. He warned that Voroshilov may say that Stalin had approved the current version. But now the position had changed. In particular, the plan for expansion of the army in the event of war was appallingly inflated.[82]

As was often Stalin's way, he saw his associates as more trusting, more easily deceived than himself. When Ordzhnonikidze tried to get an extra five million rubles of imports approved during Stalin's absence from Moscow, Stalin reproached Kaganovich for being taken for a ride:

'As best I understand, you and Rukhimovich were simply deceived.'[83] He frequently had to remind them to pay no attention to 'wailing and hysterics' from team members whose interests were affected.[84] 'You'll see, the people's commissariats will then [if their requests are refused] find [other] ways and possibilities of satisfying their needs ...'.[85]

The bureaucracies were always going to be asking for more, and more than they needed. Vesenkha wants to 'squeeze the state treasury' instead of making its own apparatus work better.[86] Narkomzem, the agricultural commissariat, was no better: the aim of local officials naturally 'is to squeeze out of the government *as much money as possible*', and the Narkomzem leadership is giving in to them.[87] Narkomsnab under Mikoian's leadership frequently came under harsh criticism: 'The bureaucratic self-esteem of Narkomsnab has no limits.'[88]

By far the most common offender in pushing institutional interest too far was Vesenkha/Narkomtiazhprom, the industrial ministry headed by Ordzhonikidze. This was in large part because it was the most powerful and well-funded institution in a period when rapid industrialization was the regime's primary goal. But it also undoubtedly had to do with Ordzhonikidze's personality. He was the team member who was most likely to insist on getting his own way and capable of throwing fits if he didn't. Molotov had a particular problem with Narkomtiazhprom because of its tendency to act as if it were totally independent of the formally superior institutions, Sovnarkom and STO, that Molotov headed. On one occasion he protested that Ordzhonikidze's institution was acting as 'a state within a state'.[89] When, in Stalin's absence, these conflicts led to open hostilities between Ordzhonikidze and Molotov in the Politburo, Stalin was indignant at Ordzhonikidze's 'hooliganism': who did he think he was, to override policy directives of Sovnarkom and the Central Committee? Equally, why couldn't Molotov and Kaganovich stop him?[90]

Given the frequency and severity of the conflicts involving Ordzhonikidze, and the fact that his death (almost certainly suicide) in 1937 followed a serious disagreement with Stalin, one might suggest that it was a liminal case – that while Stalin tolerated the practice of institutional representation, he did so only up to certain limits, and Ordzhonikidze came close to reaching them. This may be, but we should note that it was a particular type of personnel-related institutional representation that caused many of the rifts in the last years of Ordzhonikidze's life. When any of his industrial subordinates came under suspicion or were arrested by the NKVD, Ordzhonikidze's habit was to defend them passionately. (He defended his family in the same way, which soured his relations with Stalin in the final months of his life.)[91] This was regarded within the team as a non-Bolshevik trait, forgivable only in terms of Ordzhonikidze's 'Caucasian' character. For Stalin, defending suspects had always been ipso facto suspicious. It was one thing to represent an institutional interest in a fight over budget, but quite another to protect someone close to you against accusations of disloyalty.

Stalin found it natural that people would defend the interests of the institution or branch of the economy they led. Indeed, if they had not behaved in this way, he would have lost some of his edge as the team leader who was *above* special interests. He found it natural, also, that bureaucracies would give false information to protect themselves (though he considered it the duty of the Communists at their heads to sort this out before it reached the Politburo). It was part of the job description for bureaucrats to 'lie and play games (*khitriat*)' and to practise 'thin end of the wedge' tactics.[92] If you once gave in to their demands (as you sometimes had to), that became a precedent that they would then use 'as a means of *pressure*' on Moscow.[93] Stalin was proud of his skill at seeing through the stratagems of bureaucracies and local officials. He saw himself as a master decoder (particularly of written documents), able to see through the smokescreen to the real interest that was being prettified or concealed.

With regard to tempos and targets, Stalin was almost always a maximalist in these years. This has to be taken partly at face value – he thought maximum tempos and targets were the only way of achieving a quick economic breakthrough – but it was also partly an automatic response to the tendency of officials and even governmental leaders to let tempos and targets fall. Sometimes they did this out of ideological conviction, as with the Rightists, but more often because it was the line of least resistance – or would have been, but for Stalin's vigilance. When Stalin was told (by a lower official, or even by a member of his own team with an institutional interest) that something was impossible, his immediate response was to suspect the speaker of trying to protect his institution from too much exertion. He saw bureaucracies as naturally prone to entropy, falling back into inertia, retreating from radical policies into moderate 'opportunistic' ones if not constantly watched and prodded. To borrow from the Bolshevik lexicon during collectivization, it was not *peregib* (bending the stick too far) that was the constant danger in policy implementation but *nedogib* (not bending it far enough).[94] Confronted with one such *nedogib*, the suggestion that expropriated kulaks might be given the possibility of restoration of civil rights, Stalin sighed: 'I just knew that asses from the petty bourgeoisie (*meshchane*) and philistines (*obyvateli*) would have to creep into that mouse hole.'[95] In other words, you can push the officials and politicians into a radical policy like dekulakization, but after a while they always try to water it down.

This line of thinking made it natural for Stalin to take a tough rhetorical line on using force when he was addressing the rest of the team. This is not to suggest that the use of force was not congenial to him – the actions of his government make it clear that it was – but rather to point out that it fitted his conception of his role in the team, as the one whose task it was to push for the maximum against the 'line of least resistance' tendencies that were inherent in bureaucracies. Others might be squeamish; Stalin was above squeamishness. In writing to members of the team, he used stronger and more direct language about violence than the others. 'The whole group of wreckers in meat production should absolutely be shot, publishing it in the press.'[96] 'Kondrat'ev, Groman and another couple of scoundrels should definitely be shot.'[97] If hooligans on the railroads were a problem, put 'armed men on the lines and shoot hooligans on the spot'.[98]

Of course, Stalin also knew that, as a form of policy implementation, violence had its limits. He was capable of suddenly calling it off (as in the secret 1933 resolution against mass arrests in the countryside);[99] or in the comparatively rare cases where he had direct personal knowledge of a problem (making him for once not the adjudicator but the interested party), he could unexpectedly take the 'opportunistic' position. While vacationing in the south in 1931, for example, he either saw or was told of the disastrous consequences of excessive procurements for northern Georgia. He wrote to Kaganovich that the local bosses were pushing grain procurements to the maximum in a non-grain region, and asked how it was the local political leaders didn't see that 'Ukrainian' methods (that is, the maximalist ones suitable for a major grain-growing region) would not work there. 'They are arresting hundreds of people... But you don't get far just with arrests...'.[100]

Concluding reflections

In this chapter I have discussed 'Stalin and his team' at a particular point in time, the early 1930s. Later, the picture changed in many respects. Stalin's own concerns changed. By the middle of the 1930s, judging by his letters to Molotov and Kaganovich, he became less focused on industry and economics in general, and paid more attention to cultural and military questions and, particularly, foreign affairs. As the decade went on, he became a progressively more remote figure and relations with his associates became less intimate. A few of the old stalwarts still called him *ty*, but not so often 'Koba' or 'Soso', while newer members of the team like Andrei Zhdanov and Nikita Khrushchev never thought of using anything but the respectful *Vy* and 'comrade Stalin'.[101] Security concerns were increasingly to the fore in Stalin's correspondence, and the future security chief Nikolai Ezhov became one of the people Stalin regularly talked and wrote to. Ordzhonikidze was not the only team member to find colleagues endangered, and the fall in 1935 of Enukidze, a member of the inner circle socially if not exactly politically, was a worrying sign.[102] Then in 1937–8 came the bacchanalia of the Great Purges, when nobody, even those on the team, could feel themselves safe and team members found themselves powerless to save friends and family. This might well be taken to be the end of the 'team' story. But is it?

The question was first raised 30 years ago by T.H. Rigby, who cast doubt on the conventional wisdom that Stalin showed loyalty to no one and that his closest associates were in the greatest danger. It is well-known that even Politburo members were among the victims of the Great Purges. But, as Rigby demonstrates, the survival rate of the team Stalin consolidated at the beginning of the 1930s was significantly higher than that of Central Committee members as a whole, that is, of a broader political elite group. The core team membership not only survived the Purges, but kept their leadership positions. Voroshilov, Kalinin, Molotov, Andreev, Kaganovich and Mikoian, as well as Stalin, who were all elected to full membership of the Politburo at the Eighteenth Party Congress in 1939, were all still active Politburo members when the war ended.[103] There were casualties among more marginal members of the early 1930s team, as well as the Rightists.[104] In addition, even the survivors can scarcely be said to have come through unscathed, as virtually all – not excluding Stalin – lost family members and cherished assistants to the Purges. Nevertheless, Rigby concluded, it paid to be on Stalin's team. Not, he suggested, because of any tender feelings on Stalin's part, but because Stalin followed the logic of the Mafia boss: show the gang you can kill, but avoid 'so abusing that power as to drive [them] to collective desperation'. For a gang to function, members need to have 'reasonable expectations of [the boss's] continued favour and protection, or they may decide that the dangers of betraying him are less than the dangers of continued service'.[105]

We have shifted here to the terminology of 'gang' rather than 'team', which suggests that we need to consider whether 'team' remains a useful descriptor for the period after the Great Purges. It would be fully possible that, while team members survived, the old team spirit and habits did not. This might seem the more likely in that the old team members were now part of a larger group whose newer recruits were of a different generation, had never been on *ty* terms with Stalin, had not bonded in the struggles of Revolution and Civil War, and so on. The hypothesis that the team as an entity did not survive the Great Purges is plausible and may indeed be the correct one. Enough discrepancies remain, however, to suggest that the 'team' may – against the odds – have retained more than a residual existence.

In the postwar leadership patterns described by Gorlizki and Khlevniuk, there are hints of something like a team, namely a collective entity capable both of reaching consensus on policy matters and of generating some feeling of mutual solidarity among its members.[106] Strikingly, by the early 1950s this team no longer seems to include Stalin. Its consensus is not so much *against* the aging and ailing leader as *apart* from him. But it *does* include old team members Molotov and Mikoian, whom Stalin had recently accused of being British spies. By the last months of Stalin's life, the Bureau of the Presidium of the Central Committee was functioning as the equivalent of the Politburo in the 1930s, and Molotov and Mikoian had been excluded from its membership (though not from other offices), on Stalin's insistence.[107] But from the moment of Stalin's stroke in March 1953, the two of them are back at every meeting, joining the old team members Voroshilov and Kaganovich as well as 1930s recruits to the team Beria, Khrushchev and Malenkov.[108] It was this core group that immediately established a 'collective leadership' after Stalin's death. Could it be that the team not only survived Stalin, but knew how to function without him?

Notes

1   Among many biographies published before 1991, the most distinguished are Robert C. Tucker (1973), *Stalin as Revolutionary 1879–1929* (New York: Norton); Robert C. Tucker (1990), *Stalin in Power: The Revolution from Above, 1929–1941* (New York: Norton); Adam B. Ulam (1973), *Stalin. The Man and His Era* (New York: Viking Press). Tucker, in particular, set himself the task of understanding the man in terms of his background and psychological makeup.

2   T.H. Rigby (1986), 'Was Stalin a disloyal patron?', *Soviet Studies*, XXXVIII, 3, 311–24. See also Rigby's first path-breaking articles on patronage, 'Early provincial cliques and the rise of Stalin', *Soviet Studies*, XXXIII, 1, 1981, 3–28, and 'Political patronage in the USSR from Lenin to Brezhnev', *Politics*, XVIII, 1, 1983, 84–9.

3 Defined by the *Compact Oxford English Dictionary* as follows: '1. a group of players forming one side in a competitive game or sport. 2. two or more people working together. 3. two or more horses in harness together to pull a vehicle'.

4 *Fraktsiia*, usually translated as faction, was the Bolsheviks' own word to describe political groupings competing for power in the 1920s. It was used pejoratively against defeated or minority groups rather than as a self-identification of the winners. With the disappearance of factional politics at the end of the 1920s the term lost salience.

5 Rigby does not explicitly use the term 'gang', but his comparison of Stalin with a gangster boss implies it. Rigby, 'Was Stalin a disloyal patron?', p.322.

6 See the excellent article by Yoram Gorlizki and Oleg Khlevniuk, 'Stalin and his circle', in Ronald Grigor Suny (ed.) (2006), *The Cambridge History of Russia*, vol. III: *The Twentieth Century* (Cambridge: Cambridge University Press), pp.243–67.

7 I use 'government' not in the narrow sense of the activity of 'government' ('state', 'soviet') organs but in the broader sense of the exercise of legislative and executive power by all relevant institutions (party as well as state) – 'the system by which a state or community is governed', in the second of the *Compact Oxford Dictionary*'s definitions.

8 The publications are L. Kosheleva et al (comp.) (1995), *Pis'ma I. V. Stalina V.M. Molotovu 1925–1936 gg. Sbornik dokumentov* (Moscow: Rossiia molodaia); O.V. Khlevniuk et al (comp.) (2001), *Stalin i Kaganovich. Perepiska. 1931–1936* (Moscow: ROSSPEN); A.V. Kvashonkin et al (comp.) (1996), *Bol'shevistskoe rukovodstvo. Perepiska. 1912–1927* (Moscow: ROSSPEN); A.V. Kvashonkin et al (comp.) (1999), *Sovetskoe rukovodstvo. Perepiska 1928–1941* (Moscow: ROSSPEN). The first two are available in English as Lars T. Lih et al (eds) (1995), *Stalin's Letters to Molotov, 1925–1935* (New Haven: Yale University Press) and R.W. Davies (ed.) (2003), *The Stalin-Kaganovich Correspondence, 1931–1936* (New Haven: Yale University Press).

9 When archival documents have been published, I cite them from the publication. As Molotov's side of the correspondence was not included in *Pis'ma I. V. Stalin V.M. Molotovu*, I cite his letters (as well as other unpublished letters) according to their archival location in RGASPI (Rossiiskii gosudarstvennyi arkhiv sotsial'no-politicheskoi istorii – the former Central Party Archive).

10 'They [the letters] were personal, half official, when he was on leave and I replaced him [and] prepared the materials for the Politburo', Molotov told Feliks Chuev (1991), *Sto sorok besed s Molotovym. Iz dnevnika F. Chueva* (Moscow: Terra), p.277.

11 Factions had, of course, been officially outlawed at the beginning of the 1920s.

12 This is clearer in the case of Bukharin, who circa 1927 was sometimes the second addressee of Stalin's letters to Molotov, implying a leading troika. Still, Stalin used the familiar form (*ty*) writing to Rykov as well as Bukharin. See 'Dear Alesha' letter of Stalin to Rykov, 27 March 1926, RGASPI, f. 558, op. 11, d. 766, l. 96.

13 Gorlizki and Khlevniuk, 'Stalin and his circle', p.246.

14   See Iu.N. Amiantov et al (comp.) (1999), *V. I. Lenin. Neizvestnye dokumenty 1891–1922* (Moscow: ROSSPEN).

15   Quoted from Feliks Chuev (ed.) (1992), *Tak govoril Kaganovich* (Moscow), p.129, in Simon Sebag Montefiore (2005), *Stalin. The Court of the Red Tsar* (New York: Vintage Books), p.64.

16   See Bukharin's letter to Stalin of 2 March 1933 in Kvashonkin, *Sovetskoe rukovodstvo*, pp.200–1. Stalin used *ty* to Bukharin even after the latter's ouster, but less effusively. See letter of 14 October 1930 using *ty* but addressing Bukharin by name and patronymic. Kvashonkin, *Sovetskoe rukovodstvo*, p.146.

17   For Molotov, see his correspondence with Stalin in RGASPI, f. 558, op. 11, dd. 766–9; for Voroshilov, see Kvashonkin, *Sovetskoe rukovodstvo*, pp.180–1, 280–1. Koba was a legendary fighter against the Russians during the conquest of the Caucasus in the mid-nineteenth century. On Stalin's use of the nickname, see Tucker, *Stalin as Revolutionary*, pp.79–81, 132–3.

18   For Mikoian, see correspondence with Stalin in RGASPI, f. 558, op. 11, d. 765, ll. 48–9, 57–8, 68a. 'Soso', Stalin's nickname as a child, is a common Georgian diminutive for Iosif. Tucker, *Stalin as Revolutionary*, p.69.

19   Letters of 4 September 1926 and 5 December 1929, in Kosheleva, *Pis'ma*, pp.82, 169.

20   Molotov to Stalin, August 1923. RGASPI, f. 558, op. 11, d. 766, l. 15.

21   Quotations from O. V. Khlevniuk, 'Stalin i Molotov. Edinolichnaia diktatura i predposylki "oligarkhizatsii"', in G.Sh. Sagatelian et al (eds) (2000), *Stalin. Stalinizm. Sovetskoe obshchestvo: K 70-letiiu V. S. Lel'chuka* (Moscow: Institut Rossiiskoi istorii RAN), p.272, and Gorlizki and Khlevniuk, 'Stalin and his circle', pp.246–7.

22   Montefiore, *Stalin*, pp.39–40.

23   Molotov to Stalin, 28 May 1926, RGASPI, f. 558, op. 11, d. 766, l. 107, describing the Politburo incident where, out of the blue, and with Stalin out of town, Trotsky suddenly remarked: 'Molotov says he has been ordered (*emu prikazhut*)...' 'I called him a natural-born insinuator (*insinuatorom po prirode*)', Molotov reported.

24   See letter of Molotov to Stalin ('tol'ko lichno'), RGASPI, f. 558, op. 11, d. 766, ll. 26–7.

25   This consists of two letters from Stalin to Molotov, 9 and 17 April 1927, which are for some reason not included in Kosheleva, *Pis'ma*, but can be found in RGASPI, f. 558, op. 11, d. 767, ll. 17–18 and 22–9. Molotov's original letter, offering some theoretical thoughts on the dictatorship of the proletariat, is not in the file, but is referred to in a letter of 30 March 1927 (RGASPI, f. 558, op. 11, d. 767, l. 15); his curt response to Stalin's letters dated 25 April 1927 is in RGASPI, f. 558, op. 11, d. 767, ll. 31–2.

26   RGASPI, f. 558, op. 11, d. 767, l. 29.

27   See letter of Molotov to Stalin, 10 June 1927 (RGASPI, f. 558, op. 11, d. 767, l. 35) and letters of Stalin to Molotov, 23 and 24 June 1927, Kosheleva, *Pis'ma*, pp.102–3.

28   Molotov to Stalin, 10 June 1927, RGASPI, f. 558, op. 11, d. 767, ll. 35–9.

29   Stalin to Molotov, letter of 24 June 1927, in Kosheleva, *Pis'ma*, p. 103 and note. The protagonists are identified in Stalin's letter only as 'R', 'Or' and 'V', and an editorial note says that the editors have not been able to identify them. My identification is based on Molotov's letter, cited above.

30 Molotov to Stalin, 4 July 1927. RGASPI, f. 558, op. 11, d. 767, ll. 56–60. Molotov refers to the three by their first names – 'Al. [Aleksei Rykov] + Kl. [Klim Voroshilov] + Ian [Ian Rudzutak]'.

31 Molotov identifies them only as 'R + Ordzh + V' in his letter to Stalin of 21 June 1927. RGASPI, f. 558, op. 11, d. 767, ll. 45–8.

32 It is not entirely clear who voted with Molotov. Tomsky and Mikoian were absent, according to Molotov's letter of 21 June; Petrovsky and Chubar sent in absentee votes in support (though Chubar had earlier opposed: see Molotov's letter of 10 June). Bukharin, who is the joint recipient with Molotov of several letters from Stalin at this time, probably supported them on this issue. In the earlier discussion, reported by Molotov on 10 June (RGASPI, f. 558, op. 11, d. 767, ll. 35–9), those supporting expulsion were Kaganovich, Kotov, Kirov, Chudov – and, presumably, Molotov and Bukharin – to make up the total of seven.

33 Molotov to Stalin, 4 July 1927, RGASPI, f. 558, op. 11, d. 767, ll. 56–60.

34 Stalin to Molotov, 8 July 1927, Kosheleva, *Pis'ma*, p.109. (The letter was wrongly dated by Stalin as 8 July 1926.) It is not known what these reasons were. Private assurances of support? Damaging information that could be used to keep one or more of the waverers in line?

35 Stalin to Molotov, 23 June 1926, in Kosheleva, *Pis'ma*, p.102.

36 For example, Stalin to Molotov, 4 September [1926], in Kosheleva, *Pis'ma*, pp.82–4; Molotov to Stalin, 12 September 1926, RGASPI, f. 558, op. 11, d. 766, lll. 139–42.

37 Stalin to Molotov, 27 June 1926, in Kosheleva, *Pis'ma*, p.105.

38 Mikoian's response, dated 12 September 1931, is in RGASPI, f. 558, op. 11, d. 765, ll. 72–3. On the apology, see Montefiore, *Stalin*, p.62.

39 Stalin to Kaganovich, 17 August 1931, in Khlevniuk, *Stalin i Kaganovich*, p. 51.

40 Molotov to Stalin, 20 August 1928, RGASPI, f. 558, op. 11, d. 767, ll. 111–16.

41 Stalin to Molotov, undated (before 15 September 1929), in Kosheleva, *Pis'ma*, p.220.

42 Letter of Stalin to Kaganovich, 17 August 1931, in Khlevniuk, *Stalin i Kaganovich*, p.51.

43 See Sheila Fitzpatrick (2000), *Everyday Stalinism* (New York: Oxford University Press), pp.22–3.

44 Letter to Allilueva, 24 September 1930, in Iu.G. Murin (comp.) (1993) *Iosif Stalin v ob"iatiiakh sem'i. Iz lichnogo arkhiva* (Moscow: Rodina), p.33.

45 Gorlizki and Khevniuk, 'Stalin and his circle', p.248. The compromising documents were discovered in December 1928 and March 1929.

46 He seems to have been responsible for bringing a locally-generated case from the North Caucasus to Moscow and national prominence. See Stephen G. Wheatcroft (2007), 'Agency and terror: Evdokimov and mass killing in Stalin's great terror', *Australian Journal of Politics and History*, LIII, 1, 30. For the local story, see S.A. Kislitsyn (1993), *Shakhtinskoe delo: Nachalo stalinskoi repressii protiv nauchno-tekhnicheskoi intelligentsia v SSSR* (Rostov on Don: 'Logos').

47 See Sheila Fitzpatrick, 'Cultural revolution as class war', in Sheila Fitzpatrick (1992), *The Cultural Front* (Ithaca, NY: Cornell University Press), pp.119–22.

48   See Sheila Fitzpatrick (1985), 'Ordzhonikidze's takeover of Vesenkha: A case study in Soviet bureaucratic politics', *Soviet Studies*, XXXVII, 2, 160–2, and Fitzpatrick, *Cultural Front*, pp.162–5.

49   Within a few months, Ordzhonikidze replaced Kuibyshev as head of Vesenkha. Kuibyshev, although embarrassed, nevertheless remained on the Stalin team (becoming head of Gosplan); and even his two Vesenkha deputies who were directly named in the interrogations (V.I. Mezhlauk and I.V. Kosior) kept their Central Committee memberships and continued in senior industrial management positions.

50   Undated letter from Stalin to Menzhinskii, published in Diane P. Koenker and Ronald D. Bachman (eds) (1997), *Revelations from the Russian Archives. Documents in English Translation* (Washington: Library of Congress), p.243. This advice was heeded. See the sentencing of the accused in the Prompartiia trial, December 1930, quoted in Kosheleva, *Pis'ma* (editorial introduction), pp.186–8.

51   Stalin to Molotov, 2 August 1930, in Kosheleva, *Pis'ma*, p.192. This was done, as proposed by Stalin, by order of the Politburo on 10 August and 6 September 1930. O.V. Khlevniuk (1996), *Politbiuro. Mekhanizmy politicheskoi vlasti v 1930-e gody* (Moscow: ROSSPEN), p.35.

52   Stalin to Molotov, no later than 6 August 1930, in Kosheleva, *Pis'ma*, p.194.

53   Molotov to Stalin, letter of 11 August 1930. RGASPI, f. 558, op. 11, d. 769, ll. 5–11. See also Molotov to Stalin, 30 August 1930, RGASPI, f. 558, op. 11, d. 769, ll. 22–5.

54   Stalin to Molotov, 30 August 1930, in Kosheleva, *Pis'ma*, p.198. See also Stalin to Molotov, 2 September 1930, in Kosheleva, *Pis'ma*, p.211.

55   Stalin to Molotov, 30 August 1930, in Kosheleva, *Pis'ma*, p.198.

56   T.H. Rigby (1979), *Lenin's Government: Sovnarkom 1917–1922* (Cambridge: Cambridge University Press).

57   Stalin to Molotov, [July 1925], in Kosheleva, *Pis'ma*, p.36.

58   Stalin to Molotov, 30 September 1929, in Kosheleva, *Pis'ma*, p.166.

59   Stalin to Molotov, 13 September 1930, in Kosheleva, *Pis'ma*, p.217.

60   Mikoian to Stalin, undated [September 1930]. RGASPI, 558/11/765, l. 68a.

61   Voroshilov to Stalin, 8 October 1930, in Kvashonkin, *Sovetskoe rukovodstvo*, pp.144–5. Voroshilov said that his opinion was shared by Mikoian, Molotov, Kaganovich 'and partly (*otchasti*)' Kuibyshev.

62   Letter of Stalin to Molotov, 22 September 1930, in Kosheleva, *Pis'ma*, pp.222–3.

63   Molotov to Stalin, 9 October 1930, RGASPI, 558/11/769, ll. 55–62. Molotov long after the event remembered his reaction: 'Before I started to head Sovnarkom, I wrote to him... "better if it were you"', elaborating that he had told Stalin: 'If I suit, if people find that I suit, let it be so, but it would be better if you were in that position. That's what is expected, that's how it was under Lenin. Lenin was in fact the leader of the party and the chairman of Sovnarkom.' Chuev, *Sto sorok besed s Molotovym*, p.276.

64   Ordzhonikidze to Stalin [October 1930], quoted in Khlevniuk, 'Stalin i Molotov', p.275.

65   Chuev, *Sto sorok besed*, p.276.

66 Molotov to Stalin, 9 October 1930, RGASPI, 558/11/769, ll. 55–62. Apparently this was an argument against his assuming the Sovnarkom chairmanship that Stalin had used in earlier discussions.

67 Stalin held the job from 1941 to 1946. However, the correctness of his original judgement that this was not the job for him is indicated by the fact that he almost never attended its meetings. Robert Service (2004), *Stalin: A Biography* (London: Macmillan), p.526; Yoram Gorlizki and Oleg Khlevniuk (2004), *Cold Peace: Stalin and the Soviet Ruling Circle, 1945–1953* (Oxford: Oxford University Press), p.263. On the cooling of Stalin's attitude to Molotov at the beginning of the 1940s, see Gorlizki and Khlevniuk, 'Stalin and his circle', p.235.

68 The story that follows draws extensively on my article 'Ordzhonikidze's Takeover of Vesenkha'.

69 On bureaucratic interest in Soviet politics, see Fitzpatrick, 'Ordzhonikidze's Takeover of Vesenkha', especially pp.165–7; Khlevniuk, *Politbiuro*, pp.89–98.

70 *Vedomstvennost'*, the closest Russian equivalent of institutional interest, was always a pejorative word in Soviet political discourse, and Stalin often criticized people for it, while implicitly accepting it as part of the normal practice of politics.

71 This was, of course, not wholly new. Kuibyshev, Ordzhonikidze's predecessor at the head of Vesenkha, was a Politburo member too. But it was a marked divergence from the pattern of Lenin's time, when only a few heads of people's commissariats were Politburo members, and only a few Politburo members headed state bureaucracies.

72 Khlevniuk, *Politbiuro*, p.79; O.V. Khlevniuk et al (comp.) (1995), *Stalinskoe Politbiuro v 30-e gody. Sbornik dokumentov* (Moscow: AIRO-XX), p.93.

73 Khlevniuk, *Politbiuro*, p.45; Khlevniuk, *Stalinskoe Politbiuro*, pp.188–230 (attendance at Politburo meetings, 1930–33). Apart from Iakovlev, all those named were full members of the Politburo with the exception of Mikoian and (until 1934) Andrei Andreev, who were candidate members.

74 Stalin to Molotov, 29 August 1929, in Kosheleva, *Pis'ma*, p.156.

75 Stalin to Molotov, [not earlier than 6 August 1930], in Kosheleva, *Pis'ma*, p.194.

76 Stalin to Molotov [not before 23 August 1930], in Kosheleva, *Pis'ma*, p.198.

77 Stalin to Molotov, 24 August 1930, in Kosheleva, *Pis'ma*, p.204.

78 Stalin and Molotov to Kaganovich, Rudzutak and Ordzhonikidze [6 September 1931], in Khlevniuk, *Stalin i Kaganovich*, p.88.

79 Stalin to Kaganovich, 21 August 1931, in Khlevniuk, *Stalin i Kaganovich*, p.57.

80 Stalin to Kaganovich, 24 June 1932, in Khlevniuk, *Stalin i Kaganovich*, p.190.

81 Stalin to Kaganovich [after June 21 1932), in Khlevniuk, *Stalin i Kaganovich*, p.186.

82 Stalin to Kaganovich and Molotov [not later than 15 July 1932], in Khlevniuk, *Stalin i Kaganovich*, p.224.

83 Stalin to Kaganovich, 4 September 1931, in Khlevniuk, *Stalin i Kaganovich*, p.80.

84 Stalin to Kaganovich, 21 August 1931, and 14 September 1931, in Khlevniuk, *Stalin i Kaganovich*, pp.57, 104.

85   Stalin to Kaganovich, 21 August 1931, in Khlevniuk, *Stalin i Kaganovich*, p.57.
86   Stalin to Kaganovich, 30 August 1931, in Khlevniuk, *Stalin i Kaganovich*, p.72.
87   Stalin to Kaganovich, 17 June 1932, in Khlevniuk, *Stalin i Kaganovich*, p.232.
88   Stalin to Kaganovich, 19 August 1931, in Khlevniuk, *Stalin i Kaganovich*, p.52.
89   Molotov to Stalin, 21 September 1931, RGASPI f. 558, op. 11, d. 769, ll. 68–71. Stalin supported Molotov on this issue. See Stalin to Molotov, 24 September 1931, in Kosheleva, *Pis'ma*, p.238.
90   Stalin to Molotov, 1 September 1933, in Kosheleva, *Pis'ma*, p. 247 and note 2. For another example of Vesenkha's disregard for formal subordination annoying Stalin, see Stalin to Kaganovich and Molotov, 9 October 1933, in Khlevniuk, *Stalin i Kaganovich*, p.379.
91   On Ordzhonikidze's defence of his subordinates, see O.V. Khlevniuk (1993), *Stalin i Ordzhonikidze. Konflikty v Politbiuro v 30-e gody* (Moscow: Rossiia molodaia), pp.37–8 and passim; on his brother's arrest, see pp.76–82.
92   Stalin to Kaganovich, 26 August 1931, in Khlevniuk, *Stalin i Ordzhonikidze*, p.68.
93   Stalin to Kaganovich, Zhdanov, Molotov, Kuibyshev, 13 September 1934, in Khlevniuk, *Stalin i Ordzhonikidze*, p.479.
94   This, of course, runs directly counter to the argument Stalin put forward in his 'Dizzy with Success' article in 1930, which accused lower-level officials of exceeding their mandate in collectivization. But it was not uncharacteristic of Stalin to make a brazenly public untrue statement, and in this particular case it is fairly clear that the maximalism was pushed from the centre rather than being spontaneously locally generated.
95   Stalin to Kaganovich, 30 August [1931], in Khlevniuk, *Stalin i Kaganovich*, p.72.
96   Stalin to Molotov [not earlier than 6 August 1930], in Kosheleva, *Pis'ma*, p.194.
97   Stalin to Molotov [not later than 6 August 1930], in Kosheleva, *Pis'ma*, p.194.
98   Stalin to Kaganovich, 4 August 1932, in Kosheleva, *Pis'ma*, p.260.
99   Sheila Fitzpatrick (1994), *Stalin's Peasants* (New York: Oxford University Press), pp.78–9.
100 Stalin to Kaganovich [17 August 1931], in Khlevniuk, *Stalin i Kaganovich*, p.51.
101 Voroshilov and Molotov were still *na ty* with Stalin (in Molotov's case, this ended with their blow-up in December 1945): see RGASPI, f. 558, op. 11, d. 99. ll. 120, 127, 167). Mikoian had switched to *vy* by 1934 (RGASPI, f. 558, op. 11, d. 765, ll. 48–9, 57–8, 68a). Molotov dropped 'Koba' as a form of address, though in 1936 Voroshilov was still using it. See Kvashonkin, *Sovetskoe rukovodstvo*, pp.332–3.
102 On the Enukidze affair, see Montefiore, *Stalin*, pp.172–4, 242–3. Although an old friend of Stalin and other team members, Enukidze's job as secretary of the Central Executive Committee was relatively minor. He was known mainly as a distributor of favors, which made the accusations of corruption believable. When in 1936, however, the charges escalated to

oppositionism and treason, for which there was no evidence or plaus-
ibility within the team, others must have felt threatened as well.

103 Politburo membership in 1939 from Khlevniuk, *Stalinskoe Politbiuro*,
     p.934; 1945–6 membership from Khlevniuk et al (comp.) (2002), *Politbiuro
     TsK VK(b) i sovet ministrov SSSR 1945–1953* (Moscow: ROSSPEN), pp.421–4.
104 S.V. Kosior, Chubar, Eikhe, Rudzutak and Postyshev were the former Polit-
     buro full and candidate members who perished, along with Rightists Buk-
     harin, Rykov, Tomskii, and Uglanov. In addition, three members of the early
     1930s had died by the time the Purges hit their stride – Kirov in 1934,
     Kuibyshev in 1935, and Ordzhonikidze at the beginning of 1937.
105 Rigby, 'Was Stalin a Disloyal Patron?', p.322.
106 Gorlizki and Khlevniuk, *Cold Peace*, esp. pp.6, 17, 93–5, 101–8, 119–20.
     Gorlizki and Khlevniuk use the term 'ruling circle' where I use 'team'.
107 Gorlizki and Khlevniuk, *Cold Peace*, pp.150–1.
108 See attendance records in Khlevniuk, *Politbiuro TsK VKP(b)*, pp.432–7.

4

Building the Communist Future: Legitimation and the Soviet City

Graeme Gill

One of the enduring questions of political science has been that of legitimation, of what gives a regime authority, or the right to rule in the eyes of its subjects. Most discussions of this question begin from Max Weber and his three ideal types – traditional, legal-rational and charismatic[1] – but they often go beyond this typology and generate other categories of legitimation; procedural, electoral, nationalist, theocratic, and social eudaemonic are some of the modes of legitimation that scholars have at times identified when discussing communist systems.[2] This question was particularly sharp during the life of the communist states because these regimes claimed a broadly-based popular legitimacy which did not sit easily with the overwhelming and largely unlimited power that they seemed to exercise. The meaninglessness of Soviet elections in terms of the fact that they were not mechanisms for holding governments accountable seemed to call into question the whole notion of popular legitimation.

T.H. Rigby made a major contribution to this debate. Rigby introduced the notion of goal-rational legitimation.[3] This tied the acquisition of authority to the achievement, or at least the making of progress towards the achievement, of the regime's teleological goal, communism. With the achievement of the communist society being the regime's overriding goal, all actions which were directed to that end (which by definition was all of the regime's actions) were legitimate and added substance to overall regime legitimacy. The building of communism, and progress towards it, was the key. The goal-rational legitimation identified by Rigby was thus a central component of the regime's broader legitimation programme and, unlike other components of that programme, was explicitly linked with the central core of the regime's declared aim, the building of a communist society.

However it is important to recognize that goal-rationality was only one aspect of the broader regime legitimation programme. During the 1930s this aspect of the programme was particularly prominent – the claimed achievement of socialism embodied in the adoption of the new Constitution in 1936 was central here – but other principles of legitimation were also reflected in different aspects of Soviet life: charismatic in the cult of the leader, legal-rational in the new Constitution, procedural and electoral in the heightened focus on elections and democracy, and nationalist in the growing profile given to Russia and the Russians in the regime's imagery. There was also evidence of an appeal to social eudaemonic legitimation through the emphasis on increased production of consumer goods and of an improved life under socialism. It is not clear that these principles of legitimation can sit easily together; for example, the legal-rational and charismatic are basically in conflict.[4] There may also be tension between goal-rational and social eudaemonic legitimation, in the sense that the former emphasizes the achievement of a transcendent, usually longer-term goal, while the latter focuses on the provision of goods and services to the population, which is usually a short- to medium-term aim.[5] Over time, the importance of the different principles of legitimation in the programme will change, and this will be reflected in various aspects of the regime's activity. This chapter will show how one particular aspect of the regime's legitimation programme, the relationship of goal-rational to social eudaemonic principles, is reflected in the regime's policies of urban development in Moscow.

A central aspect of the programme of building communism, which was the transcendental goal, was the reshaping of the urban infrastructure of the country, especially Moscow, the 'socialist capital of the proletarian state' since its move from Petrograd in 1918.[6] Given that socialism was to be achieved in Russia, albeit prior to the announcement of its achievement in 1936 only with the help of the advanced proletariat of the West, to the Bolsheviks it was only natural that Moscow should be transformed from a centre of tsarist power and a product of 'barbarous Russian capitalism' into an advanced socialist city.[7] Throughout the life of the regime, Moscow was transformed, in large part through direct, planned changes implemented by the regime. The changing nature of the regime's programme of urban reconstruction over time not only helps to explain the way the city changed, but it also reflects the shifting shape of the regime's legitimation programme.

Early measures

The initial attempt to change the face of the city was constituted by Lenin's programme of 'monumental propaganda'. He outlined this in a letter to Lunacharsky, saying, 'You remember Campanella in his City of the Sun speaks of frescoes on the walls of his fantastic socialist city, frescoes that were to serve as graphic lessons in natural history, science....I think that this is by no means naïve and with certain modifications could be assimilated by us and realised right now...I would name what I have in mind monumental propaganda.'[8] A Sovnarkom decree of 12 April 1918 called for monuments in honour of the tsar to be pulled down and for a series of statues to be put up honouring the forerunners of the socialist revolution.[9] The programme of erecting statues to revolutionary forebears was implemented fitfully and the results were hardly encouraging. The first was unveiled in October 1918, but by the time the programme was called to a halt in 1922 it was widely seen to be a failure. Of the 25 statues that had been erected, some were so poorly made as to be unrecognizable and most were made of materials that could not withstand the Russian winter and began to deteriorate as soon as they were erected. Most statues were soon consigned to the scrap heap.[10] Rather more permanent was the removal of tsarist symbols and monuments. Tsarist regalia were prised off many of the buildings in Moscow, but this remained a patchy process. For example, the tsarist double-headed eagle was not removed from the peaks of the Kremlin towers until 1935. Major statues, including those of Alexander II in the Kremlin, Alexander III near Christ the Saviour Cathedral, and the hero of the Russo-Turkish War of 1877 General Skobelev near the Moscow Soviet, were removed, with many of them being placed in museums. This not only removed some of the tsarist sheen from the city, but their placement in museums depoliticized them and neutralized their symbolic power by transforming them into objects of curiosity. Many monuments which were not removed were hidden by red drapes or by scaffolding, especially on the regime's festive days,[11] when those parts of the city that were to witness public celebrations were also decorated with murals, frescoes, posters and appeals. At this time too, there was some changing of names of streets and squares to remove their associations with the old regime and give them a revolutionary provenance. In 1919 the first instances of places in Moscow being named after living people, in this case Lenin, occurred.[12]

An attempt was made to create a symbolic centre for the city in 1924, following Lenin's death. From 1917 the so-called 'martyrs of the revolution' were buried beneath the Kremlin wall on Red Square. This was inaugurated by a special ceremony on 10 November 1917 and marked 12 months later by erection of a bas-relief on the Kremlin wall.[13] This necropolis of revolutionary martyrs was clearly meant to be a site that evoked not just revolutionary commitment but a real sense of the sacred. This was increased following Lenin's death with the decision to inter his body in a mausoleum on this site, which transformed the site from a hallowed revolutionary graveyard into a monument to Soviet power. A temporary makeshift wooden mausoleum designed by Aleksei Shchusev was erected to take Lenin's body when he died, but this was replaced by a grander structure, again designed by Shchusev, in spring 1924. However this too was considered unsatisfactory and was replaced in 1930 by a more permanent structure made of granite, porphyry and labradorite. While more bulky than its predecessor, it did not physically dominate the Red Square space. But it did constitute the symbolic heart of both the city and the regime.[14] Its role as the symbolic centre of regime celebrations and commemorations was facilitated in 1930–31 by the removal from Red Square of the streetcar tracks, the laying of cobblestones that could carry heavy vehicles, the erection of viewing stands on each side of the Mausoleum, and the movement of the Minin/Pozharsky statue closer to St Basil's so it would not hinder mass marchers crossing the square.

During the early 1920s, there was discussion of the need for an iconic building that would represent the new regime and its ideals to the world. In the words of Sergei Kirov in December 1922 what was needed was:

> the construction of a fitting monument within which the representatives of labour could meet...This building should be a symbol of the growing might and triumph of communism not only among ourselves but also over there, in the West...We have wiped from the surface of the earth the palaces of the bankers, landowners, and tsars...Let us build in their place the palace of the workers and the labouring peasants, let us bring together everything in which the Soviet lands are rich, let us invest all our worker-peasant creativity in this monument and show our friends and enemies that we 'semi-Asiatics', we at whom the world continues to look down its nose, are capable of embellishing this wretched earth with monuments

such as our enemies could never imagine, even in their wildest dreams.[15]

Kirov argued for the building of a 'workers' palace' as this iconic building, but pressures for such an icon seemed to dissipate somewhat with the construction of Lenin's mausoleum. Nevertheless there remained within leading party ranks the feeling that a landmark building with high symbolic importance should be constructed. This sentiment culminated in the decision to build the so-called Palace of Soviets. The symbolic significance of this building was emphasized by the decision, reportedly taken by Stalin,[16] to locate the building on the site currently occupied by the Cathedral of Christ the Saviour, which had been completed in 1880 to mark the victory over Napoleon and effectively functioned as the national church in Moscow.

Design of the building went through a complicated public competition, the results of which were closely monitored by the Soviet leadership.[17] The final design was a building which, surmounted by a 100 metre tall figure of Lenin,[18] was to have a total height of 416 metres (by comparison the Empire State Building in New York is 448.7 metres). Had it been built, it would have dominated the skyline of Moscow. Its internal decoration was to be a celebration of Soviet successes and achievements.[19] It was to be the centrepiece of the redesign of Moscow and a striking symbol of the new communist world. The Cathedral of Christ the Saviour was demolished in 1931 and construction work began in 1937. Work was suspended – as it turned out permanently – in 1941,[20] in part because of the war but also because of problems with the site. The water table was too high to provide a solid foundation for such a tall building.[21]

Throughout the 1920s, despite the building of the Mausoleum and discussion about an iconic building, there was no system or coherence to the Bolsheviks' approach to the development of Moscow. Calls for the preservation of some monuments and masterpieces of the past[22] were accompanied by the widespread closure and destruction of church buildings, including major monasteries in the city.[23] For example, the Sretenskii (July 1928), Chudov (December 1929) and Simonov (early 1930) monasteries were destroyed, while the Strastnoi convent became an anti-clerical museum (it was destroyed in 1937), the Rozhdestvensky convent a museum of chemistry, and the Danilov monastery an orphans' detention centre.

At this time there was considerable debate within architectural circles about both the appropriate forms of building to reflect the new post-revolutionary conditions and the form a socialist Moscow should take. Lenin had spoken of a 'socialist city' that would be radically different from the capitalist city, but neither he nor any other leading political figure was explicit about how these types of city would differ. In the 1920s debate broke out among architects over precisely this issue. Two main general assumptions seem to have underpinned the debate. First, the gap between city and countryside should be eliminated, so that no longer would standards of living and the conditions of work and leisure be radically different in these two areas. Second, the city should be designed to serve the interests of the workers in such a way as to ensure the easy provision of services and access to employment. Various schools of thought developed over how best to achieve these goals. One important debate was between the so-called 'urbanists' and the 'de-urbanists'. The former sought the concentration of people, industry and facilities in urban conurbations, while the latter favoured a much more decentralised approach with the population being scattered and travelling to smaller urban centres to work via a highly developed transport and communications network. The most radical even favoured the complete physical destruction of Moscow as an urban centre.[24] The de-urbanists were a small minority.

Another major debate was between the formerly dominant neo-classical school of architecture which drew its inspiration from the classical and renaissance worlds, and the constructivists who were inspired by the machine age. They often combined plain flat surfaces with cylinders to evoke the imagery of the machine, and believed that a building's function should be reflected in its design. Although a number of buildings were constructed along these lines, including the Zuev Club (1927–29), Rusakov Club (1927–29), Burevestnik Factory Club (1927–29), Narkomfin apartment house (1928–30) and Narkomzem building (1928–33),[25] constructivist influence disappeared with the cultural crackdown of the early 1930s.

Regardless of these debates all sides saw the socialist city as a means of bringing about change in the mentality, values and patterns of action of its inhabitants. The city, seen as a 'social condenser' by the constructivists, was therefore part of the process of bringing about cultural change that was central to the party's message. This view of the city is reflected in the efforts architects invested in the attempt to design a new style of living space which provided for real collective common facilities – common food preparation and eating areas, common dining rooms, laundries, bathing facilities and recreation areas. This was motivated by the desire to free women from the drudgery of housework and thereby liberate them into the workforce. But such plans were not popular with many of the people who would have to live in these sorts of structures. During the 1920s a variety of planning proposals were advanced, many influenced by the garden city concept which had emerged in the West and which envisaged significant decentralization, but none of these proposals was formally taken up and implemented.[26] Only at the beginning of the 1930s was there a seeming decisive shift in the direction of town planning, something stimulated by the opportunities for this created by the construction of new towns around the industrial centres springing up as a result of the first five year plan.

A shift to planning

At the June 1931 Central Committee plenum, the Moscow city party secretary Lazar Kaganovich called for the socialist reconstruction of Moscow. Kaganovich emphasized that, unlike bourgeois cities, socialist cities must provide the best possible services and conditions for the working people.[27] All the cities in the USSR needed to be reconstructed 'materially and technically' so that they corresponded with 'the new conditions and needs of life, with the new demands of the period of socialism, with the demands of the culturally and politically mature workers and toilers'. Moscow was to be 'a laboratory to which people from all over the Soviet Union will flock to study the experience of construction'. Kaganovich emphasized the importance of housing for worker families as well as the provision of communal facilities, like dining rooms, nurseries and kindergartens, and laundries. Also needing attention were energy and water supplies (he foreshadowed the construction of the Moscow–Volga and Volga–Don canals), drainage, road infrastructure and transport, including the construction of the Metro. He also noted the importance of town planning in designing the future of Moscow, including the construction of no new large factories in the city after 1932.[28]

Kaganovich's speech and the Central Committee resolution based on it set the broad framework for the development of Moscow in the foreseeable future.[29] Three aspects of this are significant. First, this vision of the socialist reconstruction of the city gave no hint of monumentalism or of transforming the city into one dominated by prestige projects. It was a conception of socialism that was rooted in the material needs of the working people and a recognition of the strains that Moscow was currently experiencing as a result of the significant population shift into the city consequent upon industrialization and the first five year plan.[30] Second, while arguing that the city should serve the needs of the socialist era, Kaganovich acknowledged that this was a transitional period and that this needed to be reflected in urban development. Thus while new housing stock should encourage a more communal lifestyle, individual kitchens should not be eliminated until there were sufficient communal facilities in the form of public restaurants, dining halls, kitchens and laundries to satisfy demand.[31] Third, by reaffirming the importance of the urban environment, Kaganovich intervened decisively in the 'urbanist'-'de-urbanist' struggle in favour of the former. The party's position thus linked socialism, the meeting of the workers' needs, and the city in a single conception, that it was now up to the planners to realise in Moscow. That there should be heightened interest in Moscow's future at this time should not be a surprise. The commitment to the creation of a new world through the socialist transformation embodied in the five year plan naturally spawned a desire to plan how that was to be worked out in the capital.

Following the Central Committee decision, planners and architects devised a variety of plans for Moscow's future,[32] but none was taken up by the Soviet leadership. But at the same time a series of major projects were begun which had a significant impact on the city. The Moscow–Volga Canal, announced in Kaganovich's speech and opened in July 1937, was a major engineering undertaking. The canal was 126 kilometers in length and an average of 40 metres wide and five deep, and included 17 weirs and dams, 13 pumping and power stations, 11 locks, seven reservoirs and 192 other capital installations.[33] It linked Moscow to the Volga, and thereby to the Baltic, White and Caspian seas, increased the water flow in the Moscow River (thereby making navigation easier), and increased the city's water supply. It was a major prestige project, and was widely presented as emblematic of the socialist society that was being built in the Soviet Union.

But the most important of these projects was the construction of the Metro. The ground was broken on this project in March 1932, with the first line to serve the centre of the city running from Sokolniki to Gorky Park via Komsomol'skaia Square, Okhotnyi Riad and the site of the Palace of Soviets.[34] Construction of the Metro was, despite some problems, said in 1934 to be proceeding faster than similar work had been accomplished in Berlin, Rome, Prague, Tokyo, New York and London,[35] and was directly associated with such other prestige projects as Dneprostroi, Magnitostroi, Belomorstroi, and the Moscow–Volga Canal.[36] At the opening of the first line in May 1935, Kaganovich declared explicitly: 'Our metro is a symbol standing for the new socialist society.'[37] Furthermore, he said, it shows how socialism is about caring for the needs of the working people and is not, as some have claimed, a 'barracks' style of life; the Metro was built not for profit but to serve the people. The symbolic association of the Metro with socialism was also evident in the decoration of many of the stations. While a classical architectural style was common in the stations, there was also a strong reflection in their statuary and frescoes of some of the main themes of the Soviet narrative. For example, Komsomol'skaia depicted four socialist archetypes – soldier, sailor, worker and kolkhoznik – while later stations like Kievskaia and Ploshchad' Revoliutsii gave great prominence to, in the former station, the bountiful nature of Soviet agriculture, and in the latter, stereotypes of a wide variety of types of Soviet citizens. As well as soldiers, sailors, workers and kolkhozniks, there were inventors, scientists, athletes, border guards, students, and even the nuclear family.[38] But at least as important as the decoration in the symbolism of the Metro was its dimensions and the effect this had on the Moscow populace. Entry into the vestibule of many stations transported people from the streetscape with which they were familiar into a new world characterized by grandeur, space and technology. Vestibules often had high ceilings, elaborate lighting and were dominated by the long escalators which transported people into the depths of the earth. Once they reached the platforms, the island design whereby passengers going in both directions were served by the same platform created large vaulted areas that were well suited to portray the grandeur of Soviet civilisation. Rather than functional railway stations, many Metro stations were more like elaborate palaces of culture designed to service the working person, and this was how they appeared to many of those people who now lived in Moscow, especially those who were recently arrived from the country. The Metro appeared to be a genuine symbol of Soviet socialism and its raison d'etre, serving the working people and transporting them into a new world.

A General Plan for the Development of Moscow was finally adopted in July 1935.[39] It promised 'high quality buildings for the workers, so that the construction of the capital of the USSR and the architectural form of the capital fully expressed the greatness and beauty of the socialist epoch'.[40] The decision confirmed that the planned development of the city would rest on the existing historical forms (so there would be no razing of the city as some, like Le Corbusier, advocated), it would combine the best forms of classical and new architecture with more recent achievements of technology, and it would bring the different parts of the city together into a 'genuine socialist city'. The plan included proposals for greenbelts, canal construction, street-widening and housing, but the main feature of the plan was the reconstruction of the central part of the city. This involved the demolition of large numbers of buildings in Kitai Gorod, Zariad'e and the sweep from Dzerzhinsky Square to the site of the Palace of Soviets,[41] the construction of wide boulevards and significant buildings of a governmental, public or scientific character, the doubling of the size of Red Square and the construction of a gigantic building for the Ministry of Heavy Industry along one side of it in place of GUM, and the 'architectural reworking' of leading squares in the region. Not all of the plan was implemented, but significant aspects were. Much destruction of buildings noted above was carried out,[42] the widening of many major thoroughfares did take place, and a number of significant buildings were completed. Particularly important and noteworthy was the straightening and widening of Tverskaia, or as it was renamed Gorky Street, a development which involved both the destruction of some buildings and the moving of some fifty others back from their original street line to a new position.[43] The result was a broad thoroughfare fronted by grand apartment buildings with retail premises in the base of many of them, a model of the new Soviet socialist society.

While following the adoption of the plan much housing was built and services, especially in terms of transport, were improved, it is difficult to escape the conclusion that the chief result of the plan was the reworking of the centre of the city. Here the juxtaposition of the wide boulevards and the grand and imposing buildings created a real sense of monumentalism and grandeur that was a vivid expression of a confident and dynamic socialism. But it was a landscape of socialism that was populated overwhelmingly not by the working people in whose name the redesign of the city was justified, but by officials who worked for the government or party. The new apartments to be found along Gorky Street and in the sideroads off it and the new offices to be found in the buildings for state ministries were generally occupied not by factory workers but by the emergent politico-administrative elite that was developing to staff the burgeoning apparatus of Soviet rule. While the monumentalism of central Moscow may not have matched that envisaged by Speer for central Berlin or Haussman for central Paris, it was still significant and was widely seen as emblematic of a civilization on the rise; the creativity and idealism of the socialist project seemed to be embodied in the monumental dimensions of the central city scape.[44]

The monumentalism evident in late-1930s central Moscow coincided with the claimed achievement of socialism, thereby almost embodying the regime's teleological goal. The urban redevelopment reflected a mature and confident socialist state, recasting its physical environment in line with its grand aspirations for social engineering. However there was also a tension here. While the monumentalist centre might have added lustre to the sheen of socialism, in practice much of it did very little to improve the lot of ordinary workers. Certainly the construction of the Metro and other transport links and the building of housing in some parts of the city were of positive benefit to sections of the working class. But the living conditions of many remained relatively unchanged. Despite the major theme in the party's message at this time, summarized in Stalin's aphorism 'life has become better, comrades; life has become more joyous',[45] and reflected in numerous speeches, paintings and posters, the second half of the 1930s was not a time of material plenty for the ordinary Soviet population. For many regime officials, however, despite the uncertainties engendered by the Terror, this was a time of improved living conditions; the habitation of Gorky Street was part of this. So although the monumentalism did not lead to improved conditions for all, by representing the achievements of socialism and by providing practical improvement in living conditions to many politico-administrative officials, it may have helped to stabilize the regime at a time when the terror could potentially have been a destabilizing force.

The pace of development of Moscow was radically reduced during the war, with construction of the Metro the only project that was given any continuing attention. After the war, the redevelopment needs of the Soviet Union were immense. Renewal and restoration of urban infrastructure was required right across the part of the country that had been occupied by the Germans. The damage was so extensive that many believed that its rectification would hamstring the Soviet economy for many years. It was in this context that a decision was made which changed the face of Moscow: the decision to build the so-called 'vysotnye zdaniia', or 'Moscow verticals'.[46] These buildings were Soviet skyscrapers, which although differing in details shared a common structure consisting of tiers, a heavy plinth several stories up and a stepped elevation surmounted by a spire.[47] They towered over the surrounding parts of the city.[48] Originally there were to be eight of these buildings located on strategically significant parts of the Moscow topography.[49] There were to be three along an old line of fortifications on the Garden Ring: a joint office and apartment building on the highest point of the

Garden Ring at Krasnye Vorota (1949–53), the Ministry of Foreign Affairs at Smolenskaia Square (1949–52), and an apartment building at Vosstaniia Square (1949–54). The Hotel Leningradskaia (1949–53) was built on Kalanchevskaia, near the most important transportation node of the city at the termini of three railways (Kazan, Leningrad and Yaroslav). Two were built along the Moscow waterfront, the Hotel Ukraina (1949–56) on a promontory on Dorogomilovskaia Embankment, and an apartment building (1949–52) on Kotel'nicheskaia Embankment at the confluence of the Moscow and Yauza rivers. The final one was the main building of Moscow State University (1949–53), which was built on the Lenin Hills, from where it dominated the city. The un-built eighth building was to be an administrative building for the Ministry of State Security located on the waterfront in Zariad'e and would have formed a counterbalance to the Palace of Soviets on the other side of the Kremlin had it been built. These Moscow verticals became the architecturally dominant feature of the city and represented the high point of the triumphalist style.

These buildings were a major ideological statement both in terms of the fact that they were actually built and the form they took. Given the intense pressure on economic resources created by the need to rebuild after the war, added to the negation of any 'peace dividend' by the outbreak of the cold war, that so much should be spent on such buildings when cheaper and easier to construct buildings could have performed the same function suggests that the Moscow verticals were built to make a point. These buildings were a clear assertion of the power and glory of the Soviet state. Building on the conception of state greatness that emanated from the wartime message of Soviet propaganda, the creation of such structures in straitened times emphasized both the capacity of the state and its determination to trumpet its greatness. By constructing these buildings which soared to the heavens, the impression was created of a country which had been devastated by war leaping forward into the future. And by towering over the levels achieved by the previous most prominent landmarks on the horizon, the old bell towers of Moscow's churches, the Moscow verticals gave the sense of superseding and leaving behind the past. These buildings were thus meant to give a new expression to Soviet life, one of upward movement and achievement, almost of being unconstrained by the laws of earthly existence. They were meant to express the vibrancy and movement of the city, and to draw the different parts of it together, converging on the still un-built Palace of Soviets. Furthermore their inhabitation mainly by officials rather than workers was a graphic statement of the regime's recognition that its stability and future depended significantly on the growing ranks of officialdom. The earlier iconic project, construction of the Metro, continued during the time of late Stalinism. The circular line running beneath the Garden Ring was completed with 12 stations in 1950–54. These were replete with decorative motifs, celebrating victory in the Great Patriotic War as well as allusions to military achievements in Russia's past, a reflection of the increased salience of patriotic and Russian nationalist themes coming out of the war. The most striking of these was probably Komsomol'skaia-Kol'tsevaia, which opened in 1952. It included an underground 'hall of victory' that dwarfed all earlier stations. It sought to project the dominance of the Russian state through representation of the Russian past, including the great leaders Nevsky, Donskoi, Suvorov, Kutuzov, Lenin and Stalin.[50] The new stations differed from their pre-war counterparts in their greater decoration, particularly sculpture, monumental painting and mosaics.[51] Such sculptural decoration was also evident in the cultic heart of the city, the area around Lenin's mausoleum. In 1946 busts of four of the leaders buried there, Sverdlov, Frunze, Dzerzhinsky and Kalinin, were erected behind the Mausoleum; Zhdanov was added in 1948.

This period also saw renewed emphasis on the construction of housing for the people, but with many of the newly constructed apartment buildings echoing the style of the Metro by having extensive decoration designed to symbolize the ideal reality of a new and happy life. The construction of accommodation was the centrepiece of a new general plan for the reconstruction of Moscow over 1951–60 that was discussed in 1952, although little seems to have come of this.[52]

Post-Stalin ordinariness: Goal-rationalism plus social eudaemonism

The monumentalism and triumphalism of the late Stalin period disappeared after his death to be replaced by a greater sense of the mundane. The sense of excitement and of building a new world that had shown through the renewal of Moscow's centre in the 1930s ebbed away in the years of Khrushchev and Brezhnev. Despite Khrushchev's attempt to prolong the sense of movement and achievement through his emphasis on popular involvement and participation in political affairs, the result was less a widespread popular enthusiasm than a sense of ritual involvement. Khrushchev tried to keep the transcendent goal of communism to the fore, with the most important instance of this being the new party Programme adopted in 1961. However at the same time Khrushchev undercut the transcendent quality of the communist aim by tying its achievement directly to material plenty, and by seeking to measure that material plenty through comparison with the US. While the promise of material plenty had been present under Stalin, at no time was the teleological goal of communism defined in such social eudaemonic terms as it was under Khrushchev, and at no time was the US seen as an appropriate yardstick for measuring progress toward that aim. This shift toward social eudaemonism was carried even further under Brezhnev. While the ultimate goal of communism remained formally in place, it was much less emphasized than it had been under Khrushchev. It was largely replaced by a focus on the provision of material well-being to be achieved principally through the scientific and technological revolution. This combination of the effective downgrading of the teleological goal of communism and the higher profile of material well-being marked an effective replacement of goal-rationality with social eudaemonism in the regime's legitimation programme.

This shift is captured in the changes made in the Exhibition of Economic Achievements of the USSR (VDNKh). The origins of VDNKh lay in the All-Union Agricultural Exhibition which had been opened in 1939. Occupying some 136 hectares in the north of Moscow, the original exhibition was a celebration of collective agriculture. It contained working models of farms and factories but its principal theme was agricultural achievement, all presented in the shadow of Sergei Merkurov's gigantic 25 metre high statue of Stalin and the socialist realist statue 'A factory worker and kolkhoznitsa' by Vera Mukhina which topped the entrance gate. It was a celebration of plenty, and with individual pavilions for each of the ten non-Russian republics (but not Russia) and many regions, all decorated with national themes,[53] emphasized the multi-national nature of the country and of the new socialist community. The image presented was highly idealized. In the words of Jamey Gambrell, it presented an image of 'an untroubled Eden, a masterpiece of central planning, in which pristine avenues led past dramatic fountains to stately pavilions bordered by luxuriant gardens. Fabulous sculptural tableaux and dramatic paintings inside the pavilions chronicled the Soviet people's triumphant struggle to cast off the chains of the oppressive tsarist past, and showed them dancing and feasting with joy.'[54] The figure of Stalin was omnipresent, through quotations from him and representations of him in statue and painting. The exhibition was shut down following the German invasion in 1941.

When the exhibition re-opened in 1954, the original design had been substantially re-worked with many of the pavilions being reconstructed in a grander fashion. The decoration of much of the exhibition park was now even more evocative of economic plenty than it had been prior to the war, with sheaves of wheat a common decorative theme throughout the park. The overall style was a sort of 'Soviet classicism' with, in the words of one description, 'lettuce leaves instead of acanthus leaves, sheaves of wheat instead of Corinthian capitals, rams' horns instead of curly scrolls and monumental garlands of fruit...'[55] By 1956, the statues of Stalin had disappeared, as had the quotations. Later that decade, industrial themes became prominent in the Exhibition, which in 1959 became VDNKh. Four years later republican pavilions were abolished and re-assigned to state ministries, which were made responsible for the mounting of annual exhibitions about what they were doing. Now more a 'mirror of technological progress',[56] an emphasis highlighted by the transformation of the Mechanization of Agriculture Pavilion into the Space Pavilion in 1966 and the placement of a Vostok rocket in front of it where Merkulov's statue of Stalin had stood, the Exhibition lost its sense of embodying a multinational socialist community.[57] Instead it became a representation of Soviet technological prowess. The promise and hope for the future and the vibrancy of Soviet socialism that seemed so evident in its early years now seemed tired and humdrum. No longer an organic vision of Soviet society as it had been at the outset, the Exhibition had become simply a site for displays which had no intrinsic coherence and often little merit.

The retreat from Stalinist triumphalism and monumentalism and the promise it embodied was also reflected in the building programme in Moscow. In the decades following Stalin's death, construction continued on the Metro, but now for the most part the stations lacked the ornateness and grandeur of their earlier counterparts. They were functional, performing the task for which they were built, but they generally did not seek to project a distinct ideological or national message in the way that many of their earlier counterparts had done. In the 1950s and 1960s some important public buildings were built: the Luzhniki (Lenin) Stadium (1954–56), Ostankino Television Tower (1960–67), the reworking of much of Kalinin Prospekt with modern high rise buildings (1963–68), the Council of Mutual Economic Assistance building (1964–69), the TASS building (1976), and the 1960s Academy of Sciences building. There was no coherent style or unity to these structures; the CMEA building was innovative in its open book form, the high rises along Kalinin Prospekt were modern and similar to buildings in the West, while the TASS building had clear constructivist elements. Furthermore, unlike in the 1930s when so much construction took place in close quarters in the centre and thereby was able to produce a combined effect of modernist triumphalism, the scattered nature of these buildings meant that they could not produce a similar sort of impact. For the most part undistinguished, these new buildings did not convey a coherent image of the socialist metropolis, no matter how much their supporters may have said that they did. The difference compared with the 1930s is well summarized by the new Palace of Congresses built 1959–61. Although this was not envisaged as a replacement for the un-built Palace of Soviets, it was to perform many of the same functions. But the new Palace was unlike the earlier prototype that would have towered over all of central Moscow and dwarfed the Kremlin, was monumental in its architectural style, and was to be extensively decorated by representations of Soviet achievements. The Palace of Congresses was built inside the Kremlin, it was sunk into the ground so that it would not dominate its Kremlin surroundings, was clean, modern and classical in style, with some representations of Soviet symbolism (the hammer and sickle and red star) on its exterior, but in a way that did not dominate. Monumentalism and triumphalism were out and function was in.

This was also reflected in the principal part of the construction plan for Moscow in the decades following Stalin's death, the construction of apartment buildings. Khrushchev was highly critical of both architectural styles and the performance of architects under Stalin and he promoted the mass production of housing without any of the decorative embellishments characteristic of late Stalinism.[58] In the words of one scholar, he thereby launched 'the process of architecture's rapid subordination to the construction industry'.[59] The result was a standardized style of housing, principally of five storey apartment blocks made out of reinforced concrete placed all over Moscow, but especially on the ever moving outskirts of the city. Such housing was overwhelmingly bland, devoid of decoration, and designed to meet urgent housing needs rather than project the power of the state. This priority was clearly reflected in the new plan for Moscow adopted in July 1971.

This plan was prefigured in the middle of 1966 when the Central Committee and Council of Ministers adopted the so-called 'Technical-economic bases' of a general plan for the development of Moscow,[60] which was the 'symbol of the Soviet Union, Russia, socialist society'.[61] The central focus of the new plan was to be improvement in the standard of living of the people of Moscow, including the resolution of the housing problem; each family should have its own quarters and each individual their own room.[62] However in tackling the housing question, the provision of services and improvement in transport, the natural and historic features of Moscow had to be taken into account.

By the time the plan was adopted in mid-1971, the aim was to turn 'Moscow into a model communist city'.[63] Moscow was seen as 'a major centre of socialist industry, science, technology, culture and art, one of the best organised capitals in the world in terms of public amenities'.[64] The plan envisaged an expansion in quality housing stock (with taller apartment buildings), improvement in the supply of services, enhancement of the transport and communications infrastructure, expanded green space, and the preservation of historic structures. Moscow was to be developed as 'the most important administrative-political, industrial, scientific and cultural centre of the country, in the architectural face of which must be found clear expression of the progressive ideas of our society, the social and scientific progress of the Soviet state'.[65] The redevelopment of Moscow was thus meant to be representative of the growth of Soviet socialism. However although the plan envisaged wide-ranging development in the fabric of Moscow,[66] there was little about it that was either uniquely socialist or that would have differentiated it from a similar plan for urban development in the West. Improved public welfare was clearly one priority, and although mention was made of communal facilities in this regard, there was no real sense that these were to replace the stand-alone living conditions that would characterize the single-family occupancy of domiciles that had been assumed five years earlier. The architectural changes in the city may have improved living standards. But with the development envisaged in the plan both spread throughout the city rather than concentrated, and in the main devoted to the construction of functional infrastructure and what one observer called 'faceless mass construction'[67] rather than iconic buildings, they did not present a clarity of vision about either socialism or the socialist future that matched the soaring idealism evident in the 1930s.

This does not mean that ideological elements were absent from urban development in the post-Stalin period. The closure of churches, which had virtually ceased at the outbreak of the war,[68] was escalated under Khrushchev's anti-religious campaign with some 20 percent of functioning Orthodox churches closed, while the changing of street names to provide more ideologically palatable geographical place names reached a new high in 1964 when more names were changed than in any single year except 1922.[69] There were also significant changes to the cultic centre of the city. On Stalin's death, he had been interred in the Mausoleum on Red Square along with Lenin and his name had been added to the door lintel. However in 1961 his body was withdrawn from the Mausoleum and his name removed from its entrance. He was buried at the foot of the Kremlin wall just at the back of the Mausoleum. In 1969 a bust was placed over his grave. Similar busts were placed over the graves of Brezhnev, Andropov and Chernenko when they died and were buried at the foot of the Kremlin wall in 1982, 1984 and 1985 respectively. There were also changes to statuary and to the representation of leaders elsewhere in the city. With destalinization, the statues and images of Stalin that had formerly been prominent disappeared, and in line with the renewed emphasis on Lenin, representations of him multiplied throughout the city. Virtually any building that Lenin had visited was now decorated with a memorial plaque marking the event; by 1980, Moscow had 130 such 'shrines' to Lenin and 30 public statues and busts of him.[70] In 1955 Lenin's name replaced that of Kaganovich on the Moscow Metro while many placenames were similarly changed. In 1958 a statue of Feliks Dzerzhinsky was placed in front of the Lubianka, and in 1961 a statue of Marx appeared in Sverdlov Square. In May 1967 the tomb of the Unknown Soldier, with a flame carried from the Field of Mars in Leningrad, was installed beneath the Kremlin walls, but on a different side of the Kremlin to the Mausoleum and necropolis on Red Square. This development, within the context of the contemporary glorification of the Great Patriotic War,[71] created a rival cultic location in the city centre and thereby to some degree devalued the symbolism of the area of the Mausoleum.

The city and legitimation

Lenin's ambition that the bolsheviks should make the city their own, clearly distinct from capitalist cities, was shared by his successors. The attempt under Lenin to turn this aspiration into reality was unsuccessful, but under Stalin substantial steps were made in this direction. The concentration of change in the centre of the city and the monumental and triumphalist scale of much of the renovation that took place projected a strong sense both of a powerful state guiding development and of significant movement toward the communist future. The array of major projects that were announced and completed throughout the country at this time and the announcement of the achievement of socialism in 1936 added substance to this impression. Furthermore given the nature of much of the population of Moscow in the 1930s, with many newly arrived from the countryside, it is not difficult to conceive of the sense of awe and admiration that this modern city evoked. The claim to be moving toward communism, the basis of goal-rational legitimation, seemed to have real substance as the renewed city centre embodied that socialist future. This sense of movement and of creating a new civilization were reinforced by the Moscow verticals in the late-1940s and early 1950s.

But then the image became more diffuse. The geographical spread of urban renewal, the absence of concentrations of iconic structures, and the focus on the provision of infrastructure for the daily lives of Moscow's citizens consistent with the increased importance of social eudaemonism in the regime's legitimation programme clouded the apparent link between urban development and the bright future, instead linking the former with more immediate and pressing needs. With Khrushchev's reinterpretation of the meaning of communism in terms overwhelmingly of material plenty, the teleological end point of the regime was robbed of its idealism and excitement. When the approach of communism was interpreted in terms of the availability of sausage rather than the building of a new world on the basis of philosophical principles like freedom and equality, it lost its aura and became much more humdrum and mundane. The Khrushchevian and Brezhnevian programmes of urban development fitted this changed conception of the regime's goal perfectly.

In this way the urban development of Moscow during the Soviet regime was a close shadow of the regime's legitimation programme. When major work transformed the city centre, the goal-rational legitimation programme emphasized a communism that was idealistic and, like the Moscow verticals, soaring. When the urban development programme was more prosaic and crudely functional, so the legitimation programme was more banal in what it emphasized as the currency of legitimation. This was in part a function of time. The transformatory efforts associated with the first five year plan were fuelled by the enthusiasm and excitement of creating a new world, of overcoming significant odds to achieve what had not been achieved before. This endeavour to create a new civilization, much better and more just than any in the past, both stimulated the imagination to soar and encouraged the monumentalist and triumphalist approach to architectural design that was evident in central Moscow. However after Stalin's death the excitement of the creation of the new could neither be maintained nor reinvented. The issue was much more management of what existed, with some tweaking at the edges, than it was of the building of a new civilization. This is best represented in Brezhnev's concept of 'developed socialism'. Both the Khrushchev and Brezhnev leaderships tried to evoke the sorts of enthusiasms that had been evident among many at the time of the first five-year plan, but such efforts were not successful. Management of an existing reality required different qualities to the creation of something new, and these skill sets could not be easily swapped. Thus the agendas faced by the Stalin and Khrushchev/Brezhnev leaderships were very different, and this was reflected in the nature of the urban redevelopment each undertook.

Urban redevelopment was therefore a central part of the Soviet legitimation programme. For Moscow's inhabitants, as indeed for all residents of the USSR, the development of the city was a central component of the regime's search for legitimation. The city was a model of the future and embodied the regime's legitimation. In the thirties its redevelopment embodied the glory of the achievement of socialism, adding substance to that claim in a way that all who visited the centre of the city could experience. When the emphasis in the legitimation programme shifted to the supply of goods and services, and the main thrust of urban development was to make good that promise, the touchstone of goal-rational legitimation was reduced from the idealism of the earlier period to something which the ordinary people could measure, no matter how inexactly. The failure to realize those promises within the context of goal-rational legitimacy undermined belief and confidence in the regime, and the changing nature of the building programme in the capital was one marker of this.

Notes

1 Max Weber (1947), *The Theory of Social and Economic Organization* (New York: Free Press, edited by Talcott Parsons), Section III, pp.324–407.
2 For example, see Leslie Holmes (1993), *The End of Communist Power: Anti-Corruption Campaigns and Legitimation Crisis* (Melbourne: Melbourne University Press); T.H. Rigby and Ferenc Feher (eds) (1982), *Political Legitimation in Communist States* (London: Macmillan); Graeme Gill (1986), 'Changing patterns of legitimation in the USSR', *Coexistence*, XXIII, 4, 247–66.
3 See in particular, T.H. Rigby, 'A conceptual approach to authority, power and policy in the Soviet Union', T.H. Rigby, Archie Brown and Peter Reddaway (eds) (1980), *Authority, Power and Policy in the USSR: Essays dedicated to Leonard Schapiro* (London: Macmillan), pp.9–31; T.H. Rigby, 'Introduction: Political legitimacy, Weber and communist mono-organisational systems', in Rigby and Feher, *Political Legitimation*, pp.1–26.
4 The former assumes adherence to rules and laws, the latter a personalized authority that transcends rules and laws. For the classic discussion, see Weber, *The Theory of Social and Economic Organization*, pp.324–407.

5   On social eudaemonic legitimation, see Gill, 'Changing patterns', pp.249, 262; Holmes, *The End of Communist Power*.

6   Central Committee resolution 'O moskovskom gorodskom khoziaistve i o razvitii gorodskogo khoziaistva SSSR', *Pravda*, 17 June 1931.

7   'O general'nom plane rekonstruktsii goroda Moskvy', *Pravda*, 11 July 1935.

8   Cited in John E. Bowlt, 'Russian sculpture and Lenin's plan of monumental propaganda', in Henry A. Millon and Linda Nochlin (eds) (1978), *Art and Architecture in the Service of Politics* (Cambridge: The MIT Press), p.185.

9   'Dekret o pamiatnikakh respubliki', in *Dekrety sovetskoi vlasti. Tom II. 17 marta – 10 iiulia 1918g* (Moscow: Gosudarstvennoe izdatel'stvo politicheskoi literatury, 1959), pp.95–6. For further decisions, see *Dekrety sovetskoi vlasti. Tom III. 11 iiulia – 9 noiabr 1918g* (Moscow: Izdatel'stvo politicheskoi literatury, 1964), pp.47–8, 118–19. For the list of people to be honoured, see *Izvestiia*, 2 August 1918.

10   There were a few exceptions. The statues of Gogol and Herzen placed in the central city campus of Moscow University remained, as did the monument to revolutionary thinkers placed in Aleksandrovskii sad, which was fashioned out of the plinth originally designed to mark the tercentenary of the Romanov dynasty.

11   See the description in Rene Fulop-Miller (1972), *The Mind and Face of Bolshevism. An Examination of Cultural Life in Soviet Russia* (London: S.G. Putnam & Sons Ltd, trans. F.S. Flint and D.F. Tait), p.91.

12   For examples, see Timothy Colton (1995), *Moscow: Governing the Socialist Metropolis* (Cambridge, Mass.: The Belknap Press), pp.110–11. The naming after Lenin of the first places in the country actually occurred in 1917, the villages of Bogorodskoe in what became Kirov oblast and Svinarev in Rostov oblast. John Murray (2000), *Politics and Place-names: Changing Names in the Late Soviet Period* (Birmingham: University of Birmingham, Birmingham Slavonic Monographs No.32), p.130.

13   It was removed in 1948 because it had fallen into disrepair.

14   On the Mausoleum, see Aleksei Abramov (2005), *Pravda i vymysly o krem-levskom nekropole i Mavzolee* (Moscow: Algoritm); Nina Tumarkin (1983), *Lenin Lives! The Lenin Cult in Soviet Russia* (Cambridge: Harvard University Press), pp.189–206.

15   *Izvestiia*, 31 December 1922. On Kamenev's paternity of the idea, see Colton, *Moscow*, p.218.

16   F.I. Chuev, 'Tak govoril Kaganovich: Ispoved' stalinskogo apostola', in Feliks Chuev (2001), *Kaganovich-Shepilov* (Moscow: Olma-Press), p.56. For a more sceptical view, see Sona Stephan Hoisington (2003), '"Ever Higher": The evolution of the project for the palace of Soviets', *Slavic Review*, LXII, 1, 62.

17   For Stalin's view of the best proposal, see his letter of 7 August 1932 to Voroshilov, Kaganovich and Molotov, in O.V. Khlevniuk, R.U. Devis, L.P. Kosheleva, E.A. Ris and L.A. Rogovaia (eds) (2001), *Stalin i Kaganovich Perepiska 1931–1936gg* (Moscow: ROSSPEN), p.269. For the Politburo decision, see Politburo Protocol 137, 56/43, RGASPI, f. 17, op. 163, d. 981 (10 May 1933). For the designs, see *Stroitel'stvo Moskvy*, 3, March 1932, 13–34; 5–6, May–June 1933, whole issue; 3, 1934, 4–11.

18   Doubts were raised about a statue of this size, in terms of how it was to be constructed, wind resistance, and visibility. It was argued that owing to

weather conditions and air quality, the statue would be invisible from the ground for 275 days of the year. RGASPI, f. 82, op. 2, d. 504, l. 120–7. On Molotov opposing such a statue but being persuaded to go along by Stalin and Voroshilov, see F. Chuev (1991), *Sto sorok besed s Molotovym. Iz dnevnika F. Chueva* (Moscow: Terra), p.265.

19 For Politburo directions in this regard, see Politburo Protocol 64, 92, RGASPI f. 17, op. 163, d. 1199 (26 September 1938). Also see the report from construction chief Prokof'ev, RGASPI, f. 82, op. 2, d. 506, l. 26–39.

20 Although those in charge of construction continued to press into 1952 for resumption of the project. RGASPI, f. 82, op. 2, d. 506, l. 98 (1941), 99–100, 101, 104–6 (1942), 108–9, 112, 113, 115–16 (1943), 124, 125, 126, 127, 128–40, (1945), 146 (1946), 148–53, 154 (1947), 160–1 (1948), 162–3 (1949), and 164 (1952).

21 RGASPI, f. 82, op. 2, d. 506, l. 80. The site was turned into a communal swimming pool. The cathedral was rebuilt on the site in the post-Soviet period.

22 For example, see the discussions in Anatole Kopp (1970), *Town and Revolution: Soviet Architecture and City Planning 1917–1935* (London: Thames and Hudson, trans. Thomas E. Burton), p.46; Kathleen Berton (1977), *Moscow: An Architectural History* (London: Cassell & Collier Macmillan), p.199; Richard Stites (1989), *Revolutionary Dreams: Utopian Vision and Experimental Life in the Russian Revolution* (New York: Oxford University Press), pp.76–8. Also see the 1919 poster by N. Kupreianov, 'Grazhdane khranite pamiatniki iskusstva', in Aleksandr Snopkov, Pavel Snopkov, Aleksandr Shkliaruk (2004), *Shestsot' plakatov* (Moscow: Kontakt-Kul'tura), p.23.

23 Especially at the end of the 1920s. For the development of policy, see Vladimir Kozlov (1991), 'Delo ob ograblenii Tserkvi 1920–1930e gody', *Moskovskii zhurnal*, 7, 1991, 16–25. Also see Colton, *Moscow*, pp.229–33.

24 For a discussion, see Kopp, *Town and Revolution*, chapter 8.

25 On these buildings, see *Arkhitektura moskvy 1920–1960. Putevoditel'* (Moscow: Izdatel'stvo 'Zhiraf', 2006), pp.84–9, 108–11, 120–1.

26 For a survey of many of them, see Colton, *Moscow*, pp.215–47.

27 On the importance of planning in the context of the class nature of architecture, see I. Vobli (1931), 'Kak oformliat' krasnuiu stolitsu', *Stroitel'stvo Moskvy*, 3, 34–7.

28 L.M. Kaganovich (1931), *Za sotsialisticheskuiu rekonstruktsiiu Moskvy i gorodov SSSR* (Moscow: Ogiz 'Moskovskii rabochii'). Quotations from pp.51 and 16 respectively.

29 'O moskovskom gorodskom khoziaistve'.

30 For a discussion of this situation, see David L. Hoffman (1994), *Peasant Metropolis. Social Identities in Moscow, 1929–1941* (Ithaca: Cornell University Press).

31 This was an important intervention in a contemporary debate among architects about the form of housing that should be constructed. The most radical among the constructivists called for the erection of housing that only had communal facilities (kitchen, dining room, bathroom and toilet, child-minding facilities) while others argued for transitional forms between communal and private arrangements, and others purely private. Kopp, *Town and Revolution*, chapter 7. For a full discussion, see V.E. Khazanova (1980),

Sovetskaia arkhitektura pervoi piatiletki. Problemy goroda budushchego (Moscow: 'Nauka').

32   Details of some of these are to be found in Colton, *Moscow*, pp.274–7.

33   Colton, *Moscow*, p.257. For a discussion, see P. Bovin (1932), 'Samyi bol'shoi Kanal na zemnom share', *Stroitel'stvo Moskvy*, 1, 14–18.

34   For Kaganovich's announcement of preliminary plans for the first lines, see L.M. Kaganovich (1932), *The Moscow Bolsheviks in the Struggle for the Victory of the Five-Year Plan* (Moscow: Cooperative Publishing Society of Foreign Workers in the USSR), p.102. The course of construction was closely followed in the issues of *Stroitel'stvo Moskvy*, 1932–35.

35   L.M. Kaganovich (1934), *O stroitel'stve metropolitena i plane goroda Moskvy* (Moscow: Moskovskii rabochii), pp.13–14.

36   L.M. Kaganovich (1935), *Poslednii etap stroitel'stva pervoi ocheredi metro* (Moscow: Moskovskii rabochii), p.18.

37   L.M. Kaganovich (1935), *Pobeda metropolitena – pobeda sotsializma* (Moscow: Transzheldorizdat), no page numbers.

38   On the symbolic importance of the Metro and the decoration in the stations, see Andrew Jenks (2000), 'A Metro on the mount. The underground as a church of Soviet Civilization', *Technology and Culture*, XLI, 4, 697–724; Mike O'Mahony (2003), 'Archaeological fantasies: Constructing history on the Moscow Metro', *The Modern Language Review*, XCVIII, 1, 138–50.

39   *General'nyi plan rekonstruktsii goroda Moskvy* (Moscow: Moskovskii rabochii, 1936). The joint Central Committee-Sovnarkom decision, 'O general'nom plane rekonstruktsii goroda Moskvy', was published in *Pravda*, 11 July 1935.

40   'Rezoliutsiia partaktiva g. Moskvy po dokladu tovarishcha Khrushcheva N.S.', 13 July 1935, in *General'nyi plan*, p.28.

41   On Kaganovich as a major influence in the destruction of old Moscow, see Evgenii Evseev (2005), *Kaganovich. Satrap za spinoi Stalina* (Moscow: Yauza), pp.173–91.

42   Some historically significant buildings like the Sukharev Tower (1933), part of the Kitai Gorod walls (1934), Kazan Cathedral on Red Square and Bove's Triumphal gates on the road to Leningrad (both 1936) were destroyed.

43   Greg Castillo, 'Gorki street and the design of the Stalin revolution', in Zeynep Celik, Diane Favro, Richard Ingersoll (eds) (1994), *Streets: Critical Perspectives on Public Space* (Berkeley: University of California Press), p.62. For a contemporary discussion, see S.E. Chernyshev (1934), 'Rekonstruktsiia ulitsy Gor'kogo', *Stroitel'stvo Moskvy*, 4, 6–8.

44   The monumentalist and triumphalist nature of the architecture did not in itself evoke the socialist ethos because such characteristics of the architecture were present in non-socialist societies, like Mussolini's plans for the development of Rome (still clear in the design of the EUR, Esposizione Universale di Roma, region), the Hitler/Speer plans for Berlin, and the skyscrapers in the US. What evoked socialism was the ideological context within which these buildings were constructed and accordingly the sentiments attached to them. See for example, Borden W. Painter Jr. (2005), *Mussolini's Rome: Rebuilding the Eternal City* (New York: Palgrave Macmillan), esp. chapter 5; Frederic Spotts (2003), *Hitler and the Power of Aesthetics* (London: Pimlico), pp.311–98.

45 J.V. Stalin, 'Rech' na I vsesoiuznom soveshchanii Stakhanovtsev', in J.V. Stalin (1967), *Sochineniia*, tom I (xiv) 1934–1940 (Stanford: Hoover Institution, ed. Robert H. McNeal), p.89.
46 For the 13 January 1947 decision, see *Sovetskoe iskusstvo*, 28 February 1947.
47 Alexei Tarkhanov and Sergei Kavtaradze (1992), *Architecture of the Stalin Era* (New York: Rizzoli International Publishers), p.141. The hotel Leningradskaia generally lacked the stepped appearance.
48 On these buildings, see Evgeniia Gershkovich and Evgenii Korneev (2006), *Vysokii Stalinskii stil'* (Moscow: Trilistnik); A.A. Vas'kin and Iu.I. Nazarenko (2006), *Arkhitektura stalinskikh vysotok Moskvy* (Moscow: Kompaniia sputnik). They are discussed individually in *Arkhitektura Moskvy*, pp.240–55.
49 For a general discussion, including of their location, see Karl Schlögel (2005), *Moscow* (London: Reaktion Books, trans.Helen Atkins), chapter 2.
50 Tarkhanov and Kavtaradze, *Architecture of the Stalin Era*, p.165.
51 Alexander Ryabushin and Nadia Smolina (1992), *Landmarks of Soviet Architecture 1917–1991* (New York: Rizzoli International Publications), p.29.
52 See the comments by Yasnov at the Nineteenth Party Congress, *Pravda*, 12 October 1952. For discussion, see Colton, *Moscow*, pp.353–4.
53 See the discussion in Greg Castillo (1995), 'Peoples at an exhibition: Soviet architecture and the national question', *The South Atlantic Quarterly*, XCIV, 3, 727–33.
54 Jamey Gambrell, 'The wonder of the Soviet world', *The New York Review of Books*, 22 December 1994, p.30.
55 Tarkhanov and Kavtaradze, *Architecture of the Stalin Era*, p.160.
56 Gambrell, 'Wonder'. p.33.
57 Although this was still symbolized by the Friendship of Nations fountain that featured 16 gilded bronze figures (one for each republic) dressed in national costume. Castillo, 'Peoples at an exhibition', p.737.
58 For example, N.S. Khrushchev (1955), *O shirokom vnedrenii industrial'nykh metodov, uluchshenii kachestva i snizhenii stoimosti stroitel'stva* (Moscow: Gospolitizdat).
59 Catherine Cooke (1997), 'Beauty as a route to "the radiant future"', *Journal of Design History*, X, 2, 138.
60 'O general'nom plane razvitiia Moskvy', *Stroitel'stvo i arkhitektura Moskvy*, 11, 1966, p.1.
61 'Arkhitekturnyi oblik stolitsy', *Stroitel'stvo i arkhitektura Moskvy*, 11 November 1966, p.34.
62 'Osnovnye napravleniia razvitiia goroda', *Stroitel'stvo i arkhitektura Moskvy*, 11 November 1966, pp.19–20.
63 The term was adopted from Brezhnev's speech to the electors of Bauman electoral district on 11 June 1971, 'Interesy naroda, zabota o ego blage – vysshii smysl deiatel'nosti partii', in L.I. Brezhnev (1972), *Leninskim kursom. Rechi i stat'i* (Moscow: Izdatel'stvo politicheskoi literatury), vol. 3, p.387.
64 'O general'nom plane razvitiia g. Moskvy', *Stroitel'stvo i arkhitektura Moskva*, 7–8, 1971, p.2.
65 'O general'nom plane' (1971), p.2.
66 Discussion of aspects of this is to be found in a series of articles in the journal *Stroitel'stvo i arkhitektura Moskvy*, 7–8, 1971. Also see 'Prevratim Moskvu v

obraztsovyi kommunisticheskii gorod. Boevaia programma preobrazovaniia stolitsy', *Stroitel'stvo i arkhitektura Moskvy*, 9, 1971, pp.2–3.

67 Maria Kiernan (1998), *Moscow: A Guide to Soviet and Post-Soviet Architecture* (London: Ellipsis), p.11.

68 According to one, incomplete, study, of 116 churches destroyed between 1917 and 1991, 14 were destroyed before 1930, 84 in 1930–36, seven in 1936–41, and two between 1945 and 1954. Colton, *Moscow*, p.855 n.208.

69 Colton, *Moscow*, p.554.

70 Ibid., p.365.

71 For a study of this, see Nina Tumarkin (1994), *The Living and the Dead. The Rise and Fall of the Cult of World War II in Russia* (New York: Basic Books).

5
Legitimation and Legitimacy in Russia Revisited

Leslie Holmes

The 1982 volume edited by T.H. Rigby and Ferenc Fehér, *Political Legitimation in Communist States*, was a seminal work.[1] Not only did it open up a whole new dimension of Communist politics, but it also introduced the concept of goal-rational legitimation to theories of legitimacy.[2] In doing so, it alerted us to the fact that the classic Weberian three-fold approach to legitimacy was in serious need of an update and expansion, particularly if it was to apply to Communist systems.[3]

Although most Communist states are by now mere historical memories, legitimacy and legitimation continue to be hotly debated concepts, and are as relevant now as they ever were. They also constitute crucial but generally understudied aspects of post-communist transitions. This chapter begins by providing a brief overview of Rigby's argument concerning legitimacy and legitimation in Communist systems and some of the theoretical contributions to the debate since the early 1980s. Following this is an analysis of legitimation and legitimacy in Russia – the core of Rigby's primary interest in the USSR – since the collapse of Communism. It is argued that both Weber and Rigby still have much to offer in our attempts to comprehend legitimacy in post-communist Russia, though some of their key concepts need to be reworked and supplemented if they are to be convincingly applied to the contemporary political system.

Rigby on legitimacy and legitimation

Much of Rigby's introductory chapter in the Rigby and Fehér collection referred to above is an elaboration of Max Weber's classic study of legitimacy. Rigby starts by reminding us that the concept of legitimacy in political analysis pre-dates Weber by not merely centuries, but millennia. Thus Pharaoh Amenhotep IV (father of Tutankhamen) understood the concept and the importance of legitimacy almost three and a half thousand years ago, while both Plato and Aristotle wrote on the subject. Nevertheless, it is Weber who really placed the issue of legitimacy on the contemporary social science agenda. He identified three ideal-types (or 'pure types', as Weber calls them) of legitimation – traditional, charismatic and what is usually called legal-rational. Since all three will be cited in our analysis of contemporary Russian legitimation, it is worth repeating Weber's description of the bases of system legitimacy. Rigby himself cites Weber's analysis in *The Theory of Social and Economic Organisation*, but another valuable and slightly more detailed version will be used here:

> First, the authority of the 'eternal yesterday', i.e. of the mores sanctified through the unimaginably ancient recognition and habitual orientation to conform. This is 'traditional' domination exercised by the patriarch and the patrimonial prince of yore.
>
> There is the authority of the extraordinary and personal *gift of grace* (charisma), the absolutely personal devotion and personal confidence in revelation, heroism, or other qualities of individual leadership. This is 'charismatic' domination, as exercised by the prophet or – in the field of politics – by the elected war lord, the plebiscitarian ruler, the great demagogue, or the political party leader.
>
> Finally, there is domination by virtue of 'legality', by virtue of the belief in the validity of legal statute and 'functional competence' based on rationally created *rules*. In this case, obedience is expected in discharging statutory obligations. This is domination as exercised by the modern 'servant of the state' and by all those bearers of power who in this respect resemble him'.[4]

As Rigby notes, Weber himself acknowledged that the pure types are 'rarely found in reality'; rather, actual systems typically exhibit elements of two or even all three of these types in unique balances.

Having highlighted problems in Weber's analysis of legitimacy, Rigby goes on to argue that the concept of legitimation was relatively neglected until the late 1960s and early 1970s, when the alleged legitimacy crisis of capitalism resulted in 'greatly increased scholarly interest' in legitimation.[5] But most of the new material focused on Western democracies, and Rigby believed that the time had come to consider the issue of legitimacy and legitimation in Communist systems. He argued that as Communist systems had moved away from the overt coercion of earlier periods, they had placed more emphasis on the need to legitimate their systems. But none of Weber's three pure types applied to mature Communist systems. Rather, the dominant mode was what Rigby called 'goal-rationality':

> ... the legitimacy claimed for the commands issuing from this system and for those holding office under it is framed in terms of 'goal-rationality' rather than the formal-legal rationality of Western 'capitalist' systems.[6]

Rigby then proceeds to elaborate what this goal-rationality entails. His analysis starts by emphasizing a distinction between different types of bureaucracies, based on their different orientations. For Weber, bureaucracies in a legal-rational state were mainly concerned with the application of abstract rules. But Rigby argues – correctly – that while most bureaucracies in modern Western states are primarily 'rule-applying', some are more focused on task achievement. For him, the latter orientation typifies most Communist bureaucracies:

> Consonant with this, the legitimacy claims of the political system, of those holding office under it, and of the latters' commands, are validated in terms of the final goal ('communism') from which the partial and intermediate goals set by the leadership are allegedly derived.[7]

In short, late-Communist legitimation was primarily teleological, geared towards the end-goal of communism. However, Rigby recognizes that many of the goals of late-Communism were more immediate – yearly and five-year plans are a prime example. Yet even these more immediate goals were justified in terms of the final goal, and had to be presented as basically compatible with them. Goal-rationality was thus a pervasive component of state ideology.

Some subsequent contributions to the debate

T.H. Rigby's focus on legitimacy in Communist systems led various scholars to engage with and develop an interest in it. In addition to the numerous contributors to the volume he edited with Ferenc Fehér – R.N. Berki, Georg Brunner, Graeme Gill, Agnes Heller, Henry Krisch,

Maria Markus, and Robert F. Miller – various Australian scholars from both sociology and political science joined the debate. One of the most influential was sociologist Jan Pakulski. In a controversial and thought-provoking article, Pakulski maintained that it was inappropriate to analyse Soviet-type societies in terms of legitimacy. Instead, he argued, mass compliance – and hence the absence of overt mass unrest – should be interpreted not in terms of the systems' underlying legitimacy, but rather from the perspective of what he called 'conditional tolerance' on the part of the citizenry.[8]

But not everyone accepted that legitimacy was an irrelevant concept in the context of Communist systems. For example, Agnes Heller – who was at the time living in Australia – accepted that Communist systems could be seen as legitimate if one section of the population considered the social order legitimate and the rest of the populace did not clearly favour or envisage an alternative one. In adopting this position, she was explicitly agreeing with Weber. She also made it clear that she considered the USSR legitimate, but not Communist Czechoslovakia, Poland or Hungary, since most citizens in these latter states did have an image of an alternative political order.[9]

In a 1993 book, building on Weber and Rigby, the present author argued that there were at least ten discernible modes of legitimation operating in the contemporary world, many of which were to be found in Communist states. In addition to the four already considered – traditional, charismatic, legal-rational and goal-rational – there were three further domestic modes, plus three external modes; since producing that list, I have added a fourth domestic mode. In order to make sense of these, it is necessary first to focus on four aspects of legitimation that have not yet been considered here.

The first relates to the agencies according legitimacy. Weber was clear that the citizens constitute only one of the agents that can grant legitimacy to a political system; their authorization of state power can be called popular legitimation. In addition, legitimacy can be granted by state apparatuses of various kinds (staff legitimation), and by the political elites themselves (self-legitimation).[10] Several theorists of revolution have been very aware of this three-fold distinction, and have argued that if what Tilly calls a revolutionary situation is to lead to a successful revolutionary outcome, popular legitimacy is less important than staff or elite legitimation.[11] In other words, if the state apparatuses and the elites believe in their right to rule or dominate, they will usually be able to counter popular delegitimation. Rigby also maintained this.

The second aspect focuses on what is being legitimated. In theory, a clear distinction can be drawn between a political system and a political regime.[12] Thus the Australian *system* is a parliamentary liberal democracy with a traditional monarch as the head of state, whereas – at the time of writing – the regime was a Labor one headed by Kevin Rudd. In other words, the regime is the leadership team that runs the system. It is equally clear in most theory that legitimacy should refer to the system rather than the regime. But this theoretical distinction is often difficult to sustain or defend in the case of actual polities – *especially transition ones*. This is because the system has by definition not yet consolidated, so that citizens – and often the staffs and even the elites – are still forming their views on the optimal long-term arrangement. In such a situation, the new regime will typically advocate a particular type of system and work to ensure that the citizens become convinced of the desirability of this system. But many citizens will ultimately assess the desirability of the system being constructed by the performance of the regime. Such a conflation of system and regime would be disapproved of by some political theorists. But the world is rarely as tidy or rational as many would prefer, and transition states require us to re-visit established norms.

It is a moot point whether or not most citizens really legitimize a system rather than a regime in the modern world; many would find the distinction precious or unrealistic. And what is putatively the principal legitimation mode of the modern state, the rule of law, has been under attack from many quarters in recent years anyway, as even developed democracies, such as the USA under George W. Bush, have often placed security concerns above it. But developments in the advanced democracies are not a focus of the present chapter. The concern here is only with a new type of political arrangement in Russia, one less than two decades old at the time of writing.

Our third aspect is the time-frame of legitimation. The fact that systems were seen to move from one dominant legitimation mode to another in Weber's analysis demonstrates that his approach to legitimation was dynamic. His advocacy of legal-rationality as the only legitimation mode suitable for a truly modern state can be read as a teleological approach, akin to Fukuyama's notion of the 'end of history'. It also shows that Weber perceived the first two legitimation modes as ultimately temporary, even if the traditional mode is much more durable than the charismatic. But the fact that neither is permanent brings fuzziness to these concepts and unpredictability about their duration in the real world. Moreover, the fact that Weber argued that charismatic legitimation is typically short-lived and thus temporary is evidence that legitimacy can be a contingent and fickle phenomenon. Had Weber argued that legal-rationality is the *only* form of legitimation, then it would be difficult to sustain the argument that his conception is fuzzy, and that it is all the better – more realistic – for being so.

The final dimension to be highlighted here builds on this notion of fuzziness. This is that Weber's emphasis on the fact that his three legitimation modes were ideal or pure types, and that actual political systems typically display unique blends of two or even all three of them, means that analysis of the power arrangements in a given country need not start from the assumption that the system will display most or all of the characteristics of any one legitimation mode exclusively.

Rigby's conception of goal-rational legitimation as a teleological mode might have meant that it was intended to be a permanent phenomenon, or at least a long-term one. However, the sudden collapse of Communist power is proof that goal-rational legitimation can also be relatively short-lived, and is contingent.

The main reason for the emphasis here on fuzziness and contingency in both Weber's and Rigby's conceptions is that they allow us to consider aspects of legitimation that some purist theories of legitimation reject. For instance, explicit recognition that charismatic legitimacy is short-lived permits consideration of other transient legitimation modes. Given this, we return to the claim that at least four domestic modes of legitimation can and should be added to the four already identified by Weber and Rigby.

If it is accepted that *performance* can legitimate at least a regime, and that in transition states the borderline between regime and system is blurred, then our fifth mode of legitimation is *eudaemonism*, that is, happiness inducing, or legitimation based on satisfying the populace. This is usually interpreted to refer primarily to economic performance, such as impressive growth rates and development, the provision of a wide range of public goods and services, low unemployment and inflation rates, etc. This legitimation mode would not be accepted by Seymour Martin Lipset, who explicitly contrasted legitimacy and effectiveness in a four-cell matrix (the two axes being legitimacy-effectiveness and positive or high level/negative or low level). For Lipset, legitimacy was an evaluative concept, whereas effectiveness was an instrumental one.[13]

Eudaemonic legitimacy *might* also be rejected by Rigby, since it does not at first sight appear to be normative in his sense. Thus he makes it clear that popular legitimacy involves 'the notion that [political authorities] have the *right* [emphasis added] to make ... demands' that citizens will comply with their orders. In the same passage, he also explicitly rejects the notion that 'hope of reward' is a basis for legitimacy. This could be interpreted as a rejection of eudaemonism as a legitimation mode.[14] However, such an interpretation can be challenged. As used in the present analysis, the concept of eudaemonic legitimation does not mean that citizens obey the authorities simply in the hope of improving their living standards ('hope of reward'), for instance. Rather, they obey because they believe that the authorities know what they are doing – are running 'the system' well – as reflected in system performance. They are thus willing to grant the authorities the right to make decisions on their behalf. This accords well with most normative approaches to legitimacy, which focus on the *consent* of the ruled.

Certainly, a number of well-regarded analysts of Communist politics have argued in favour of recognizing what is here called eudaemonism as a potential legitimation mode.[15] More recently, head of the World Bank Robert Zoellick has made it clear – though not specifically in the context of Communist or post-communist systems – that he too recognizes eudaemonism from this perspective: 'Legitimacy must be achieved through performance. It needs to be earned by delivering basic services, especially visible ones. Clean up the garbage.'[16] If many citizens judge a regime (and system) at least to a significant degree in terms of its capacity to give them what they want, then they are likely to treat that regime as legitimate if it *is* delivering those goods and services. And it is not unreasonable to assume that popular legitimation of a regime can over time develop into legitimation of the type of system advocated by that regime and that it claims to be constructing. Conversely, the precipitate decline of popular and possibly other forms of legitimacy if performance seriously falters is perfectly compatible with the Weberian (and Rigby's) approach to legitimacy.

The rapid collapse of both the Soviet Empire and the Soviet Union itself between 1989 and 1991 resulted in an identity crisis in Russia. Throughout the 1990s, many Russians experienced difficulties both in identifying just with Russia itself as distinct from the Soviet Union, and in accepting that Russia had suffered a quintuple loss – viz. its outer empire, its inner empire, the Cold War, its status as a superpower, and its status as the home of the principal challenge to the liberal democratic capitalist model. In this type of situation, leaders will sometimes invoke *official nationalism* in their attempts to unify society and enhance state legitimacy; after all, legitimizing a state will be substantially more difficult if citizens do not relate to the political unit in the first place. Official nationalism is thus the sixth mode identified here. Like charisma, this cannot be an effective long-term *dominant* legitimation mode. While official nationalism can be used long-term as one part of the legitimation process, it can be dangerous to political elites to attempt to make it the primary source of legitimacy for more than relatively short periods, since it can increasingly be seen as exclusionary and a threat to other states.

The seventh domestic mode is *new traditional* legitimation. Here, a leadership will seek legitimacy in part through identification with predecessors known to have been very popular and assumed to have been legitimate. A prime example from the Soviet era is Mikhail Gorbachev, who sometimes likened his own approach to that of Lenin; a postcommunist example from Central Europe is Czechia's former president, Vaclav Havel, who often compared himself with Thomas Masaryk.

Our final domestic mode is *contrasting with the past*; it is almost the opposite of new traditional legitimation.[17] Here, a leadership will seek legitimacy by explicitly contrasting its own style and/or policies with those of a past regime or system it believes to have been delegitimized. This is a common legitimation mode in transition states, in which leaders seek to distance themselves from the previous system. It often manifests itself in forms of retrospective and retributive justice that are common in and largely peculiar to transition states, notably lustration. Like the charismatic and official nationalist modes, this form of legitimation can only be relatively short-lived.

Ultimately, it is domestic legitimacy that matters most to a system or regime. But it would be remiss to overlook the fact that external legitimation can be and often is another important variable in the overall legitimacy equation. In many cases, it relates primarily to self-legitimation, and three types can be identified. The first and most obvious form of external legitimation is official recognition of a regime by other states and by international organizations, notably the UN. The second is support from foreign leaders. Gorbachev provides an example of this form of self-legitimation. By 1990, the Soviet leader was aware that he had lost the support of much of the population. But influential foreign leaders continued to support and encourage Gorbachev, which helped to convince him that his approach was legitimate, even if unpopular. The third form of external legitimation is the most abstract, opaque and indirect. It applies where leaders of a given state continue to believe in their own legitimacy because of their faith in an external role-model they consciously emulate. As long as the leadership of that external role-model retains faith in its own model, leaders in other countries copying it can continue to believe in themselves. Like the second mode of external legitimation, this one focuses on *self-legitimation*.

Legitimation in post-communist Russia

At the time of writing, Russia had recently installed its third post-communist president, Dmitrii Medvedev. Although Medvedev has committed himself to making Russia less presidential than it has been since December 1993, it remains a basically presidential system. Indeed, many have called it a super-presidential system, since the formal powers of the Russian president surpass those of most presidents. In light of this, the analysis here will be primarily of the presidency as the principal focus of the legitimation process.

Boris Yeltsin became the first popularly elected president of Russia in 1991, and the initial stages of his presidency were legitimized above all in terms of charisma and a claim to be building legal-rationality. Russia was in a revolutionary situation at the beginning of the 1990s, even in the absence of violent revolution. While many theorists maintain that revolutions necessarily entail violence,[18] this is not the case. If a country moves within the space of a few short years from having a one-party quasi-dictatorship with a centrally-planned, largely state-owned economy to a multi-party arrangement with a serious commitment to the introduction of an increasingly marketized and privatized economy, it has undergone a revolution. Since Weber and Rigby agree that it is primarily in a revolutionary phase that a charismatic leader is most likely to emerge, it is not surprising that Yeltsin was initially seen as a charismatic leader. His resistance to those who sought to reinstate an authoritarian USSR in August 1991 greatly enhanced his charismatic image.

But Yeltsin's charismatic legitimacy was already beginning to wane by 1993. State power is always exercised through a combination of coercion and legitimacy, and late-1993 witnessed a clear move away from the latter and towards the former, as the president ordered troops to fire on the White House (Russia's parliamentary building). Over the next few years, Yeltsin became an increasing embarrassment to the Russian citizenry, as his frequent inebriation resulted in some serious diplomatic gaffes. By the time he was pressured to resign – 31 December 1999 – power was being exercised neither through legitimacy nor much coercion; it was dispersed, and central state power was barely being exercised at all. This demonstrates that coercion and legitimacy do not invariably co-exist in a zero-sum relationship, an important point to which we return below. When Putin succeeded Yeltsin, he was initially only the acting president. But to the extent that his power was legitimated in any classic Weberian sense, it was partly in having been named and approved as successor by the previous president. However, this form of legitimation is associated with Weber's 'traditional' mode, rather than with either legal-rationality or charisma. In this sense, it was an inappropriate form of legitimation for a country claiming to be modern and democratizing. But Putin soon ran for election as president, and by March 2000 had won in a more or less genuinely competitive election. This could be argued to have granted him a form of legitimacy typically associated with modern democracy and legal-rationality. However, the overwhelming majority of developed democracies are parliamentary, while a small number are mixed.[19] As scholars such as Fred Riggs and Juan Linz have pointed out, there is only one presidentialist established liberal democracy, the USA.[20] So this legitimation mode for Putin begins to look problematic, and the source of any legitimacy he might have enjoyed has to be sought elsewhere.

Early in his first term of office, Putin stated that he favoured a 'dictatorship of laws'. This can be and sometimes is interpreted as indicating that the new president favoured the rule of law. That is certainly how Putin himself sought to present his position. Yet many analysts have argued that the concept of a 'dictatorship of laws' was either mere rhetoric or else should be interpreted as meaning that the state will use the judicial and law-enforcement systems to enforce a de facto dictatorship. It is worth returning here to Rigby's summary of Weber, since this emphasises that Weber's interest in the rule of law was more oriented towards the *Rechtsstaat* (law-based state) than towards democracy:

> Even more striking is Weber's oft-noted failure to discuss modern 'bourgeois' democracy in the context of his analysis of the rational-legal system, and its relegation to an appendix to his treatment of the routinization of charisma ... If, then, it was not in the liberal democracies of his day that Weber saw the 'pure type of rational-legal rule with bureaucratic administrative staff' historically most closely approximated, where was it? The answer, as has frequently been noted, is of course the bureaucratic *Rechtsstaat*.[21]

Moreover, as Rigby goes on to point out, while Weber's preferred system was one in which the bureaucratic order would be subject to some form of parliamentary oversight, the German theorist was equally clear that such a system should still have strong leadership – '... in [Weber's] growing pessimism he found his one hope in a new form of charismatic rule which he termed "plebiscitary leader-democracy"'.[22] Thus if Putin really meant that Russia was to move towards the rule of law under his strong and charismatic leadership, which was more important than democracy, but in which there would be some semblance of the latter, he could be argued to have been acting completely in line with Weber's conception of legal-rationality.

To this point, the word transition has been employed but not defined. There continues to be heated debate about the meaning of transition, and especially about identification of the point at which transition begins to mutate into consolidation. But the issue of how to define and identify transition is essentially sidestepped here; that argument belongs elsewhere. All that is suggested here is that, in the context of post-communist states, transition was in the 1990s closely related not only to the concept of democratization in the political sphere, but also to marketization and privatization in the economic. Few would dispute this.[23] If this uncontroversial premise is accepted, it can be used as another component of our argument about post-communist legitimation in Russia.

There is plenty of evidence that many citizens in early post-communism – generally, not only in Russia – had only a vague understanding of democracy. For many, it was a system that was above all fundamentally different from its predecessor and that delivered prosperity. In the minds of many citizens, democracy and capitalism were at least closely linked and interactive, if not actually identical. Two of the key components of capitalism were taken to be marketization and privatization. Numerous post-communist politicians throughout central and eastern Europe and the CIS contributed to this notion of near-identification of democracy and capitalism; in this, Russia was no exception. For reasons brilliantly explained by Joel Hellman,[24] many politicians in Russia wanted economic reform – but only to the point where their personal interests were maximized and subject to least risk. Part of the reason for the major conflict between Yeltsin and the Russian parliament in the early 1990s was that his acting prime minister, Yegor Gaidar, wanted to take reform beyond the point of maximum interest to members of the elite and into the risk zone. He was in a real sense Russia's equivalent of Poland's Leszek Balcerowicz – *except* that Gaidar's plans were hijacked before they could progress very far, unlike those of Balcerowicz. While some dispute this, it is argued here that the fact that Poland was the first post-communist state to start to grow its economy is largely attributable to Balcerowicz's early and powerful 'shock therapy'.[25] The relevance of all this to legitimation is that poor *economic* performance in a transition state can damage the image of the *political* system being advocated by those running that state.

That the emphasis on the economy can damage the development of the rule of law – and implicitly democracy – was recognized by none other than quintessential free marketeer Milton Friedman in the early 2000s. Having argued in the 1990s that the most important objective for post-communist states was to 'privatize, privatize, privatize', he acknowledged in 2002 that, 'It turns out that the rule of law is probably more basic than privatization. Privatization is meaningless if you don't have the rule of law'.[26]

At this juncture, let us return to President Putin. Several legitimation modes could be seen to be operating in the early Putin era, of which only two have so far been identified – old traditional (in having been named a successor) and legal-rational (more or less legitimately elected; emphasis on the dictatorship of laws).[27] But there were others. An obvious one was charisma. After the national humiliation the drunken Yeltsin was seen to have brought to his country, his clean-living judo expert successor was admired by many Russians. Putin exemplified the plebiscitarian ruler identified by Weber. Another mode was eudaemonism. There is no question that overall living standards rose substantially under Putin. It is equally indisputable that Putin was fortunate in this. Had it not been for the significant increases in global oil prices following 9/11 and the subsequent invasion of Iraq, Russia – which is reputed to have the world's second largest oil reserves – would not have enjoyed the impressive economic growth it enjoyed in the 2000s until the Global Economic Crisis began to impact upon it. This is not to deny that there were also potentially delegitimizing aspects of this economic 'miracle'. Notably, the distribution of wealth led to much discontent among many ordinary Russians, as the Gini coefficient that had already increased under Yeltsin continued to climb. But the significance of such discontent can be exaggerated; as long as most citizens believe that some of the new wealth will eventually trickle down to them, widening Gini coefficients do not necessarily act as a serious delegitimator.

The list of legitimation modes employed by the Putin regime has still not been exhausted. Arguably the most significant of all was the use of official nationalism. Whereas Yeltsin only succeeded in humiliating Russians when they needed their leader to help them out of their identity crisis, Putin succeeded in giving them back a sense of pride and identity. Unfortunately, this was – as nationalism so often is – partly at the expense of others. Thus Putin was able to play on the Russian imperial tradition through various forms of leverage, most notably energy, over other countries. While this might have upset many Germans and been seen by them as an act of corruption or humiliation, the appointment of former Chancellor Gerhard Schroeder as chair of the shareholders' committee of the company responsible for managing the gas pipeline between Russia and Germany (Nord Stream) was symbolically a major coup.[28]

Finally, further exploration of the old traditional mode is warranted, since some have argued that *this* was the primary legitimator of the Putin regime. According to Russian commentator Stanislav Belkovsky,[29] Putin's legitimacy was based on 'the ritual of Russian monarchy'. Belkovsky argues that the legitimacy of a Russian Tsar manifests itself in two key factors. One is that there are no alternatives. Certainly, while Putin was formally challenged for the presidency in the presidential elections of both 2000 and 2004, none of his competitors constituted a serious challenge to him. In this sense, the notion of 'no alternatives' applies to Putin. The other factor is that the monarch can do no wrong. While it would be quite misleading to claim that Putin did no wrong, or that the Russian citizenry never criticized him, he was at least as much a 'Teflon' president as President Reagan was said to have been.[30] Belkovsky claims that Putin did not permit any criticism of himself; while this is an exaggeration, the second Russian president did ensure that criticism in the media, particularly the electronic, was severely limited.

Like Putin before him, current Russian president Medvedev owes his position largely to his predecessor, even if he too has been popularly mandated. According to the analysis outlined in the previous paragraph, this continues old traditionalist legitimation, since 'The next czar can only be a person chosen by the czar – not an outsider'.[31] But the measures taken to legitimate Medvedev's presidency involve several other legitimation modes. These include renewed emphasis on Russian official nationalism (seen for instance in the way the Georgia crisis of mid-2008 was handled and presented) and at least as much stress placed on the importance of the rule of law as Putin did in the early stages of his tenure.

One of the clearest signs that Russia was moving away from its putative commitment to both democracy and the rule of law would have been if Putin had had his presidency extended, as many other CIS presidents – notably in Central Asia and Belarus – have done. Many assumed that Putin would do this. But once again confounding most analysts, Putin cleverly managed to hold on to much of his power without acting in any way unconstitutionally. By essentially nominating a close and presumably trustworthy associate as his successor, then having that protégé name him prime minister, Putin was able to retain much of his status and power. Since Medvedev formally assumed office in May 2008, he has so far proved more or less willing to share power with his predecessor, so that Russia currently has a bicephalous or dual executive leadership. While there were signs by early 2009 that Medvedev was becoming more assertive vis-à-vis Putin, he had not yet clearly become *the* leader at the time of writing. But as noted above, Medvedev – a former law professor – has also proved in some ways to be even more committed to the rule of law than was Putin.

Arguably the best evidence to this effect is Medvedev's determination to reduce corruption in Russia. Both Yeltsin and Putin promised to introduce an anti-corruption law but failed to do so. Indeed, in terms of 'doing no wrong' discussed above, Putin acknowledged in his final press conference as Russian president that corruption had been 'the most wearying and difficult to resolve' of all the problems he had faced during his presidency.[32] This was close to admitting failure. In contrast, Medvedev made it clear in his first major presidential campaign speech (22 January 2008) that, were he to be elected, he would clamp down on corruption, as part of a larger project to enhance the rule of law in Russia. The future president did not mince his words – 'Russia is a country of legal nihilism ... Not a single European country can "boast" of such a level of disdain for the law.'[33] Once elected, he made good on this promise, signing a decree in May designed to counteract corruption[34] and a National Anti-Corruption Plan at the end of July, and then submitting four draft anti-corruption laws to the Duma in early October. In marked contrast to earlier anti-corruption bills introduced during the Yeltsin and Putin presidencies, the Medvedev versions were soon adopted, and with relatively few amendments. The new laws became effective from the beginning of January 2009. While it cannot be denied that some of his actions are a cause for concern – the treatment of Khodorkovsky, for example – President Medvedev has taken some significant steps in the right direction in terms of strengthening the rule of law in Russia.

Legitimacy in post-communist Russia

The focus in the previous section was primarily on the ways in which the three post-Soviet Russian presidents (have) sought to legitimate their rule. This section will seek to address the much more difficult issue of how effective such legitimation attempts have been. In short, the focus switches from legitimation to legitimacy – or, to use Rigby's terminology, from 'legitimating intent' to 'legitimating force'.[35]

Legitimacy is a notoriously difficult phenomenon to measure. Lipset, following Gabriel Almond, maintains that one useful indicator of a high level of legitimacy is a 'secular political culture', manifested mainly in national rituals and holidays.[36] This is highly ethnocentric, and far from convincing. For instance, several Communist states could be seen to have enjoyed a high level of legitimacy by this criterion, whereas coercion may have been more salient in them much of the time. Meyer's 'ultimate test' of no or little legitimacy has already been mentioned, and is more convincing. But it does not help us in attempting to determine levels of legitimacy in non-crisis periods. Beyond this test, legitimacy can usefully be approached in terms of a 4×3 matrix, with the four-point horizontal axis representing legitimacy (none; low; medium; high) and the three-point vertical axis representing legitimating agencies (elite; staffs; populace). Various measures can be employed to produce ultimately subjective assessments of the level of system legitimacy accorded by each of the three agencies, which can then be used for marking the appropriate cells. A system can be said to enjoy a high level of legitimacy in the following permutation:

	None	Low	Medium	High
Elite				X
Staffs				X
Populace				X

Conversely, the system looks set to collapse in the following permutation, since not only the masses, but even the staffs and elite have lost faith in it, and in themselves as rulers:

	None	Low	Medium	High
Elite	X			
Staffs	X			
Populace	X			

Unfortunately, a level of subjectivity or arbitrariness – and certainly care – is required not only in deciding in which cells to place our crosses, but also on how to interpret or classify permutations other than the extreme and straightforward cases just outlined. To demonstrate this, let us assume for the sake of argument that the following matrices represent the situations in two Communist states during 1989:

China, early-June 1989

	None	Low	Medium	High
Elite				X
Staffs				X
Populace	X			

Romania, late-December 1989

	None	Low	Medium	High
Elite				X
Staffs	X			
Populace	X			

The two matrices are similar; the cross in only one cell (staffs) has changed position – albeit from one end of the axis to the other.[37] In this sense, we might initially be tempted to use similar terms to describe the overall pattern of the two matrices. Yet the practical implications of relatively small changes in these two abstract portrayals of the level of legitimacy in actual countries are highly significant. In the Chinese case, the leaders and a key section of the staffs (that part of the military brought to Beijing to suppress the Tiananmen protesters) still believed in the system, and were thus able to suppress the mass unrest; the system survived, and in fact went on to prosper. In Romania, in contrast, Ceauşescu and his immediate entourage apparently still believed in their right to rule, while much of the citizenry was quite alienated from the Communist system by 1989. But it can be argued that it was neither the views of the elite nor of the citizenry that ultimately mattered. Rather, the fact that the military and an important section of the security police (*Securitate*) lost faith in the Ceauşescu regime and turned against it was in many ways the crucial factor leading to both regime and system collapse.

What conclusions can be drawn from these abstractions? While *overall* assessments of the level of legitimacy in two (or more) cases may look rather similar, what appear to be relatively small differences can have profoundly significant implications. Before making any references to the overall level of legitimacy in any particular country, it is clearly important to disaggregate *at least* to the three types of agency identified here. In fact, the two concrete cases used here to make an abstract point suggest that the staffs, at least, should sometimes be further disaggregated into coercive (military, police) and administrative agencies; the attitudes of the former are typically more significant than those of the latter. This said, the rest of this part of the analysis will focus on only three types of agency.

Having disaggregated in terms of the three potentially legitimating agencies, it is possible to assign a numerical value to each of the levels of legitimacy (none = 0; high = 3), and then score a particular state in terms of the three agencies. In the case of China, the score would be 6, whereas Romania's would be 3. Having done this, there could then be a somewhat arbitrary decision on cut-off points (e.g. total score 1 to 3 = low level of legitimacy; 4 to 6 = medium level of legitimacy; 6 to 9 = high level of legitimacy). *However*, while such a method would often be a satisfactory way of assessing legitimacy levels, we must also be aware of potentially misleading permutations. If the aggregate score includes a 0 or 1 for either the elite or the staffs, then what might initially seem like a medium or high level of overall legitimacy needs to be challenged. For example, a given system might score 6 or 7 (3 each for elite and populace, 0 or 1 for staffs), when it is in fact in a serious legitimacy crisis because of staff hostility. Awareness of the importance of disaggregation should help analysts to make a more accurate assessment of the legitimacy situation in a given state and the likelihood of regime and/or system collapse.

Most of the preceding argument has been theoretical, and much of it speculative. It might therefore appear worthwhile considering survey evidence relevant to the issue of legitimacy in Russia. Unfortunately, one of the potential problems with mass surveys is that certain concepts familiar enough to professional political scientists may be almost unknown among the general population. Legitimacy and legitimation fall into this category. Pilot surveys on corruption run by the author in four European states (including Russia) in 2003 revealed that both the terms 'legitimacy' and 'state' were problematic for many respondents. Consequently, a question that originally sought to elicit popular views on 'the legitimacy of the state' had to be reworded to refer to the 'authority of the government'. Many surveys that may be cited to gauge popular legitimacy – on trust in or respect for particular politicians or political institutions, for example – may in fact be reflecting popularity and/or be referring to the regime rather than the system. However, this confusion only endorses the argument here that the distinction between these two concepts is often an artificial one in transition states. With this caveat in mind, it is worth briefly considering what surveys reflect in terms of the possible level of legitimacy of various Russian presidential regimes and, by implication given the blurred line between regime and system in transition states, of the Russian political system.

Numerous surveys conducted in Russia in the 2000s indicate that Putin was a highly popular president, and that a majority of Russians were more than willing to give him their consent to rule Russia; while popularity and legitimacy are not synonymous, nor are they mutually exclusive. In one 2004 survey cited by Willerton, 50 percent of respondents indicated that they trusted President Putin, compared with just 1 percent that trusted political parties.[38] A February 2009 survey conducted by VTsIOM revealed that some 70 percent of respondents approved of President Medvedev, while Prime Minister Putin was approved of by 74 percent; the same survey suggested that 43 percent of Russians trusted (or had confidence in – the Russian word is *doverie*) their president, whereas 59 percent trusted the prime minister.[39] If the results of such normative assessments are combined with the presidential electoral results of 2000, 2004 and 2008, it becomes difficult to disagree with Richard Sakwa's conclusion that the Russian leadership does enjoy popular legitimacy.[40]

Nevertheless, some sceptics argue that Russians still live in fear of their political masters, so that surveys are not an accurate measure of the citizenry's 'real' evaluations and attitudes. A simple reply to such sceptics is that they need to provide alternative evidence. Mattei Dogan is among those analysts who believe that surveys are in general poor reflectors of the actual level of state legitimacy in a society (generally, not specifically in Russia). He therefore advocates measuring legitimacy through the use of proxy methods. His starting point for assessing the degree of legitimacy is to assume that 'the lower the degree of legitimacy, the higher is the amount of coercion'. From this he argues that the degree of legitimacy can be assessed by considering 'some indicators of coercion, such as the absence of political rights and of civil liberties'. According to Dogan, a country can be ranked according to a number of variables designed to assess the level of coercion. However, it must be acknowledged that most of the variables are highly subjective, and that two analysts could reach quite different conclusions in assessing the level of coercion based on factors such as 'free competition among parties' or 'freedom of expression'. It is therefore fortunate that Dogan proposes another proxy measure of the level of legitimacy – the level of corruption: 'A high level of corruption is one of the best symptoms of delegitimation.'[41]

Despite the numerous problems involved in measuring corruption, most analysts nowadays accept that if using several different methods – multi-angulation – yields similar results, then we can be reasonably confident that the level of corruption has been assessed with an acceptable degree of accuracy. If there is indeed a correlation between corruption levels and the level of legitimacy, what can be said about post-Soviet Russia?

Most of the techniques used nowadays for assessing corruption levels are relatively new, so that multi-angulation is not possible for the whole period since 1991. For instance, the most frequently cited global assessment, the Transparency International Corruption Perceptions Index (TICPI), dates only from 1995, and Russia was first assessed in 1996.[42] Space limitations and the fact that I have recently produced detailed analyses of this elsewhere mean that only the briefest summary of the corruption situation in Russia will be provided here.[43] Using various techniques produces similar results, viz. that Russia appears to be among the most corrupt states in the world, and compares particularly badly with other industrial and post-industrial states. The corruption situation did improve somewhat during Putin's first presidential term of office, but then deteriorated again. It will be interesting to track the situation under Medvedev.

According to Dogan's argument, the corruption situation in Russia suggests a low level of legitimacy. But it must be acknowledged that Dogan appears to be considering only popular legitimacy; his whole approach strongly suggests this. Moreover, his argument about the relationship between coercion and legitimacy is framed in terms of a zero-sum situation. Yet ever enigmatic Russia means that such an assumption must be questioned.[44] It has already been argued that the late-Yeltsin era casts doubt upon the common assumption that lower levels of legitimacy will necessarily mean higher levels of coercion. While it is true that there were odd signs of increasing coercion in the late-1990s, such as a deteriorating score in Freedom House's assessment of press freedom, these were relatively marginal.[45] Even more significantly, surveys conducted in the early-2000s suggested that most Russians were pleased that Putin appeared to be taking a strong line against groups that many ordinary Russians believed had taken unfair advantage of the relatively more liberal Yeltsin era. Expressed another way, the Putin regime appeared to be increasing its popular legitimacy in part by increasing coercion.

Conclusions

It has been pointed out that a number of analysts – possibly including T.H. Rigby himself – are unwilling to accept concepts such as eudaemonism and official nationalism as legitimation modes. Clearly, I disagree with this position. This is to no small extent because the clear distinction often drawn between system and regime is increasingly difficult to sustain in the contemporary world – particularly in transition states, with which neither Rigby nor Weber was explicitly concerned. But the argument here that eudaemonism, new traditionalism, etc. should be added to the list of legitimation modes does not mean that all modes should be treated as equals. It has already been argued that official nationalism, for example, should only ever function short-term as a principal legitimator. Since Weber himself saw charismatic legitimacy as relatively short-term, and legal-rationality as the only appropriate long-term legitimator of the modern state, the notion of a hierarchy of legitimation modes is perfectly compatible with his classic approach.

Acknowledging that legitimation modes are not all equal is useful, inter alia, for analysing the stability of a polity. Ceteris paribus, polities that are highly dependent on either charisma or eudaemonism, for example, are more likely to experience significant challenges from their populations than are polities firmly grounded in legal-rationality. This point is highly relevant to the current (2009) situation in Russia. While President Medvedev made it clear immediately upon taking office that he was committed to the development of a rule of law culture in Russia, and hence signalled his intention to move towards legal-rational legitimation, it will take years for such a culture to develop. Yet the Global Economic Crisis and the massive decrease in the price of oil hit Russia just months after Medvedev took power, undermining the capacity of the Russian state to be legitimated on the basis of eudaemonism. Does this mean that Russia is facing a legitimacy crisis?

While there is no doubt that Russia *could* experience a full-blown legitimacy crisis – and soon – this is not a *necessary* scenario, for two reasons. First, the country's leadership could simply revert to the centuries-old tradition of exercising its power more on the basis of coercion than on legitimacy. Such an overt move to coercive dictatorship can from some perspectives be interpreted as a legitimacy crisis, since it indicates that the political leadership has essentially given up – at least on a temporary basis – its attempts to rule primarily on the basis of legitimacy. On the other hand, it suggests that the leadership has not lost faith in itself and its right to rule – i.e. that *self*-legitimation is still effective. This would therefore constitute only a *partial* legitimacy crisis, one of popular legitimacy.

Even the suggestion that a move towards greater coercion would be a sign of a crisis of popular legitimacy may be a Western-centric assumption. As Sil and Cheng Chen have argued, there is probably a weak correlation between legitimacy and democracy in Russia.[46] If many Russians are more concerned about order than democracy, then it should not be assumed by Western liberal democrats that leaders who offer and provide the former, with scant regard for the latter, are necessarily experiencing low levels of popular legitimacy. Indeed, quite the opposite might pertain in the Russian case; if democracy is associated with chaos, corruption and criminality, then leaders tending towards the authoritarian end of the political spectrum who can offer (and eventually provide) order, and far more manageable levels of corruption and criminality, may enjoy a high level of popular legitimacy. The reader is reminded at this point that Weber himself was more concerned with legitimacy than democracy. Contemporary analysts who assume that only the latter type of political system is compatible with the former are entitled to their opinion, but must acknowledge that they have departed from Weberian analysis.[47]

The second reason that a legitimacy crisis in Russia might not occur relates to what I have in earlier work called the 'legitimating effect of legitimation shifts'.[48] According to this argument, a regime's leadership can become aware that it is losing popular legitimacy, but seeks to reverse this decline by shifting its emphasis from one or two dominant legitimation modes to one or two others. For example, if economic crisis in Russia means that eudaemonism is no longer going to be an effective legitimator, then a shift in emphasis to official nationalism and/or the development of the rule of law may avert a major decline in popular legitimacy.

The official nationalist notion of 'making Russia great again' could act as a medium-to-long-term *telos* (goal) for Russia – though for reasons already elaborated, this would be risky. A safer bet would be to emphasize the notion of *developing* the rule of law, as distinct from actually achieving it. This would not have been possible in the Soviet era, since Marxist-Leninist ideology and practice were ultimately incompatible with the rule of law. But there is no such impediment in contemporary Russia. Were this focus on developing a rule of law culture to become either a or the dominant legitimation mode, the possibility that legal-rationality and goal-rationality could blur – or at least overlap – arises. While it is unlikely that T.H. Rigby would have ever envisaged his innovative concept of goal-rationality merging with legal-rationality,[49] Russian developments since the collapse of the Communist system have created new scenarios that in turn have required us to revisit and refine notions of legitimation and legitimacy. While he may not have realized it at the time he devised the concept of goal-rationality, Rigby's contribution to theories of legitimation has more traction and applicability than simply to Communist states.

But what no analyst can predict with any degree of conviction is whether or not a merging of goal-rationality and legal-rationality would avoid a legitimacy crisis in Russia. If Medvedev uses his fight against corruption as the principal method for developing a rule of law culture in Russia, it could backfire on him. Russian staffs have proven very capable in the past – including during the Communist era – of blocking the implementation of the leaders' wishes and policies if these are perceived by those staffs to be against their own interests. If the current anti-corruption drive is perceived by large sections of the Russian staffs to threaten their position, they could seek to counter it and could lose respect for the leadership (i.e. Russia would have moved into one of the problematic '6' or '7' legitimacy situations identified above). A smart if cynical approach by Medvedev would be to implement the anti-corruption measures with enthusiasm among the administrative staffs but weakly among the coercive staffs. Whether or not that would be sufficient to avoid a legitimacy crisis would depend largely on the actual circumstances at the time. In the current uncertain global situation, it would be foolhardy to speculate on what those might be.

Notes

1 I am indebted to the Australian Research Council (ARC) for funding that has facilitated those aspects of the research for this project relating to cor-

ruption (ARC Large Grant No. A79930728 and ARC Discovery Grant No. DP0558453).

2 T.H. Rigby, 'Introduction: Political legitimacy, Weber and communist mono-organisational systems', in T.H. Rigby and Ferenc Fehér (eds) (1982), *Political Legitmation in Communist States* (London: Macmillan), pp.1–26. It should be noted that Rigby had already begun to develop this concept in an earlier work – see T.H. Rigby, 'A conceptual approach to authority, power and policy in the Soviet Union', in T.H. Rigby, A. Brown, P. Reddaway (eds) (1980), *Authority, Power and Policy in the USSR: Essays Dedicated to Leonard Schapiro* (London: Macmillan), esp. pp.19–21. However, his introductory chapter in the 1982 volume provides a much fuller elaboration and has been more influential.

3 Weber died in 1920, not long after the October Revolution in Russia, but before Communist power had been consolidated in what at that time was the only nascent Communist state. In line with a common convention, Communist refers here to the practice of states, whereas communist refers to the theories of Marx, Lenin and others. However, for both stylistic and convention-related reasons, the term post-communist is used here, rather than post-Communist.

4 H. Gerth and C. Wright Mills (eds) (1970), *From Max Weber: Essays in Sociology* (London: Routledge and Kegan Paul), pp.78–9.

5 The best-known analyses are J. Habermas, 'What does a legitimation crisis mean today? Legitimation problems in late capitalism', in W. Connolly (ed.) (1984), *Legitimacy and the State* (Oxford: Blackwell), pp.134–79; J. Habermas (1976), *Legitimation Crisis* (London: Heinemann).

6 Rigby, 'Introduction', p.10.

7 Ibid., p.12.

8 J. Pakulski (1986), 'Legitimacy and mass compliance: Reflections on Max Weber and Soviet-type societies', *British Journal of Political Science*, XVI, 1, 35–56. The reference here to overt mass unrest relates to the observation by Alfred Meyer that we can only really be certain a communist state is illegitimate or close to being so if it collapses, or if there are clear signs of a danger of this; overt mass unrest is one such sign. A. Meyer, 'Legitimacy of power in east central Europe', in S. Sinanian, I. Deak and P. Ludz (eds) (1972), *Eastern Europe in the 1970s* (New York: Praeger), p.67.

9 A. Heller, 'Legitimation', in F. Feher, A. Heller, G. Márkus (1984), *Dictatorship over Needs* (Oxford: Blackwell), pp.137–8.

10 For analysts advocating an essentially similar threefold division to Weber's, see, for example, Rigby, 'Introduction', pp.14, 17; P. Lewis, 'Legitimation and political crisis: East European developments in the post-Stalin period', in P. Lewis (ed.) (1984), *Eastern Europe: Political Crisis and Legitimation* (London: Croom Helm), p.6; F. Teiwes (1984), *Leadership, Legitimacy and Conflict in China* (London: Macmillan), pp.44–5; Pakulski, 'Legitimacy and mass compliance', p.36.

11 For example, T. Skocpol (1979), *States and Social Revolutions* (Cambridge: Cambridge University Press), p.32; C. Tilly (1993), *European Revolutions 1492–1992* (Oxford: Blackwell).

12 Not everyone agrees with the nomenclature used here. Thus James Malloy's preferred term for what is here called a regime is 'government', while he uses the term regime to refer to what is here called a system. J. Malloy,

'Contemporary authoritarian regimes', in M. Hawkesworth and M. Kogan (eds) (1992), *Encyclopedia of Government and Politics*, Vol.1 (London: Routledge), pp.229–46.

13 S.M. Lipset (1960), *Political Man* (New York: Doubleday), pp.77–83.

14 Rigby, 'Introduction', p.1.

15 G. Gill (1986), 'Changing patterns of systemic legitimation in the USSR', *Coexistence*, XXIII, 249; S. White (1986), 'Economic performance and communist legitimacy', *World Politics*, XXXVIII, 3, 462–82.

16 From a September 2008 speech available at http://www.cfr.org/publication/ 17228/zoellicks_speech_at_the_international_institute_for_strategic_ studies.html (accessed 14 January 2009).

17 I am indebted to one of my former PhD students, Dr. Matt Killingsworth, for having triggered this idea in my mind through his work on lustration in Poland.

18 A.S. Cohan (1975), *Theories of Revolution* (London: Nelson), p.25.

19 The term mixed is used here in preference to the more common terms, semi-presidentialism and semi-parliamentarism. This is because the latter two terms skew conceptualization towards either the president or the parliament; while the practice of particular systems does orient more towards one agency or the other, the generic term should not.

20 F. Riggs (1988), 'The survival of presidentialism in America: Para-constitutional practices', *International Political Science Review*, IX, 4, 247–78; F. Riggs (1997), 'Presidentialism versus parliamentarism: Implications for representativeness and legitimacy', *International Political Science Review*, XVIII, 3, 253–78; J. Linz, 'Presidential or parliamentary democracy: Does it make a difference?', in J. Linz and A. Valenzuela (eds) (1994), *The Failure of Presidential Democracy: Vol. 1 – Comparative Perspectives* (Baltimore: Johns Hopkins University Press), pp.3–87.

21 Rigby, 'Introduction', p.8.

22 Ibid., p.9.

23 Though see T. Carothers (2002), 'The end of the transition paradigm', *Journal of Democracy*, XIII, 1, 5–21.

24 J. Hellman (1998), 'Winner takes all: The politics of partial reform in post-communist transitions', *World Politics*, L, 2, 203–34.

25 Inverted commas are used here because the term shock therapy can be misleading. There is no question that Balcerowicz rapidly introduced a number of radical economic reforms. On the other hand, Poland's privatisation process – a key component of the move towards capitalism – was slower than in some of the other central and eastern European states.

26 J. Gwartney and R. Lawson (eds) (2002), *Economic Freedom of the World: 2002 Annual Report* (Calgary: Fraser Institute), pp.xvii–xviii.

27 Those who criticize Russian presidential elections and claim they have been undemocratic need to bear in mind the US situation. Technically, US presidents are not *directly* elected by the people. More significantly, George W. Bush won in 2000 only because of a questionable Supreme Court ruling; in terms of the majority will, Al Gore should have won that election.

28 It is acknowledged that this appointment led to much criticism in both Russia and Germany. Some Russians considered it wrong to appoint a foreigner, especially a German, to such a key position, while many Germans sus-

pected Schroeder of having cut a deal with the Russians shortly before the German elections to ensure he had a secure and well-paid position were he to lose. However, an SPD parliamentarian more or less convinced me over dinner in Berlin in December 2008 that Schroeder accepted this position for ultimately honourable rather than selfish reasons – viz. wanting to maximise the likelihood that his fellow Germans would have a reliable energy source in an unreliable world. As for Russian critics – while not all were placated, many apparently did eventually accept that it was prestigious to have a former German Chancellor as the chair of a major Russian project, and that it made sense to have a German in a high position in the project, given that the pipeline terminated in Germany.

29 S. Belkovsky, 'What's the secret of Vladimir Putin's legitimacy?', *New Times*, 8 October 2007.
30 Teflon is a non-stick coating material, so that a Teflon president is one to whom criticism and scandal do not adhere. For an analyst using this term with reference to Putin, see J. Willerton, 'Putin and the hegemonic presidency', in S. White, Z. Gitelman, R. Sakwa (eds) (2005), *Developments in Russian Politics* (6th edn) (Basingstoke: Palgrave Macmillan), p.37.
31 Belkovsky, 'What's the secret'. A similar point is made by Vice-President of the Russian Centre for Political Trends Vitalii Ivanov, who calls Medvedev 'the younger Tsar' and maintains: 'His legitimacy derives from Putin's legitimacy.' V. Ivanov, 'Suverenitet obiazyvaet', *Izvestiia*, 4 February 2008.
32 V. Putin (2008), 'Transcript of Annual Big Press Conference', 14 February 2008, http://www.kremlin.ru/eng/speeches/2008/02/14/1011_type82915_160266.shtml (accessed 19 February 2008).
33 D. Medvedev, 'Ianvarskie tezisy Dmitriia Medvedeva', *Rossiiskaia gazeta – Nedelia*, 24 January 2008 (accessed 20 October 2008).
34 D. Medvedev, 'Ukaz Prezidenta Rossiiskoi Federatsii ot 19 maia 2008 g. N 815 "O merakh po protivodeistviiu korruptsii"', *Rossiiskaia gazeta*, 22 May 2008 (accessed 20 October 2008).
35 Rigby, 'Introduction', p.11.
36 Lipset, *Political Man*, p.80.
37 The assessment of the level of popular legitimacy in China in mid-1989 is wittingly contentious, and it is accepted here that a good case can be made for moving the cross to the 'low' cell. But the Chinese authorities certainly perceived a serious problem, as witnessed by their treatment of Zhao Ziyang and the fact that the Chinese capital was placed under martial law until January 1990. Moreover, the primary intention here is to make a *theoretical* point that may or may not accurately reflect the actual situation in a given country at a particular juncture.
38 Willerton, 'Putin', p.37.
39 *Interfax*, 17 February 2009, as cited in *Johnson's Russia List*, 18 February 2009 and checked on the VTsIOM website.
40 R. Sakwa, 'Politics in Russia', in S. White, Z. Gitelman, R. Sakwa (eds) (2005), *Developments in Russian Politics* (6th edn) (Basingstoke: Palgrave Macmillan, p.16.
41 M. Dogan, 'Conceptions of legitimacy', in M. Hawkesworth and M. Kogan (eds) (2004), *Encyclopedia of Government and Politics* (2nd edn) (London: Routledge), pp.114–15.

42 Other well-known Transparency International assessments, notably the Bribe Payers Index and the Global Corruption Barometer, are even more recent, dating only from 1999 and 2003 respectively.
43 L. Holmes (2008), 'Corruption and organised crime in Putin's Russia', *Europe-Asia Studies*, LX, 6, 1017–37; L. Holmes, 'Corruption, governance and democratic practice in Russia: From Putin to Medvedev', International Conference on State Governance and Democratic Practice in Russia, National Chengchi University, Taipei, 8–9 November 2008 (available on request from the author).
44 Churchill's 1939 quip that Russia 'is a riddle, wrapped in a mystery, inside an enigma' still resonates 70 years later!
45 Thus, while Russia's score for press freedom did decline between 1994 and 1999, Freedom House continued to categorize the Russian press as 'partly free' until well into the Putin era (2003) – at which point it was downgraded to 'not free'.
46 R. Sil and Cheng Chen (2004), 'State legitimacy and the (in)significance of democracy in post-communist Russia', *Europe-Asia Studies*, LVI, 3, 347–68.
47 While this issue is not central to the present analysis, it is noted that most Western analysts accept that Russia has its own limited – what is often called Schumpeterian, minimalist or electoralist – version of democracy anyway. Common terms used to describe this include 'managed' and 'guided' democracy.
48 L. Holmes (1993), *The End of Communist Power: Anti-Corruption Campaigns and Legitimation Crisis* (New York: Oxford University Press), pp.23, 40.
49 Rigby, like Weber, accepts that two or more legitimation modes may co-exist and jointly operate in any actual polity. However, the phenomenon being described here is not one of parallel or simultaneous modes, but rather of possible merging.

6
Perestroika as Revolution from Above

Archie Brown

Perestroika is an ambiguous concept. The term was chosen by Mikhail Gorbachev partly because the word 'reform' had been taboo in Soviet ruling circles ever since the 'Prague Spring' of 1968, the unfolding of which also put paid to Aleksei Kosygin's modest attempt to reform the Soviet economy. Gorbachev had used the word *perestroika* in speeches and writings on a number of occasions even before he became General Secretary of the Central Committee of the Communist Party of the Soviet Union (CPSU) in March 1985. What he meant by it, however, changed over time, especially during the period of less than seven years in which he was Soviet leader. In 1985 he believed that the Soviet system was reformable and 'perestroika' was for him essentially a synonym for reform. The imprecision of the word had the initial advantage that almost everyone could be in favour of perestroika because they meant so many different things by it. In retrospect, conservative Communists felt they had been hoodwinked. Given their political outlook, they should have opposed the reforms of the perestroika era more vigorously and earlier than they did. They were kept on board not only by the hierarchical nature of Soviet politics and the power and authority which accrued to the general secretaryship. What also wrongfooted them was Gorbachev's success in establishing the dividing line in Soviet politics as lying between a pro-perestroika progressive majority and a reactionary anti-perestroika minority.

Perestroika was linguistically as well as politically ambiguous. The word means reconstruction, and reconstruction in turn can mean anything from restructuring an existing edifice to constructing a building anew from the foundations up. At the beginning of the period in which Gorbachev headed the CPSU, perestroika had for him the first and narrower of these two meanings, notwithstanding the fact that he was the only serious reformer in the Politburo he inherited. In contrast, from the middle of 1988 Gorbachev was dismantling Soviet political structures, adopting policies designed to replace them with something new. He had essentially embraced the second and more radical meaning of perestroika. As Viktor Kuvaldin has put it: 'Gorbachev came increasingly to believe that what was needed was not a renovation or even an overhaul of the System but its replacement'.[1] When Kuvaldin added that this became 'a full replacement, from the roof to the foundation', the word order was not accidental.[2] Elena Bonner quotes her late husband, the physicist and leading dissident Andrei Sakharov (who died in December 1989) as saying: 'We began to create our new house, not from the basement but from the roof'.[3]

In due course that meant calling into question the Leninist foundations of the Soviet system. This was not, however – and could not be – Gorbachev's starting-point. Quite apart from the fact that it would have been suicidal for even the party leader to challenge the wisdom of Lenin, Gorbachev held the USSR's principal founder in high esteem. He has written that 'perestroika began under the sign of the late Lenin'.[4] He meant the Lenin of the NEP period when Lenin had some second thoughts on what had been constructed thus far, although that reconsideration did not extend to the Bolsheviks' monopoly of power. By the mid-way point of his less than seven years in the Kremlin, Gorbachev was breaking with Lenin*ism*, but continuing to cite Lenin selectively in support of the changes taking place. While still holding the office of General Secretary of the Central Committee of the CPSU, Gorbachev evolved into the kind of democratic socialist to be found in Western Europe – the type of social democrat, in fact, whom Lenin despised.[5] It was in 1988 that Gorbachev's reforms took on a system-transformative character, moving beyond mere reform. And by February 1990 he had explicitly endorsed the principle of 'political pluralism', thus going beyond the 'socialist pluralism' he had embraced as early as 1987.[6] Much later he was to write that the essence of the system on the eve of perestroika was 'the totalitarian control of one party'.[7]

There was plenty of dissatisfaction in Soviet society in the years immediately prior to the launch of perestroika but no serious pressure from below for change. There were no mass strikes, no significant disorder, and no rebellion within the ranks of the party, military, KGB or the population as a whole. In spite of a long-term decline in the rate of economic growth from the 1950s to the first half of the 1980s, the system of rewards and sanctions, the apparatus of coercion, and the monopoly of power of the Communist Party were all in place. Dissident groups were weaker, not stronger, than they had been one or two decades earlier. No movement from outside the party's ranks posed a threat to the leadership of the Communist state. Nor was there any civil society in the sense of autonomous organizations which could exert influence and act independently of the party-state authorities.[8]

Diversity behind the monolithic façade

There were, however, undercurrents within the Communist Party itself which were flowing in very different directions. Behind the monolithic façade which the party, with some success, presented both to the outside world and to Soviet citizens, its membership included Stalinists, nationalists, conservatives, liberal reformers (both those who favoured cultural and political liberalization and those whose primary concern was with introducing market elements into the economy), anti-Stalinists who looked to the late Lenin or the purged Bukharin as a source of inspiration, as well as socialists of a more social democratic disposition. Gorbachev's initially successful coalition-building brought together all except the first of these categories under the umbrella of perestroika.

Gorbachev, if we apply Isaiah Berlin's terms, was a fox, not a hedgehog (although Berlin's subject was writers, not politicians).[9] He was open to many ideas rather than being bound by one. He was ready from early on in his general secretaryship to make some concessions to the market, although he only gradually came round to the view that the market, rather than a plan, should be the main operational basis of the economy. Even in the last years of the Soviet Union, it was, however, a regulated market economy he favoured, for which he was much ridiculed by market fundamentalists. He hoped that the Soviet Union would be able to move to a market modified by governmental intervention of the kind practised in the Scandinavian social democracies. He was attracted also by the West German model of a 'social market economy' (although not by the more unconstrained capitalism favoured by Ronald Reagan and Margaret Thatcher).

Acceptance in principle of a market economy, as distinct from market elements within an essentially command economy, came, however, only in the last two to three years of Gorbachev's leadership, partly under the influence of Nikolai Petrakov who served as Gorbachev's economic aide throughout 1990. Until then Gorbachev had not had a professional economist on his personal staff. In spite of the fact that the slowdown in the rate of Soviet economic growth was one of the stimuli to perestroika, economic reform was rarely Gorbachev's top priority.[10] For his first five years in power, he left economic management very largely in the hands of the Chairman of the Council of Ministers, Nikolai Ryzhkov, whom he had placed in that post in succession to the veteran Brezhnevite, Nikolai Tikhonov. Gorbachev's own priorities were political reform and putting an end to the Cold War.

Gorbachev favoured also a cultural liberalization. He did not side with just one school or clique of Russian writers. One of his favourite contemporary authors was the Kirghiz novelist Chingiz Aitmatov who wrote in Russian and whom Gorbachev appointed to the short-lived Presidential Council.[11] Uniquely for a Soviet leader, Gorbachev admired both talented Westernisers and Russophiles within the intelligentsia as well as writers who did not fit neatly into the one category or the other. If politically, he was essentially a Westerniser, his cultural tastes were much more eclectic. Gorbachev's liberalism did not mean that he favoured only liberal writers. On the contrary, he was also attracted to the 'village prose' school of Russian writers, many of whom were, to a greater or lesser degree, Russian nationalists. One of the village prose authors, Valentin Rasputin, was, indeed, appointed to Gorbachev's Presidential Council, although he was not a member of the Communist Party. Perhaps more surprisingly, Gorbachev was supportive of the Russian nationalist painter, Ilia Glazunov. This was not because he approved of his political views, but because he admired his art. He was conscious also that it was art which appealed to a wide Russian public. Indeed, Aleksandr Iakovlev has recalled Gorbachev's anger in 1986 after he refused permission for Glazunov to have an exhibition of his paintings in the Manezh, the main exhibition hall in central Moscow. Gorbachev told Iakovlev that the exhibition must be allowed to go ahead. He added that if Iakovlev did not mend his ways, 'we will not in future be able to understand each other'.[12] Iakovlev described this as the 'sole direct threat' he received from Gorbachev during all their time working together.[13]

It is perhaps not surprising, then, that even Russians of a nationalist disposition could initially welcome the energetic new leader. For those nationalists who identified Russian greatness with a mighty Soviet state, perestroika appeared to offer the promise of a revitalization of their country. For those who believed that Soviet rule had displayed a reckless disregard for Russian's cultural heritage and natural environment, some of the early policies of the Gorbachev leadership offered encouragement. Especially following the disaster at the Chernobyl nuclear power plant in April 1986, Gorbachev and his allies in the Soviet leadership became increasingly sensitive to environmentalist concerns.

For example, the plan, hatched in the 1970s, to divert major Siberian rivers – risking grave ecological damage – was formally abandoned on 14 August 1986.[14] Informed scientific criticism played a significant part in influencing the decision, but similar objections had already been raised in Brezhnev's time without halting the project in its tracks. The campaign against the river diversion, which might have benefited Kazakhstan and Central Asia at the expense of Siberia, had involved Russian writers as well as scientists.

Prominent among the former was Sergei Zalygin, who grew up in Siberia. He was appointed editor of the influential monthly journal *Novyi mir* (New World) in August 1986 and before long it was publishing materials that even its great editor in the 1960s, Aleksandr Tvardovskii, could not get away with. A spate of appointments of new editors to journals which were, in their different ways, to acquire great importance during the perestroika period occurred in 1986. The conservative editor of the party's theoretical journal, *Kommunist*, Richard Kosolapov, was replaced by the philosopher of science and more open-minded intellectual, Ivan Frolov. The literary monthly *Znamia*, under its new editor Georgii Baklanov, rivalled *Novii mir* in its boldness in breaking Soviet taboos. *Moskovskie novosti* (Moscow News) and *Ogonek* (Little Light), saw their circulations take off dramatically under their bold new editors (also appointed in 1986) Yegor Iakovlev and Vitalii Korotich. These two weeklies were quickly in the vanguard of glasnost, pushing the boundaries of the new openness ever wider. Although there were also journals of an ever more openly nationalist and conservative orientation, it was the more liberal publications mentioned above which became forums for serious discussion of extending the scope of perestroika, with some of the more radically reformist members of the Soviet intelligentsia contributing. In turn, these journals and weeklies, which consistently outsold their Russian nationalist competitors, influenced public opinion more broadly.[15] In the face of this liberal advance, many of the Russian nationalists were by 1987–88 making common cause with the party conservatives in opposition to the radicalization of perestroika.

Thus, the political process, even in the years of an ever more radical reform agenda, 1986–88, was not entirely top-down, but increasingly involved a revitalized society and an openly argumentative intelligentsia. However, it was the power of appointment and the benevolent protection extended by Gorbachev and Iakovlev to editors and publications that were soon to be the subject of regular attack from conservative Communists which changed the terms of political discourse.

The new political leadership

The role of Aleksandr Iakovlev has sometimes been exaggerated – as, for example, when he is described as the 'architect of perestroika'. In reality his growing influence was entirely dependent on Gorbachev's goodwill and the fact that the general secretary needed an experienced party official capable of implementing policies he himself favoured. Nonetheless, especially since Gorbachev made some bad appointments as well as good ones, his speedy elevation of Iakovlev through the highest ranks of the party was of great importance.

Iakovlev had been not only one of Gorbachev's earliest appointments but also his most significant choice when in 1985 he brought him back into the Central Committee apparatus as head of the Department of Propaganda. He had been First Deputy Head and acting head of that department from 1965 to 1973. Iakovlev then spent a decade in Canada as Soviet Ambassador. It was Gorbachev's 1983 visit to Canada as head of a Soviet delegation which brought them into close contact and to the speedy realization that they shared much common ground – in particular, the belief that the Soviet system was in need of radical reform. Iakovlev's evolution to a reformist position had been a gradual one. His lengthy stay in a prosperous and democratic Western country profoundly influenced the development of his thinking. Earlier, he had played a far from enlightened role in 1968, presiding over the distorted propaganda about the Prague Spring which emanated from Moscow. However, by late 1972 he was already displaying a growing independence of mind when he published a newspaper article that he did not first clear with higher authority, in which he attacked all forms of nationalism and chauvinism, including Russian nationalism. It enraged both conservative Communists and Russian nationalists and was condemned by Brezhnev within the Secretariat of the Central Committee.[16] Iakovlev was ejected from the Central Committee apparatus, although the Soviet Embassy in Ottawa provided a soft landing.

His return to the Central Committee – and in a far more influential position than he had ever held before – meant that, with Gorbachev's full approval, he was able to supervise the appointments of new editors of the weeklies and monthlies already mentioned, publications which went on to provide a far sharper critique of the Soviet past and present than had ever been permitted before. Iakovlev's exceptionally speedy promotion would have been unthinkable but for Gorbachev's own support for the cultural liberalization and broadening of political debate that Iakovlev was encouraging. Immediately after his election to membership of the Central Committee, Iakovlev became in March 1986 a Secretary of the Central Committee. By July 1987 he was one of the senior secretaries – that is to say, he belonged to the tiny group of people who combined a Secretaryship of the Central Committee with full membership of the Politburo.

Within a consolidated Communist state, especially one such as the Soviet Union (or China) where the system was established indigenously rather than by foreign imposition, the successful initiation of change is more likely to come from within the ruling party rather than from outside its ranks.[17] And, given the hierarchical organization of the party, it is extremely difficult for change to get underway unless it is promoted – or, at a minimum, supported – by the party leader. Thus, Gorbachev's reformism and open-mindedness were of crucial importance in the radicalization of the political agenda between 1985 and 1988. One element of that was his power of appointment. He did not have an unconstrained power to change the membership of the Politburo. This, in the post-Stalin era, was more a matter of collective co-option, but it was a process in which the General Secretary's opinion counted for much more than anyone else's. An unusual feature of Gorbachev's use of his power of appointment was that it was almost totally devoid of clientelism.

No one has done more than T.H. Rigby to show how important were patron-client relations in Soviet politics.[18] Over many pre-perestroika decades it was possible to come to a judgement on how strong a particular Politburo member was, and especially on the extent to which a General Secretary was increasing his power, by examining how many people who had worked with him in the past – in the republics or regions of the Soviet Union – he was able to bring into the top leadership team, whether as a Secretary of the Central Committee, candidate or full member of the Politburo. Unlike most of his predecessors, Gorbachev had not moved around the country. Before he was appointed a Secretary of the Central Committee in 1978, he had spent the whole of his career as an official, first in the Komsomol and then in the Communist Party apparatus, in his native territory of Stavropol'. He did not, however, appoint any of his numerous subordinates from his time as *kraikom* first secretary to the top leadership team in Moscow. The one near-exception was Vsevolod Murakhovskii, a Ukrainian by nationality, who was Gorbachev's successor as head of the Stavropol' territorial party organization and who doubtless owed his appointment as head of a newly-created State Committee for the Agro-Industrial Complex (Gosagroprom) in 1985 to Gorbachev. However, Murakhovskii was promoted no further, and the new organization itself was so far from being a success that it was wound up in 1989.

Gorbachev lost little time in dispensing with the services of the most spectacularly unreconstructed members of the Politburo and succeeded in substantially reducing the average age of the top leadership team. His confidence in his own powers of persuasion as well as his awareness of the deference that would be shown to the General Secretary, given the hierarchical norms of the system, meant that he was content to appoint to – or keep within – the Politburo people of different political dispositions. He had removed the more obvious deadwood and potential enemies by the end of 1986 – most notably, the other senior secretary at the time of Konstantin Chernenko's death, Grigorii Romanov; the veteran Chairman of the Council of Ministers, Nikolai Tikhonov; the Moscow party first secretary Viktor Grishin; and the first secretary of the Kazakhstan party organization, Dinmukhamed Kunaev. In addition to Iakovlev, two significant reformers promoted were Eduard Shevardnadze and Vadim Medvedev. However, Gorbachev also elevated Yegor Ligachev to be second secretary of the party from April 1985, a position he retained until September 1988. Although Ligachev was initially an energetic supporter of Gorbachev, his reformism was within narrow limits, and before long he was at loggerheads with Iakovlev and closer in his views to the more conservative members of the Politburo, such as the Chairman of the Council of Ministers of the Russian republic, Vitalii Vorotnikov.

Another strand within the Politburo was represented by the former factory managers, Nikolai Ryzhkov, who succeeded Tikhonov as Chairman of the Council of Ministers of the USSR, and Lev Zaikov, who supervised the military-industrial complex. Politically, they occupied technocratic, centrist positions, but Gorbachev reposed great trust in both Ryzhkov and Zaikov during the first five years of perestroika. From 1985 until 1988 a leading Soviet traditionalist Andrei Gromyko remained a member of the Politburo as the formal head of state – Chairman of the Presidium of the Supreme Soviet. Gromyko had served as Soviet Foreign Minister under five different Soviet leaders – Khrushchev, Brezhnev, Andropov, Chernenko and, briefly, Gorbachev. When, less than four months into his general secretaryship. Gorbachev moved Gromyko to the headship of state (as had been tacitly agreed between the two men at the time of Gorbachev's succession), Gromyko was very satisfied with what could be viewed as a promotion, yet constituted a less onerous role for a man in his mid-seventies. He was far from happy, though, when he discovered that Gorbachev's choice to replace him at the ministry was the foreign policy neophyte Shevardnadze. He had expected to be succeeded by one of his own former subordinates and to continue to wield significant influence over foreign policy. In fact, there was soon to be a sharp break with the style and substance of diplomacy favoured by Gromyko.

Boris Yeltsin attended Politburo meetings from June 1985 until October 1987, first as a Secretary of the Central Committee and subsequently as a candidate member of the Politburo. From December 1985 Yeltsin was First Secretary of the Moscow city party organization. He had been backed for that post by Ligachev who had earlier pressed for Yeltsin's transfer from Sverdlovsk to Moscow. Ligachev had hoped that the beneficiary of his support would then be 'his man' within the leadership, but Yeltsin ploughed a more independent furrow. He did not at this stage of his career have a distinctive reformist policy, but he made it very clear that he was not one of nature's subordinates. His relationship with second secretary Ligachev became strained on personal as well as political grounds, for both men were domineering by disposition and intent on getting their way.

What these various examples should make abundantly clear was that the top leadership team Gorbachev partly inherited and partly assembled was not a body of like-minded people. It was, moreover, one in which Gorbachev did not always prevail. He sometimes took one step back, although not long after he would usually take two steps forward. Within the Politburo Gorbachev's own views were closest to those of Iakovlev, Shevardnadze and Medvedev. They were reformers of varying degrees of radicalism, but all owed their places within the inner leadership entirely to the general secretary. Yet they constituted only a minority within the Politburo. Gorbachev's political antennae led him to keep within the top leadership team quite formidable representatives of different tendencies that were to be found within the higher echelons of the party. He sometimes made concessions to the conservative majority, and had an acute political sense of how far he could go at any given time.

Debate within the Politburo

A case in point is the document prepared for the 70th anniversary of the Bolshevik revolution which was discussed in the Politburo on 15 October 1987. Assessing Soviet history was always a politically charged exercise for the leadership and this was an opportunity for Gorbachev to temper the celebratory nature of the event with a further break from the complacency of the Brezhnev era. The draft report evoked a wide variety of different responses. Some of the more radical wording, which had been endorsed by Gorbachev before the rest of the Politburo had their say, was toned down or omitted.[19] Mikhail Solomentsev, the veteran Chairman of the Party Control Committee, was among those who complained that the draft report contained too much criticism of the Soviet past. He expressed concern about the effects of this in Eastern Europe and wanted more emphasis on the achievements which, he said, greatly outweighed the 'shortcomings' and 'mistakes'.[20] The draft had also mentioned the need for a new Constitution. Solomentsev was just one of the majority – they included not only Ligachev and Ryzhkov but also Yeltsin – who said that it would be premature to embark on such a project or to mention it in the report. Solomentsev complained, additionally, about attacks in the press, which had included the statement that the older generation of party officials were Stalinists. Gorbachev's response was to say that 'the criteria for evaluating cadres today, party workers of all ranks' should be reduced to one: their 'relationship to perestroika'.[21]

Vitalii Vorotnikov wanted more stress on the need to inculcate feelings of Soviet patriotism and also observed that more attention should be paid in the report to economic questions. Gorbachev said that Vadim Medvedev had been 'bombarding him all morning' about the neglect of the economy in the draft document.[22] The Chairman of the KGB, Viktor Chebrikov, was among the Politburo members who objected to the statement in the draft that an 'authoritarian-bureaucratic model of socialism' had been constructed in the Soviet Union. This, he complained, was a Western formula. Gorbachev responded that Bukharin had used this terminology before anyone in the West, but he met the objection by saying that, perhaps, the word, 'model' should be changed and replaced by 'methods' or 'means'.[23] Heidar Aliev, who was shortly afterwards to be removed from the Politburo by Gorbachev, disapproved of the inclusion of the concept of 'socialist pluralism' in the report, since he regarded 'pluralism' as an alien concept.[24] Anatolii Luk'ianov, who at that time was the Secretary of the Central Committee with oversight of the KGB and the military, likewise objected to this phraseology. He was prepared to tolerate the word 'pluralism' but only if it were rephrased as a 'socialist pluralism of opinion in society'. Putting a full stop after 'socialist pluralism' would be understood in the West to mean a 'pluralism of power', but 'we, Communists, the party', he added, 'will not divide power with anyone'.[25]

El'tsin made a curious and far from radically reformist contribution to the Politburo discussion. Its oddity lies in the fact that just six days later, at a Central Committee meeting held to approve the report as amended by the Politburo, he delivered a famously critical speech, in defiance of protocol, and so began the process of his alienation from the Communist Party, although he remained a nominal member of the Central Committee until 1990.[26] At the Politburo meeting of 15 October, he complained that the anniversary report laid too much emphasis on the February revolution of 1917, which had been 'bourgeois-democratic', and there was a need to say more about the October revolution. He referred to 'the genius of Lenin' but would have liked more material in the document on Lenin's close comrades-in-arms. When Gorbachev asked him whom he had in mind, he named Sverdlov, Dzerzhinskii, Kalinin and Frunze. However, the draft report as a whole, said El'tsin, makes 'a very powerful impression and, of course, it is possible to accept it'.[27]

Each stage of the radicalization of the reform process in the Soviet Union during perestroika was wholly dependent on Gorbachev's ability to manoeuvre successfully within the top leadership team, a majority of whom were not in the least well disposed towards far-reaching political reform. The policy of glasnost and the changes in editorial boards of journals and the leadership of the 'creative unions' played a part in the process. But while giving articulate critics of the status quo platforms in which to press the case for further change was in some ways advantageous for Gorbachev, it also meant that complaints in the Politburo about the supposed irresponsibility of press criticism were aired with increasing frequency. Yegor Iakovlev and Korotich kept their editorial posts, but thanks only to the support of Gorbachev. The backing of Aleksandr Iakovlev was important but, given that there was a majority in the Politburo who believed that press criticism was getting out of hand, that was not enough. Although Gorbachev sometimes voiced impatience at particular articles that appeared in the press, he used the authority of the general secretaryship to sustain editors such as Yegor Iakovlev who were pushing the boundaries of glasnost to the point at which it became virtually indistinguishable from freedom of speech and publication.

What became known as the 'Nina Andreeva affair' illustrated the strength of the opposition within the Politburo itself to perestroika in its radical form. There is no need to discuss the episode in great detail here, for it is well enough known. The essence of the matter is that a polemical composition which began its life as an attack on the post-1985 changes by a neo-Stalinist Leningrad lecturer, Nina Andreeva, was worked into a major article for the newspaper *Sovetskaia Rossiia* and published on 13 March 1988, just as Gorbachev and Iakovlev were leaving on separate trips abroad. The article attempted to rehabilitate Stalin as well as concepts such as the class struggle and the leading role of the proletariat which had been essentially discarded by the perestroika-era 'New Thinking'. The article deplored what it saw as an unjustified emphasis on the terror and repression in recent discussions of the Soviet past. In that and, as it turned out, most other respects the Andreeva article was fully in tune with the thinking of more than half the members of the Politburo.

In an unpublished book manuscript which Gorbachev wrote in 1988 and in the early months of 1989, he noted that many regional party officials received telephone calls from the Central Committee of the Communist Party telling them to republish the Andreeva article and to publicize it.[28] The piece had appeared with the blessing of Ligachev who at the time was still second secretary of the party. It was praised in informal discussion by him and by other Politburo members – Vorotnikov, Gromyko and Solomentsev, among them.[29] The publication of the Andreeva polemic had been a deliberate attempt to turn the clock back and put an end to the expansion of political freedom which was already occurring under the banner of perestroika. Since there was no immediate response from the party leadership, the article was taken by many to signal a change of course at the top of the political hierarchy. In the period of three weeks between the publication of the Andreeva article and its detailed rebuttal in an unsigned article in *Pravda* on 5 April, few people challenged what they supposed was – or, at least, might be – the new line. Many intellectuals, who were two years later to criticize Gorbachev for what they called his 'half-measures', maintained a discreet silence until the general secretary, with the help of Iakovlev in particular, had persuaded and browbeaten the top leadership team into agreeing to denounce the article as an 'anti-perestroika manifesto'. The authoritative *Pravda* article which followed was drafted mainly by Iakovlev, with Gorbachev's participation.[30] After this rebuttal, Russian and other Soviet intellectuals found their voice again, but the episode illustrated the extent to which the direction of change in the country still depended, three years after the launch of perestroika, on the political disposition and political will of the holder of greatest institutional power within the system.

The run-up to the Nineteenth Party Conference

The party conservatives had intended the Andreeva article to be a turning-point and, in fact, it was, but of a very different nature from what they had in mind. Realizing the strength of the opposition to perestroika within the existing political structures, and having seen off the challenge of those who stood behind Andreeva, Gorbachev went on the offensive. As early as the January 1987 plenum of the Central Committee of the CPSU, which put political reform squarely on the agenda, it had been decided that an all-Union party conference (the second most authoritative gathering after a party congress) would be held in June 1988 to consider the further democratization of the party and society. It was during the preparatory work for that conference, in the immediate aftermath of the Andreeva controversy, that the agenda of Gorbachev and his closest allies was radicalized. Various commissions were charged with working on different areas of policy – Aleksandr Iakovlev, for example, headed the commission charged with elaborating the policy of glasnost – but Gorbachev also presided over small group discussions to which the main contributors included Iakovlev, Vadim Medvedev, Evgenii Primakov, Georgii Shakhnazarov, Ivan Frolov and Anatolii Cherniaev.

However, Gorbachev was aware that even though he intended to spring a few surprises at the party conference, he had to prepare the ground in advance to some extent by bringing his powers of persuasion to bear on the key office-holders within the Communist Party. He met with all the republican and regional party secretaries – who were divided into three groups – on 11, 15 and 18 April 1988. In light of later developments, it is hardly likely that Gorbachev convinced a majority of them of the need for radical political reform, but they could be left in no doubt of *his* commitment to it. Given the norms of obedience to higher authority, and especially to the general secretary, which still prevailed within the CPSU, this in itself was important.

Knowing that these party secretaries had very recently been encouraged from within the Central Committee apparatus to propagate the line purveyed in the Andreeva article, Gorbachev made a point of telling them that, on his initiative, the Politburo, its candidate members, and Secretaries of the Central Committee had considered that article (which, he noted, would not have mattered if it had been Andreeva's work alone) and had unanimously (*edinodushno*) evaluated it as 'harmful, anti-perestroika and, in parts even, as reactionary'.[31] Gorbachev did not add that this 'unity' was not present at the outset, although the regional party secretaries might have inferred that from Gorbachev's telling them that the discussion took place over two days as well as from their very recent memory of being recommended to distribute the self-same article. With conflicting signals coming from the Secretariat of the Central Committee in the persons of Ligachev and Iakovlev, party secretaries, as well as newspaper and journal editors, could take a lead from the one or the other, according to their disposition. The authoritative line, to the extent that such a thing still existed, became clear only when the general secretary weighed in.

Without telling the regional party secretaries that within his inner circle there was discussion of the desirability of moving to contested elections for the all-Union legislative organs as well as for the soviets at lower levels, Gorbachev mentioned that if a first secretary was not elected to the soviet, he should leave his party post. That would enhance, not detract from, the authority of the party. He also held up as a good example for the Soviet Union the practice in the American Congress of having the legislature consider and – only when satisfied – confirm the fitness for office of candidates for senior executive posts. He contrasted this with the Soviet Union where people could simply find out from the newspapers that they had been appointed.[32] Gorbachev lectured the assembled republican and regional party secretaries on the crimes of Stalin, mentioning also Molotov's culpability.[33] More strikingly, he said that, while cadres were necessary, the nomenklatura had been 'anti-democratic from its very birth'.[34]

One of the important breaks with the past in the Soviet Union during the second half of the 1980s was the support of the reformist wing of the party leadership for genuine social science. This had been at worst repressed and at best circumscribed in the pre-perestroika years (although with some partial exceptions such as mathematical economics, since the party leaders and ideologists could not make head or tail of it). Some of the social scientists combined an overly optimistic belief in their ability to offer salvation to Soviet society with an unashamed promotion of their discipline. Thus, when a Politburo session on 12 May 1988 was devoted to 'raising the role of sociology in the solution of major problems of Soviet society', Tat'iana Zaslavskaia, one of the social scientists invited to participate in the meeting, said: 'Today there are 6 thousand sociologists in the country and we need to have 60 thousand'.[35]

Zaslavskaia, who had already demonstrated her independence of mind and character in pre-perestroika times, had the kind of evangelical zeal about sociology's potential contribution to fashioning a better society that was to be found in Western countries in the 1960s (but had subsequently receded there). Nevertheless, she became the first director in 1988 of a truly significant institution – VTsIOM, the All-Union Centre for the Study of Public Opinion (established with the approval of Gorbachev and by decision of the Politburo). Its importance lay not only in the fact that it conducted survey research professionally but also in its contribution to the process of democratization. Next to the contested elections which were agreed upon in principle by the Nineteenth Party Conference in mid-1988 and introduced in practice in March 1989, nothing was more important for democratization than the publication of research on political opinion conducted by such a reputable body as VTsIOM.

Political discourse was altered in important ways when public opinion, elicited in surveys, could be contrasted with the views which party officials attributed to the mass of the people. Once VTsIOM began to track the rise and fall in popularity of particular politicians, its research impinged even more directly on political life. That did not happen, however, until after 1988. By the second half of 1989 and especially in 1990–91 opinion polls had become more part of pressure from below than of revolution from above. However, VTsIOM was established in 1988 with the explicit aim of making both the party leadership and the country as a whole better informed about opinion within Soviet society. Its foundation was the direct result of the desire of reformers at the top of the political hierarchy for such reliable information. Their political support was all the more necessary when it came to the publication and dissemination of the results of survey research.

The Nineteenth Conference

The key event, however, in what Aleksandr Iakovlev and others have rightly called the 'revolution from above' – or what, on several occasions, Gorbachev described as the pursuit of 'revolutionary goals by evolutionary means' – was the Nineteenth Conference of the CPSU, held from 28 June to 1 July 1988.[36] The terminology 'revolution' can, of course, be questioned, since Gorbachev, and, indeed, his closest associates, were not revolutionaries by temperament. Moreover, they had begun, as noted earlier, with the intention of reforming the system rather than changing it fundamentally. The justification for using the word 'revolution' is that from the time of the Nineteenth Conference, Gorbachev and his allies were actively engaged in the task of systemic transformation. They were consciously dismantling the pillars of the Soviet political system as it had existed hitherto, although they had no intention of dismantling the Soviet state. When that statehood disintegrated, it was as an entirely unintended consequence of political transformation and of the fundamental change in Soviet foreign policy. Even for internal developments within the USSR, the latter was scarcely less important than the former, since the example of East European countries acquiring their independence in the course of 1989 was a crucial factor in emboldening the most disaffected nationalities within the Soviet Union to follow suit. They subsequently moved beyond prudential arguments for greater self-government within the USSR to a demand for separate statehood.[37]

The Nineteenth Conference was of huge significance both for the signals it sent out concerning the new Soviet foreign policy and for its opening the way to the pluralization of the Soviet political system. The 'theses' which were prepared for the Conference raised numerous concerns in the Politburo. Solomentsev, Chairman of the Central Auditing Commission Ivan Kapitonov, and Gromyko were among those who said that there needed to be more in the documents on the leading role of the Communist Party. Gromyko also wanted more emphasis on the principle of the 'class character' of the Soviet system.[38] Those who wished to amend the documents in a conservative direction did not, however, have things all their own way. Indeed, Gorbachev noted that an earlier draft of the report he was to give to the conference had said that the threat of nuclear war had been removed 'thanks to our strength (*sila*)'. That had been changed to 'thanks to the new thinking' which was 'more correct'.[39]

When the Conference was held, there were, among the many innovations announced, two momentous policy declarations. One concerned foreign policy. Gorbachev more explicitly than hitherto stressed each country's freedom to choose its political and economic system and the impermissibility of armed intervention to uphold or impose a system they did not want. He emphasized the 'universal applicability' of this and said that the concept of freedom of choice occupied a 'key place in the new thinking'.[40] This passage in Gorbachev's speech got rather less attention at the time than it deserved. It had a greater resonance when he made essentially the same point in his speech to the United Nations on 7 December 1988. There was, he declared in New York, no excuse for denying people's freedom of choice and there should be no exceptions to this universal principle.[41] This had clear implications for the peoples of Eastern Europe. They took Gorbachev at his word over the next 12 months. Although, Gorbachev had in mind existing countries, he used at the UN the term *pravo narodov*, meaning the right of peoples (or nations) to 'freedom of choice'. Accordingly, although this was far from his mind, that principle could be applied also to the different nationalities within the Soviet Union itself. Gorbachev's intention in December 1988 was, however, to render obsolete the ideological foundation of the Cold War, and in this he succeeded.[42]

The Nineteenth Conference took place less than a month after Ronald Reagan's historic visit to Moscow as American President. When the United States Ambassador, Jack Matlock – in Helsinki to meet with Reagan and brief him in advance of his discussions with Gorbachev – was faxed the newly-published 'theses' for the Conference, he was astonished. Matlock had expected a rehash of reforms that had already been discussed in Central Committee plenums and in Gorbachev's speeches. He wrote:

> But as I read and discovered one new element after another, my excitement grew. Never before had I seen in an official Communist Party document such an extensive section on protecting the rights of citizens or such principles as the separation of powers, judicial independence, and presumption of a defendant's innocence until proven guilty. ... What had passed for 'socialism' in Soviet parlance had dropped from sight. What the 'theses' described was something closer to European social democracy.[43]

Matlock summarized the document for Reagan and told the president that if the 'theses' turned out to be real, 'the Soviet Union could never again be what it had been in the past'.[44] This indeed turned out to be the case. The most fundamental change affecting the domestic political system, to be endorsed by the Nineteenth Conference, was the move to contested elections for a serious legislature that would be capable of criticizing the executive and calling it to account. After seven decades of a rubber-stamp assembly that rarely met, and passed legislation retrospectively and on the nod when it did, this was movement in the direction of a qualitatively different political system. The principle of competitive elections had been accepted and established by Gorbachev, in consultation with his advisers, well ahead of the conference. They had also agreed to begin the process of moving executive power from the party to the state, although the party was still meant to provide the broad guidelines for policy. One element of that movement was the decision to abolish half the departments of the Central Committee, including almost all which dealt with different sectors of the economy. A new post of Chairman of the Supreme Soviet was to be created, designed for Gorbachev. It turned out to involve him in presiding over the new working legislature – in effect, adding the Speakership to his already manifold responsibilities. It was an impossible burden, and it became a stepping-stone to a further movement of executive power from the party machine to the state, when the office of President of the USSR was created in March 1990, with Gorbachev as its first – and last – occupant.

While the delegates to the 1988 Conference had accepted the principle of a reduction in the day-to-day power of the party apparatus, a clearer separation than hitherto of the functions of the party and the state, and even the declaration that there should be competition among several candidates in elections to soviets and for the new all-Union legislature, they had assumed that all these things would take time. Some of them doubtless hoped that there would be a change of leadership and of policy which would prevent the changes ever taking place at all. Gorbachev, however, bounced them into accepting a concrete and imminent timetable for these changes just as they were getting ready to go home. At the end of his speech winding up the Conference on 1 July, Gorbachev said there was just one more resolution he wished to put to them. It was called 'On some urgent measures for the practical implementation of reform of the political system of the country'.[45] The measures included reorganizing the party apparatus and implementing the decisions about the division of functions between the party and soviets 'before the end of the present year'.[46] Even more importantly, the resolution stressed the necessity of altering the USSR Constitution in order that elections for the new legislature, the Congress of People's Deputies, could be held and that body brought into existence by April of the following year.[47]

The elections for the Congress of People's Deputies took place, in fact, on 26 March 1989. This was not fully-fledged democracy, but it was, nevertheless, a democratizing measure of immense significance. A third of the seats had been reserved for candidates from 'public organisations', which enabled a hundred senior members of the CPSU to enter the new legislature without the inconvenience of facing the electorate, but the smaller electorates in some of these public bodies chose strikingly non-conformist deputies. They included Andrei Sakharov, chosen by the Academy of Sciences, after the bureaucracy of the Academy had made a vain attempt to exclude him. A majority of the remaining two-thirds of the seats had two or frequently more candidates contesting them. Even when an official managed to run unopposed, it was no guarantee of election. If over half of the electorate voted against the candidate, he was not elected – a fate which befell the First Secretary of the Leningrad regional party committee (and candidate member of the Politburo) Yurii Solov'ev. That led to his removal from the party leadership, both locally and nationally. This illustrated the point that, in yet another diminution of the party's unaccountable power, the people as a whole could now make a party official's position untenable by rejecting his candidature for the legislature.

Even more important in the transfer of power from the party to the state had, however, been the abolition of many of the party departments which supervised governmental bodies, along with the de facto replacement of the Secretariat of the Central Committee (which for over a year ceased to meet as a body and subsequently met only irregularly) by commissions of the Central Committee. Ligachev had to exchange his position of second secretary of the party for the very poor substitute of chairing the commission on agriculture. Presenting his proposals to the Politburo on 8 September 1988, Gorbachev placed them in the context of the transformation of the political system, saying:

> The reorganisation of the apparatus is connected with the formation of a rule-of-law state. The entire structure of our society and state must work on a legitimate basis, i.e. within the limits of the law. No-one has the right to go beyond the boundaries of the law, to break the law. And the most important violator, as I have more than once had to say, is sitting here, at this table – the Politburo, and also the Secretariat, of the Central Committee.[48]

Gorbachev both in public and private placed the changes in the party's structure and its relationship with governmental organs in the context of movement to a state based upon the rule of law. For 70 years the party had been above the law, so the change was, to say the least, overdue. Gorbachev made a distinction, however, between the party's power and its authority. He did not present the reduction in size and functions of the apparatus as constituting a reduction in the authority of the party. Rather, he said, that authority would be enhanced. As the United States Ambassador Matlock aptly put it: 'He had to pretend that he was preparing the Party for an even more effective role, one that would determine policy, leaving the grubby day-to-day management to lesser figures in the government structure'.[49] But as Matlock added: 'I had been around bureaucracies long enough to know that a "policy-making" job that does not include authority over those who carry out the policy is a sham'.[50]

Conclusions

The elections for the Congress of People's Deputies and the functioning of that body – and of the inner body, the Supreme Soviet, which it elected – are beyond the scope of this chapter, for those elections and the convening of the First Congress (which lasted from 25 May until 9 June) marked the point at which movement from below became more important than the revolutionary change by evolutionary means from above. Democratic centralism became a dead letter, for although the overwhelming majority of candidates in the elections were members of the Communist Party, they stood against each other, espousing very different policies. The most striking victory was that of Boris El'tsin, contesting a constituency that embraced the whole of Moscow, in which he gained almost 90 percent of the votes and defeated Evgenii Brakov, the manager of the Zil car-manufacturing plant who had the backing of the party apparatus. Indeed, in the cities especially, the support of the party apparatus could be more of a hindrance than a help to a candidate. Oleg Bogomolov, the long-serving head of one of the most reformist of Soviet research establishments, the Institute of Economics of the World Socialist System, was one of three candidates for a Moscow suburban seat in which all the resources of the apparatus were put behind his chief opponent, the local party boss. In the face of this, Bogomolov was at times pessimistic about his chances. Yet he received more than 60 percent of the votes, and later remarked: 'I didn't realize what a great advantage it would be to run *against* the party'.[51]

Once the proceedings of the legislature got underway, it was clear that conservative Communists were in a majority, but that a talented and articulate minority of deputies of varying degrees of radicalism were ready to criticize the executive and to hold ministers and Politburo members alike to account. Gorbachev's earlier invocation of the desirability of following the American example of seeking the approval of the legislature for candidates proposed for major governmental office was accepted with alacrity by the newly-empowered assembly. The Chairman of the Council of Ministers Nikolai Ryzhkov was in the end quite relieved when 'only' nine out of his 69 nominations for ministerial office were rejected.[52] The new political pluralism gave opportunities for the voicing of grievances and demands which had been wholly stifled prior to perestroika and only partially articulated before these first Union-wide competitive elections. Thus, for example, in several republics – notably the Baltic states and Georgia – the election provided the opportunity for voters to choose candidates who would espouse the national cause.

This point would not, however, have been reached in the absence of a minority within the highest echelons of the Communist Party who had moved from a desire to reform the system to a determination to pursue system-transformation. That minority succeeded partly because they had more supporters among the party intelligentsia than had their conservative counterparts in the top leadership team. Above all, however, they succeeded because they had the general secretary on their side. While making tactical concessions along the way, Gorbachev had up until the contested elections of 1989 wielded more power, and been granted more authority, than anyone else within the Soviet Union. He and his major allies – with Iakovlev playing a role second only in importance to that of the general secretary in the radicalization of perestroika during its first four years – used the political resources of the system they had inherited to dismantle the pillars of that system. By doing so – and this applied to Gorbachev, in particular, from the moment the Congress of Peoples' Deputies met in its first session – they were diminishing their own power and authority.

Yet the system was such that it was only from within the leadership of the ruling party, albeit a divided leadership, that the breakthrough to pluralization of a long-consolidated, highly authoritarian political system could be brought about. The paradox was noted by Iakovlev in the 'theses' he prepared for his contribution to the Politburo session of 8 September 1988 which considered Gorbachev's proposals for reducing the size and functions of the party apparatus. As Iakovlev put it:

> In the implementation of the perestroika of the party apparatus we now come against a contradiction that is inherent in perestroika as a whole. Namely: the establishment of the new must still proceed in many respects through old forms and methods, but at a certain stage lead to a full and irrevocable repudiation of them.[53]

In that sense, perestroika in the years 1985 to early 1989 was, indeed, a revolution from above, and from within – from within the highest echelons of the ruling party whose own monopoly of power it was repudiating.

Notes

1 Viktor Kuvaldin (2005), 'Three forks in the road of Gorbachev's Perestroika', in Andrei Grachev, Chiara Blengino and Rossella Stievano (eds), *1985–2005: Twenty Years that Changed the World* (Turin: World Political Forum and Editori Laterza), pp.337–51, at p.343.
2 Ibid.
3 In Grachev, Blengino and Stievano (eds), *1985–2005*, p.175.

4   Mikhail Gorbachev (2006), *Poniat' perestroiku … pochemu eto vazhno seichas* (Moscow: Al'pina), p.16.

5   Among all his Western interlocutors, those whom Gorbachev felt closest to politically were Felipe González, the Spanish prime minister, and the president of the Socialist International and former German Chancellor, Willy Brandt. See Andrei Grachev (1994), *Kremlevskaia khronika* (Moscow: EKSMO), p.247; See also Mikhail Gorbachev, 'Delaet li chelovek politiku? Delaet li chelovek istoriiu?', *Svobodnaia mysl'*, No. 17, 1992, pp.17–21. In this article, following Brandt's death, Gorbachev pays warm tribute to him, emphasizing the closeness of their ideas and their personal friendship. The same issue of the journal contains a transcript of the conversation between Brandt and Gorbachev of 17 October 1989.

6   *Pravda*, 15 July 1987, p.2. For Gorbachev's embrace of 'political pluralism', see his speech to the Central Committee published in *Pravda*, 6 February 1990, pp.1–2.

7   Gorbachev, *Poniat' perestroiku*, p.18. It is worth adding that Gorbachev does not make a clear distinction between totalitarianism and authoritarianism in this book. He uses the terms more or less interchangeably. The distinction he does make sharply is between totalitarianism/authoritarianism, on the one hand, and pluralism and democracy, on the other.

8   The dissident groups were too miniscule and too persecuted to come into the category of civil society. The nearest approximation to activity which could be deemed a manifestation of civil society was environmentalist campaigning, especially the efforts in the post-Stalin era to save Lake Baikal and the opposition to the Brezhnev-era grandiose scheme to divert Siberian rivers for the benefit of Kazakhstan and Soviet Central Asia. See Douglas R. Weiner (1999), *A Little Corner of Freedom: Russian Nature Protection from Stalin to Gorbachev* (Berkeley: University of California Press).

9   Isaiah Berlin (1957), *The Hedgehog and the Fox: An Essay on Tolstoy's View of History* (New York: Mentor).

10 Yegor Gaidar has produced an account of the policies of perestroika that is as economically determinist as the Marxism he earlier jettisoned. He is particularly unconvincing in attributing virtually every major policy of Gorbachev to a concern that the Soviet Union was going financially bankrupt. Gaidar provides, however, much valuable information on the growing economic crisis after 1988, exacerbated as it was by the sharp fall in the price of oil during the second half of the 1980s. See Yegor Gaidar (2007), *Collapse of an Empire: Lessons for Modern Russia* (Washington, DC: Brookings Institution).

11 That body was created in March 1990 and wound up in November of the same year. Any expectation that it would become the successor organ to the Politburo was dashed by its being essentially an advisory body rather than an executive committee and by its lack of institutional underpinning – in contrast with the Politburo which stood at the pinnacle of a hierarchy of party committees and had party secretaries on all the rungs of the ladder ready, throughout almost the whole of the Soviet period, to do its bidding.

12 Aleksandr Iakovlev (2003), *Sumerki* (Moscow: Materik), p.398.

13 Ibid.

14 Ibid., pp.426–7.

15 Yitzhak Brudny, the author of an important study of Russian nationalism during the last four decades of Soviet rule, notes that as the 1980s drew to a close 'the main thick journals of the Russian nationalists proved incapable of competing against their liberal-reformist rivals in the battle for readers'. See Yitzhak M. Brudny (1998), *Reinventing Russia: Russian Nationalism and the Soviet State 1953–1991* (Cambridge, Mass.: Harvard University Press), p.230.

16 'Zasedanie Sekretariata TsK KPSS, 20 noiabria 1972 goda. Kratkaia rabochaia zapis', p.5, Volkogonov Collection, R 10325, National Security Archive (NSA), Washington, DC.

17 See Archie Brown (2009), *The Rise and Fall of Communism* (London: Bodley Head), pp.593–8.

18 See, for example, Rigby's introduction to T.H. Rigby and Bohdan Harasymiw (eds) (1983), *Leadership Selection and Patron-Client Relations in the USSR and Yugoslavia* (London: Allen & Unwin); and Rigby (1990), *Political Elites in the USSR: Central Leaders and Local Cadres from Lenin to Gorbachev* (Aldershot: Edward Elgar).

19 Gorbachev made it clear during the Politburo meeting that he had seen and discussed several previous variants of the draft report. See 'Zasedanie Politbiuro TsK KPSS, 15 Oktiabria 1987 goda', Volkogonov Collection, NSA, p.162.

20 Ibid.

21 Ibid., p.165.

22 Ibid., pp.158 and 160.

23 Ibid., pp.149–50.

24 Ibid., p.155.

25 Ibid., p.176.

26 Yeltsin's speech even at the Central Committee meeting was more a breach of protocol than the presentation of a radical reform agenda. Moscow rumour rendered it more critical than it actually was. However, he did point to the lack of improvement in economic well-being and accused some other members of the top leadership team of sycophancy towards the general secretary. For the official transcript of Yeltsin's speech, published for the first time some 18 months after it was delivered, see *Izvestiia TsK KPSS*, No. 2, 1989, pp.239–41.

27 'Zasedanie Politbiuro TsK KPSS, 15 Oktiakbria 1987 goda', pp.137–40.

28 M.S. Gorbachev, 'Perestroika – ispytanie zhizn'iu' (unpublished book manuscript, Gorbachev Foundation archives), pp.46–7.

29 A.S. Cherniaev (ed.) (2008), *V Politbiuro TsK KPSS...Po zapisiam Anatoliia Cherniaeva, Vadima Medvedeva, Georgiia Shakhnazarova (1985–1991)* (2nd ed.) (Moscow: Al'pina), pp.305–7.

30 Iakovlev had gone to the Politburo with a carefully argued, typed document which provided the basis for the later *Pravda* unsigned article. For the full text of his presentation to the Politburo, see 'Tezisy k vystupleniiu A.N. Iakovleva na Politbiuro TsK KPSS po povodu stat'i N.A. Andreevoi v gazete "Sovetskaia Rossiia"', 25 March 1988, in Aleksandr Iakovlev, *Perestroika: 1985–1991. Neizdannoe, maloizvestnoe, zabytoe* (Mezhdunarodny Fond 'Demokratiia', Moscow, 2008), pp. 192–200.

31 'Vstrecha Gorbacheva so vtoroi gruppoi sekretarei TsK kompartii respublik, obkomov i kraikomov partii, 15 aprelia 1988 goda', in Chernaiev (ed.), *V Politbiuro TsK KPSS....*, pp.322–36, at p.325.

32 Ibid., p.329.

33 At a meeting with newspaper editors and writers on 7 May 1988, Gorbachev asked rhetorically why people could not get it into their heads that if, instead of Stalin, someone else had been there during the Second World War, 'we would have won the war more quickly and with fewer losses'. See 'Vstrecha s redaktorami gazet, pisateliami, deiateliami kul'tury, 7 Maia 1988 goda', Ibid., p.361.

34 'Vstrecha Gorbacheva so vtoroi gruppoi sekretarei...', *V Politbiuro TsK KPSS...*, p.334. The leading Western analyst of the nomenklatura over many years has been T.H. Rigby, starting with his University of London doctoral thesis, 'The Selection of Leading Personnel in the Soviet State and Communist Party' (1954) and including his chapters on 'The origins of the nomenklatura system' and 'The nomenklatura and patronage under Stalin', in Rigby, *Political Elites in the USSR* (1990), pp.73–126.

35 'Politbiuro 12 Maia 1988 goda, O povyshenii roli sotsiologii v reshenii uzlovykh problem Sovetskogo obshchestva', in *V Politbiuro TsK KPSS...*, p.375.

36 For the published transcript of the proceedings, see *XIX Vsesoiuznaia konferentsiia Kommunisticheskoi Partii Sovetskogo Soiuza 28 iiunia – 1 iiulia 1988 goda* (2 volumes, Politizdat, Moscow, 1988).

37 I have discussed this in some detail in Chapter 8, 'The national question, the coup, and the collapse of the Soviet Union', in Archie Brown (1996), *The Gorbachev Factor* (Oxford: Oxford University Press), pp.252–305; and in Chapter 27, 'The break-up of the Soviet State', in Brown, *The Rise and Fall of Communism*, pp.549–73.

38 'O proekte tezisov k XIX partkonferentsii, Politbiuro, 19 maia 1988 goda', in *V Politbiuro TsK KPSS*, pp.377–8.

39 'Obsuzhdenie proekta doklada Gorbacheva v XIX partkonferentsii, Politbiuro, 20 iiunia 1988 goda', *V Politbiuro TsK KPSS...*, p.391.

40 *XIX Vsesoiuznaia konferenstsiia Kommunisticheskoi Partii Sovetskogo Soiuza: Stenograficheskii otchet*, Vol. 1, p.43.

41 M.S. Gorbachev, 'Vystuplenie v organizatsii Ob"edineinykh natsii, 7 dekabria 1988 goda', in Gorbachev, *Izbrannye rechi i stat'i*, vol. 7 (Politizdat, Moscow, 1990), pp.184–202, at p.188.

42 See Andrei Grachev (2008), *Gorbachev's Gamble: Soviet Foreign Policy and the End of the Cold War* (Cambridge: Polity), pp.166–8; and Archie Brown, *The Rise and Fall of Communism*, pp.522–8.

43 Jack F. Matlock, Jr (1995), *Autopsy on an Empire: The American Ambassador's Account of the Collapse of the Soviet Union* (New York: Random House), p.122.

44 Ibid.

45 *XIX Vseoiuznaia konferentsiia Kommunisticheskoi Partii Sovetskogo Soiuza*, vol. 2, p.185.

46 Ibid.

47 Ibid.

48 'O reorganizatsii partiinogo apparata, Politbiuro 8 sentiabria 1988 goda', *V Politbiuro TsK KPSS...*, p.416.

49 Matlock, *Autopsy on an Empire*, p.131.

50 Ibid.

51 Ibid., p.210.
52 Nikolai Ryzhkov (1992), *Perestroika: Istoriia predatel'stv* (Moscow: Novosti), p.291.
53 Iakovlev, 'Tezisy k vystupleniiu A.N. Iakovleva na Politbiuro TsK KPSS o roli i meste partii v obshchestve', in Aleksandr Iakovlev, *Perestroika: 1985–1991*, pp.223–9, at p.227.

7
How Much Did Popular Disaffection Contribute to the Collapse of the USSR?

Peter Reddaway[1]

How much did popular disaffection with communism, Soviet imperialism, and the Establishment in general contribute to the collapse of the USSR? This complex question has not, as yet, been sufficiently researched by scholars. Why not? First, few researchers have studied closely the at least partially visible roots of some sorts of disaffection – expressed by so-called dissidents – in the period from the mid-1950s to 1987. Second, when a wider range of types of discontent came into public view in 1988–89, some observers tended to misperceive them as being mostly reformist and pro-Gorbachev in nature,[2] rather than, in large measure, anti-Establishment, anti-imperial, or opposed to communism – at least in its familiar, oppressive form. And third, when the Soviet Union disintegrated in 1991, some scholars like Martin Malia misinterpreted events in an opposite way. They saw the disaffection as constituting an authentic, popular, anti-communist revolution,[3] not as being, mostly, waves of anti-Establishment protest against a corrupt elite class that was failing to deliver what it promised. This disaffection made an important contribution to the collapse of an empire. But it was not, in my opinion, an authentic revolution. Not only was Russia's class structure changed only at the margins. In addition, personnel turnover in the higher levels of the political institutions and the government bureaucracy was limited, with new members coming mostly from within the existing privileged elites. Moreover, while many of the senior communists at each level lost their official positions, only a handful of them were imprisoned, and then only for a few months. Also, no-one was excluded from the upper levels of society. In general, former officials kept their housing and their property, and obtained respectable, well-paying jobs.

Why, then, did most Sovietologists not consider the nature and significance of popular disaffection in the Soviet Union? In search of some clues, let us look at a characteristic episode. In the United States in 1983 a major effort of cooperative research and discussion culminated in the publication of the volume *After Brezhnev*, edited by Robert Byrnes. It charted current trends in the USSR and considered how they were likely to play out over the subsequent ten years. Thirty-five scholars took part, many of them widely respected in academic and public circles. Eight of them wrote the extended essays that made up the book.[4]

In the preface, Byrnes wrote that 'the volume as a whole reflects to a large degree the views of all participants'. Further, 'all of us agree that there is no likelihood whatsoever that the Soviet Union will become a political democracy or that it will collapse in the foreseeable future'.[5] Seweryn Bialer, in a contribution which contained many perceptive points and discussed, if only briefly, the dangers of increasing worker alienation and sharpening ethnic tensions, nonetheless dismissed such notions as 'the coming revolution in Russia' and the imminent 'revolt of the nationalities'. He concluded that the Soviet Union 'does not now and in all probability will not in the next decade face a systemic crisis that endangers its existence. It has enormous unused reserves of political and social stability. Gigantic economies such as the Soviet Union's, presided over by intelligent and educated professionals, do not go bankrupt. They become less effective, stagnate, or experience an absolute decline for a period, but they do not disintegrate.' All in all, Bialer wrote, 'I am drawn inescapably to the conclusion that we will witness the external expansion of an internally declining power.'[6]

For a long time there will be debate over why observers were slow to doubt the viability of the Soviet system, and why they were un-impressed by the views of a minority who believed that the USSR's foundations were built largely on sand, and also, in some cases, that by 1989 its system was showing signs of beginning to come apart.[7] But one broad reason may be that the majority held views not very different from those expounded in *After Brezhnev*. To put it simply, the book's authors maintained that while the Soviet regime faced numerous problems, including popular and intellectual discontent, its leaders were determined and experienced men who had, using the Party and police apparatuses, skilfully divided, cowed, or bought off all sections of the population, and would anyway act firmly to suppress any dissenting political or ethnic group that might emerge. Moreover, Bialer in particular was absolutely convinced that they would expand their foreign empire.

Why then *did* the USSR break up?[8] Let me summarize my views suc-
cinctly, and then expand on them. A small group around Gorbachev
concluded in the early 1980s that increasing economic stagnation posed
a medium-term threat to the party's rule.[9] From 1985–6 on, the group
tried to generate economic dynamism through economic and political
reforms. The various economic reforms caused dislocations, inflation,
and increased popular discontent. The political reforms soon escaped
from the Kremlin's control, because they released longstanding popular discontent that was more widespread than the leadership anti-
cipated. Sharpened by deteriorating economic conditions, including
the falling world price of oil,[10] by official manipulation of trumpeted
new freedoms such as free elections, and by brief, periodic political
crackdowns, much of the disaffection was channeled into both anti-
Union emotions and ethnic nationalisms. These emotions and nationalisms were, in large measure, at least implicitly anti-communist and
proved to be potent. When the pro-Union forces staged a desperate rally
in August 1991, it was too late, and they unwittingly precipitated the
USSR's almost instant demise. Powerful, politically connected mafias
also played a role. Although at times they sided with the conservative
party leaders who had protected them since at least the Brezhnev era,
they ultimately found the business opportunities in a more decentral-
ized system too tempting and switched sides.

Elite reformers

Let me now expand on these points. Leaving aside discussion of important 'external' factors, like the growing gap between Soviet and Western
advances in science, technology, and weaponry, Soviet overextension
abroad, and the USSR's substantial diplomatic isolation, I believe that
the first initiative inside the USSR which set the ball rolling towards the
system's collapse was a strategic decision made by Gorbachev and a few
colleagues within the party leadership. The decision derived partly from
these external factors, and partly from concern over their primary causes,
the deepening economic and political stagnation at home. The decision was to try to make communist rule secure in the USSR for the
indefinite future by launching, from above, a series of economic and
political reforms to be known collectively as perestroika.

The man often called the chief architect of perestroika, Aleksandr
Iakovlev, was, I believe, correct to describe the strategy as a 'revolution
from above'. 'There is no escaping the simple truth', he holds, 'that *perestroika* was launched by a very small group of party and government

leaders... In Poland, the instrument of change was the opposition ... In my country it was the "apparatchiks". We created an opposition to ourselves.' Elsewhere he clarified this thought by pointing to perestroika's intellectual origins: 'The idea of *perestroika* had long been fermenting in the minds of intellectuals, but it began to be implemented by people belonging to the top echelon of the Party hierarchy.'[11]

Dissent and disaffection

The fermenting process had gone on at two closely connected levels. The first was that of heterodox (in varying degrees) but party-oriented intellectuals operating on the fringes of the Establishment, and the second was that of openly dissident intellectuals and their friends and colleagues. Individuals could, and often did, move from one level to the other, or even straddle both levels. Andrei Sakharov, for example, though never a party member, started on the first, Establishment level in the early 1960s, moving in circles whose ideas and activities were reflected in Roi Medvedev's *Political Diary*.[12] In 1968 he wrote his well-known essay 'Progress, Coexistence, and Intellectual Freedom'.[13] This circulated widely in samizdat, was broadcast to the USSR many times from the West, influenced a wide range of Soviet intellectuals, and was a forerunner of many of the perestroika ideas of 1986–7. However, in 1968 it angered the authorities, and this led – in the context of a general crackdown on dissent – to reprisals against Sakharov and to his gradual move to the second level.[14] People here were more outspoken and often prepared to go to jail rather than compromise their views. They occupied the political 'danger zone'. They drew the KGB's fire, thus giving the first level some security and breathing space. Individuals on the first level appreciated their service and their courage.[15] Certainly the courage of dissidents facilitated the quieter work of heterodox party-oriented intellectuals, such as the Novosibirsk economists and sociologists described by one of their number, Tat'iana Zaslavskaia.[16] Zaslavskaia also relates how in 1982, prior to Brezhnev's death, Gorbachev, as the Central Committee secretary designated to liaise with party intellectuals, began to invite her and scholars like her to present their papers at confidential, private seminars in Moscow.[17]

Thus within most professions there were a number of dissidents whose ideas or moral example influenced many colleagues – and also, in some cases, at least from 1982 on, reached reformist party leaders through party-oriented dissidents like Zaslavskaia. In physics and mathematics, among many independent dissidents, well-known examples were

Sakharov, Valentin Turchin, and Yuri Orlov. In biology, examples were Sergei Kovalyov and Zhores Medvedev, in history – Aleksandr Nekrich, Pyotr Yakir, and Mikhail Gefter, in philosophy – Grigory Pomerants and Aleksandr Zinoviev, among lawyers – Sofia Kalistratova and Dina Kaminskaya, among writers – Aleksandr Solzhenitsyn, Joseph Brodsky, Viktor Nekrasov, and Vladimir Voinovich, among popular protest singers – Aleksandr Galich, Bulat Okudzhava, and Vladimir Vysotsky, among artists – Oskar Rabin and Ernst Neizvestny, among church intellectuals – Anatoly Levitin-Krasnov, Gleb Yakunin, and Sergei Zheludkov, in military circles – Pyotr Grigorenko and Genrikh Altunyan, and so on. For each of these individuals there were scores of semi-dissidents who were influenced and, in effect, at least partially protected by this one, more outspoken colleague. In addition, there was a much larger number of Soviet citizens who listened on Western radio stations to samizdat materials written by or about such individuals, and were influenced by them.

The scholar honoured by this Festschrift, Harry Rigby, has expressed these points well. His fruitful research on both empirical and theoretical topics led him to the helpful definition of the USSR as 'a mono-organizational society', in which all public activity, except that of a few dissidents, was controlled by one organization, the communist party. However, this did not prevent Gorbachev's reforms of the late 1980s from being overtaken by 'the pent-up force of the "shadow culture" which had grown and matured under the carapace of coercive controls since the 1950s'. This culture was powerful, because, 'while a few thousand active dissidents played a vital role, underestimated at the time by many Western Sovietologists, the present author included, there were also millions of outwardly conforming *passive* dissidents who largely shared their values'.[18]

Thus when glasnost was proclaimed in 1986 – to stimulate policy-relevant debate and also generate enthusiasm among a population that would be implementing or cooperating with many of the reforms to be introduced from above – there were plenty of intellectuals who were ready to respond. Among other things, they were keen to express and debate the same sort of ideas that the dissidents had written about in samizdat over the preceding two decades, even if they knew little or nothing about these writings. The ideas concerned such topics as the separation of powers, the rule of law, judicial reform, civil and political freedoms, the right to emigrate, removal of discrimination against particular peoples and religious denominations, reform of the penal system, an end to abuses of psychiatry, and so on.

Thanks to glasnost and democratization, these issues soon became the stuff of politics and legislation, some of the dissidents were publicly honoured, and, from 1989 on, in cases like those of Sakharov, Kovalyov, Altunyan, Yakunin, and Revolt Pimenov in Russia, Vyacheslav Chornovil in Ukraine, and many others, they became elected politicians at the national, regional, or local level.[19]

At first, while glasnost was a policy that produced almost complete freedom of expression at the grass-roots of society, at the level of the mass media it was closely controlled by the Party.[20] However, by 1989 this control was slipping, and a widening range of groups and individuals were able to use the print and broadcast media to try to mobilize different sections of the public behind their viewpoints. Gorbachev's attempt in late 1990 to tighten the censorship of television in ways detrimental to democrats went against this trend, but had only slight effect.

While stressing the enthusiasm for debate, we should also note that as regards the mobilizing of support, the political actors in an increasingly free society had little or no genuinely political experience. Communists had never been compelled to seek voluntary support. Dissidents had always been suppressed if they began to organize any clearly political group, let alone a party: even a human rights group usually suffered arrests and suppression. And the general public – except for individuals who had belonged to dissident ethnic or religious groups – had no experience at all of organizing themselves autonomously to express their long-standing demands and grievances. Moreover, remembering the empty propaganda of the communists, they were instinctively distrustful of politicians making promises.[21]

This raises the difficult question of how discontented and ready for change ordinary people were in the Gorbachev period – a theme on which Donna Bahry has shed useful light. After comparing the results of opinion surveys conducted in the late Stalin period, the late Brezhnev era, and the Gorbachev years, she reaches the conclusion:

> *In the aggregate*, the desire for reform under Gorbachev was similar to that of the late Stalin years on many questions: most people wanted some political liberalization and some tolerance of private enterprise. However, the composition of the reform constituency changed over time, and relatively modest cleavages under Stalin grew into substantial ones by the end of the Brezhnev era.[22]

Against this background, dissidents stood out mainly because they dared to say openly what most people said only in private. In some cases, though, they held more radical, even openly anti-communist views.

The discussion to date has sought to explain why, at first, the perestroika programme received substantial support. It seemed to offer the sort of political liberalization and tolerance of private enterprise that most of the public wanted, its ideas were more or less in tune with those of mainstream dissidents and semi-dissidents, and there was a small but powerful group in the party which favored perestroika as being the best way to secure party rule for the long-term.

By 1989–90, however, the Gorbachev group had not received, or retained, *enough* support for perestroika from either the *nomenklatura* or 'the people'. Thus, although the group was remarkably skilful at neutralizing *nomenklatura* opposition, it soon proved unable to keep control of the effects of the reform process on society. Once glasnost, democratization and perestroika had gained a certain momentum, the key development was the leaders' loss of control over it. In more concrete terms, control was lost partially due to the emergence, from below, of numerous independent groups espousing programmes that were nationalist, populist, egalitarian, libertarian, anti-Establishment, or simply opposed to communism, at least of the *apparat* type.

A further key was the fact that in the face of this mounting challenge, important parts of the *nomenklatura* in most of the republics, including Russia but excluding Central Asia, abandoned the supposedly strict communist principles of 'democratic centralism', that is, absolute obedience to central commands, and paid little attention to the increasingly frantic appeals of Gorbachev and the federal government to hold the country together. Instead, each such leader sought to preserve his own power – and with it, that of the local mafia or mafias on which he depended – by suddenly embracing the centrifugal nationalism of his own republic, thus greatly accelerating the union's disintegration. At the same time, these leaders claimed to Moscow that this was the only feasible way of trying to keep their republics within the union. Thus much self-serving flouting of party discipline occurred. The fact that no republican leaders were seriously punished at any stage may, as noted earlier, be at least partly explained by the agreement apparently reached between the leaders and the mafia organizations that the union was probably doomed, and a smooth transition with maximum continuity of leadership was the best course to aim for.

Let me elaborate now on my earlier point about the relative lack of attention paid by many Sovietologists to the force and significance of these developments. Perhaps the most basic cause was the pervasive neglect or distrust of non-official sources of information on the USSR, that is, materials produced by samizdat authors, defectors, or emigrants, or uncensored, first-hand accounts by foreigners. Much of this neglect and distrust seems to have stemmed from an overly mechanistic application to the USSR of social science methods devised for non-communist systems, or from a fear that the use of such sources might jeopardize the approval of visas needed to visit the Soviet Union, or from anti-Western or pro-Soviet biases, or from some combination of these factors. But whatever the explanation in any individual case, the neglect was not, in my view, justified by common-sense criteria for objective research.

Taking the argument further, serious study of a semi-closed society like the USSR required spending a significant amount of time in it, to get to know its people and institutions well at first-hand. This was likely to show that many Soviet citizens lived double lives in which they said orthodox things in public, but were more critical of the existing order in private. It also made it easier to note that when the press admitted that 'in individual places' (*v otdel'nykh mestakh*) matters were not as they should be, in reality these 'shortcomings' (*nedostatki*) were often widespread.

From this perspective, it was not difficult to understand the importance of non-official Soviet sources. Most of the interviews, articles, and books by new emigres and defectors, for example, though their contents diverged sharply from the images portrayed by official sources, rang, by and large, true. While such sources had to be scutinized for bias and exaggeration like any other source, the widespread corruption, the pervasive hypocrisy in public, and the private cynicism of officials about ideology that the sources described, were all things that direct experience of Soviet life would have already at least partially revealed to foreigners with the necessary linguistic skills and powers of observation.[23] Likewise, when *samizdat* materials began to proliferate in the mid-1960s, it was clear enough that their authors – soon to be known as dissenters or dissidents – had simply decided to write and circulate more or less what they really thought, and not just to say it to trusted friends in private.[24]

The small number of scholars who read non-official sources carefully were still faced, of course, with the difficult task of assessing the collective weight and significance of these materials. Did the dissident groups, for example, have a stronger social base than the often small number of signatures on their documents might suggest? Were some of the groups seed-beds of future political opposition, or were they too marginal or eccentric to be seen in this light? The history of the last two decades suggests that, indeed, they did contain future oppositionists, and their social base was often significant and tended to widen over time. However, more research on these questions is needed.[25]

The issue of exactly how dissidents were viewed by the Soviet authorities has become clearer in recent years. Strong evidence, including statistical material, that the leadership obsessively feared dissent comes from a wide range of official archival documents, which scholars have now begun to analyse.[26] These documents show beyond question that the Kremlin took popular and intellectual disaffection very seriously. For example, the total number of prosecutions between 1958 and 1986 under two of the political articles of the Criminal Code (numbers 70 and 190–1) was about 6,000; for the eight years from 1967 through 1974, 121,406 individuals were formally warned that they were on the verge of being charged under these two articles; between 1975 and 1988 the annual number of anonymous protests handled by the KGB varied between a low of 8,723 and a high of 22,502; and in this period 2,438 of the authors of these anonymous documents were – although in most cases probably mentally healthy – forcibly confined to mental hospitals as punishment (while thousands more were jailed).

From the Kremlin's point of view – which gave absolute priority to maintaining unchallenged rule by the Communist Party – the Soviet leaders were right to treat dissent seriously. Anti-imperial, anti-communist, and just anti-Establishment views and emotions did indeed pose a real potential threat to party rule.[27] The fact that these views and emotions were less developed and perhaps less widespread in the USSR than in Eastern Europe does not affect this judgment. 'Compensation' for that fact is the equally important circumstance that unlike Eastern Europe, the USSR had no outside power that would come to the rescue of its communist party, if the latter's rule were to falter and – the supreme fear of totalitarian rulers – be threatened by collapse. Thus, from their viewpoint, the Soviet leaders had good reason to nip all forms of disaffection in the bud, before they gathered strength. And not surprisingly, the Kremlin did this with extra zeal in the wake of each eruption in Eastern Europe – in Hungary in 1956, in Czechoslovakia in 1968, in Poland in 1980–81 – because these eruptions significantly increased disaffection inside the Soviet Union.[28]

Disaffection and Gorbachev

Why then did Gorbachev, soon after his accession to power in 1985, diverge from this traditional and rational enough view of the dangers posed by popular disaffection? Initially, in fact, he did not diverge from it. Whipping up a considerably exaggerated sense of economic crisis, when the problem was really one of stagnation,[29] he prescribed as the main cure for it the Andropov recipe of streamlining economic management and imposing tougher discipline on the whole population. This helped him to make his personal power more secure, but did not, except briefly, produce impressive economic results. So he decided, after a year and a half in office, to change his strategy. He spelled it out for the first time in an intellectually comprehensive way in two famous, mutually complementary speeches of January and June 1987. Now the main goals became market socialism (though the actual term was too risky for him to use at that time) and – to overcome the inevitably fierce resistance to such radicalism from the party and ministerial hierarchies which employed almost 20 million officials – a partial democratization of the political system. This democratization would also serve two further purposes. It would release many pent-up tensions in society, caused in part by the crackdown of 1979–85 on all forms of dissent and deviance. This, Gorbachev hoped, would gain him popular support. And it would also impress the West, making its governments more inclined to cooperate with him on economic matters and on the radical arms control measures which were essential if he were ever to reduce his military budget and free up resources for consumer industries.

But why did Gorbachev not think that democratization would be dangerous for the party's monopoly on political power, a monopoly to which he was certainly devoted – in both private and public until at least 1988 and in public until 1990?[30] The answer for 1986–8 can be summed up thus: he believed that popular gratitude for his democratization and the dramatic economic advances that it would facilitate, would neutralize any ungrateful oppositional agitators who might try to cause trouble. He had confidence because he also believed, without saying it, that democracy could, ultimately, be steered and controlled by society's leaders. In a speech of 1987 that was an eloquent paean to democracy, he repeatedly rejected the view that democracy might subvert socialism or public order. A few extracts illustrate the point:

> Those who have doubts about the expediency of further democratization apparently suffer from one serious failing ... they do not believe in our people. They claim that democracy will be used by our people to disorganize society and undermine discipline, to undermine the strength of the system ... Democracy is not the opposite of order. It is order of a higher degree, based not on ... the

mindless carrying out of instructions, but on whole-hearted, active participation by the whole community in all of society's affairs... Democracy means self-regulation by society, confidence in the civic maturity of Soviet people and in their awareness of their social duty... The more democracy we have ... the more order and discipline we shall have in our socialist house.

So it is either democracy, or social inertia and conservatism. There is no third way, comrades.[31]

In another speech he expressed the communitarian view espoused by the writer Aleksandr Solzhenitsyn and some Slavophiles, and known as *sobornost'*. This holds that any community can reach agreement, even on contentious issues, through honest discussion between its members. If there should be one malicious hold-out, he would be so isolated after the discussion that he would not be able to cause damage and could safely be ignored.[32] Thus, as Gorbachev made clear later, there was no need for opposition parties, which would only foment artificial divisions in society.

There were, it seems, several sources for the naïvete of these views. First, in provincial Stavropol, where Gorbachev was a communist official for almost a quarter of a century (1955–78), there was too little in the way of openly expressed political dissent for him to get a feel for it at first-hand. Thus he did not learn that, as Dmitri Glinski has acutely noted, people were bound to dislike him for his utopian communitarian rhetoric, because it portrayed them as being morally better than they saw themselves as being.[33] Second, his Politburo colleague Aleksandr Iakovlev, a party intellectual, fed him roughly the views sketched above, which were also supported by another Politburo member, his friend Eduard Shevardnadze, and by liberal party intellectuals whom he consulted on economic and social problems from about 1982. He also knew something of the West-oriented democratic views of the exiled Andrei Sakharov, whom he persuaded the Politburo to release. In December 1986 he called Sakharov back to Moscow to resume his 'patriotic work'.[34]

Beyond these factors – which highlight Gorbachev's high regard for the West and his almost exaggerated respect for certain intellectuals – he had in his personality an over-confidence about his admittedly formidable powers of manipulation, a characteristic that occasionally amounted to recklessness. This made him believe that he would be able to change course, as in the past, if things went wrong. According to his chief-of-staff, Valerii Boldin, on a number of occasions he calmed Boldin's fears that his policies were leading the country towards calamity by saying: 'Just wait and see what I can do.' And in 1990 he assured Boldin: 'As long as I am president of the USSR, I shall not allow the destruction of the Union.'[35] Later he often admitted there was one key factor that he had not foreseen – the rise and the power of ethnic nationalism.

The dramatic release of Sakharov was the prelude to the release in 1987–8 of most of the country's political prisoners. Gorbachev also addressed another major source of popular disaffection when he got the Politburo to agree to remove all Soviet troops from Afghanistan by early 1989. By this time it was understood in the Politburo that military intervention in Eastern Europe had become unthinkable, since it would only re-create the sort of popular alienation caused by nine years of struggle and death in the Afghan quagmire.[36] All these developments were intended to facilitate, in Gorbachev's above quoted words, the 'wholehearted, active participation by the whole community' in the patriotic programme of perestroika.

Prior to 1989, Gorbachev apparently hoped that although party hardliners hated most of these policies and were therefore trying to organize against him, the policies were building for him a much bigger constituency of supporters that would swamp and neutralize the hardliners. But now, in 1989, the unforeseen consequences of his liberalism began to weaken his control over events. To see how, and to try to weigh the contribution of popular disaffection to the process, we shall separate out the most significant episodes in chronological sequence.

In 1988 some of the 'popular fronts' and analogous groups which had developed with Gorbachev's tacit encouragement (via articles by Boris Kurashvili and Tat'iana Zaslavskaia) in order to mobilize both communists and non-communists in support of perestroika had begun to cut their teeth. They were particularly provoked by two events. The first was the anti-perestroika thrust by party conservatives that was spearheaded by Nina Andreeva's article in *Sovetskaya Rossiya* of 13 March and parried by the Gorbachev forces only three weeks later. And the second was the Party Conference called for June. The shock to Gorbachev of the first episode made it all the more important that his forces should regain the upper hand at the Party Conference. This consideration strengthens the circumstantial evidence suggesting that Gorbachev supporters, probably operating from the Central Committee Secretariat, clandestinely encouraged and assisted certain unofficial groups in their efforts to prevent the conference delegations representing their cities from being stacked with conservatives. In Yaroslavl, for example, the group of activists who soon formed the local Popular Front suddenly found it rather easy to organize rallies, and were also given compromising material (*kompromat*) about the most powerful local conservative, Fedor Loshchenkov, the first party secretary of the region, which probably came from KGB files. As a result, Loshchenkov was soon ousted and the Yaroslavl delegation to the Party Conference was more to Gorbachev's liking.[37] The fact that somewhat analogous events occurred only, apparently, in a few other cities suggests that the growth of unofficial activity nationwide was probably less dramatic than it was in these selected cities, and that the difference may perhaps be explained by veiled official support given by Gorbachev forces to the popular fronts in those locations.

By 1989, some of these fronts had become, above all in the Baltic republics, vehicles for nationalism. Nationalist dissidents who had recently been released from jail assumed prominent positions in them. In the partially free elections of early 1989 for the revamped, quasi-democratic Congress of People's Deputies of the USSR (CPDU) the Baltic popular fronts caused a sensation by trouncing the communists and winning three quarters of the Baltic seats. Meanwhile, in a number of larger cities of Russia and Ukraine some of the official communist candidates, including a few big names, lost to former dissidents, other liberals, and – in one especially important case in Moscow – to a disgraced former Politburo member, Boris Yeltsin. In the preceding months Yeltsin had rebuilt the popular support base he had gained when, as Moscow city party chief in 1986-7, he had used fiery populism to unleash popular discontent, firing officials and exposing official abuses. Eventually, however, he went too far in his attacks on the conservatives in the Politburo, and Gorbachev opted to remove him from his post and humiliate him.[38]

This brings us to the difficult question of how to interpret the results of the CPDU elections, as well as those of the republican and regional elections of 1990 and the RSFSR presidential election of 1991. More particular questions, only some of which can be touched on in this chapter, are: What sorts of popular disaffection were being expressed, how strong was the disaffection, how much did it change from 1989 to 1991 and from area to area, and, above all, how exactly did officials obstruct the free expression of electors' preferences? All three elections served as barometers of popular views and mechanisms for real change. But no systematic exit polls were conducted, most candidates ran on personal, politically vague platforms,[39] and the political context in which the elections took place was so volatile and fast moving that the results were hard to interpret. Some analysts concluded that the CPDU elections of 1989 constituted an organized, revolutionary overthrow of the communist regime.[40] Others saw the key in the fact that glasnost allowed the formation of unofficial organizations (*neformaly*), which then mobilized popular discontent to bring about change through the ballot box.[41]

My own inclination is to modify the second interpretation by stressing an additional dimension that could, and apparently did operate in most areas except especially conservative ones like Central Asia. My interpretation starts from Bahry's strongly argued case, discussed earlier, that a generalized, non-revolutionary, but mounting level of political and economic discontent existed in the Soviet population from the late Stalin period onwards. In his quasi-populist phase from late 1986 through early 1989 Gorbachev deliberately tapped into this discontent, to harness it. He used speeches like the hymn to democracy quoted earlier, and toured the country to urge the popular masses – like Yeltsin in Moscow – to throw out officials who could not reform themselves, for example, by responding to the needs of society as expressed 'from below' by ordinary people.

In the run-up to the CPDU elections of 26 March 1989[42] – the first to feature more than one candidate for most of the popularly contested seats – various public media elaborated on this message. They also explained didactically the socially useful functions of genuinely democratic elections, and discussed how Soviet elections had been fundamentally abused in the past.[43] These themes were also of course espoused by the *neformaly*, but these groups had little or no access to the media, and, in the cities where they existed, local officials often blocked their efforts to hold rallies and circulate literature. So, outside a few big cities and the Baltic republics they probably had a rather small impact,[44] almost certainly much less than that of Gorbachev, his allies, and official, democratically inclined publications like *Ogonek* and *Argumenty i fakty*.

How then did ordinary people respond to the pre-election campaign and manoeuverings? First, although most of them had, as Bahry suggests, long been at least somewhat discontented, they were intrigued enough by the programme of perestroika, by the fact that Gorbachev and parts of the media had raised their hopes for a fair vote, by having lost their fear of voting their conscience, and by the innovation of multicandidate elections – to want to take part. Second, the more politically aware, especially among party members, had been put on their guard by the undemocratic ways in which many of the delegates to the Party Conference of June 1988 had been selected.

Third, ordinary people noticed how, in most locations, local officials tried, usually successfully, to manipulate the procedures for nominating and then registering the candidates for popular election. This was done through undemocratic manoeuverings at factories and other work places, where officials rammed through the candidacies of a more or less uniform slate of individuals, which had been secretly approved in advance by the party. This practice provoked a large number of formally filed complaints from citizens. In those cases where undesirable candidates were put forward by residents' groups, officials often refused to grant permits for the required nomination meeting (with its minimum attendance of 500 voters), or did so only at the last moment, so that the quorum would be unattainable. Or they stacked such meetings with 500 of their own supporters, then locked the doors. If, despite everything, undesirable candidates somehow got nominated, then the local electoral commissions often found ways to avoid registering them – usually for 'technical reasons'.

All these obstacles were of course overcome in the exceptional case of Boris Yeltsin, who received massive support from *neformaly* in Moscow, and greatly profited from the persistent efforts by the party apparatus to discredit and impede him. True, access to the Soviet media was difficult even for him, but on the day before the poll he was allowed to reply in *Moskovskaia pravda*,[45] edited by his ally Mikhail Poltoranin, to a letter which had attacked him. He summed up the problems which had thwarted most 'undesirable' candidates by criticizing the Moscow City Party Committee for 'putting pressure on the labor groups that nominated me as their candidate, making it difficult for me to organize meetings with voters, disallowing nomination documents, and selecting the participants in election-district meetings'.

Fourth, ordinary electors could easily notice, from the media, how the 750 'corporate' seats (one third of all the seats) in the Congress of People's Deputies were filled. The Communist Party, for example, nominated 100 candidates for its 100 'reserved seats', and the Council of Collective Farms likewise nominated 58 candidates for its 58 seats and approved them all in half an hour.[46] Ordinary people thus saw that not only were the members of these corporations given extra representation in the new parliament on top of their representation as citizens, but their corporate representatives had clearly been chosen in the old way – by the Establishment in secret, and not in any free election. *Pravda* even reported that it had received a number of letters from party members complaining about this abuse of the electoral principle by the party.[47]

Fifth and finally, voters in over one quarter of the electoral districts (399 out of 1,500) noted that in spite of all Gorbachev's rhetoric about the need for electors to have a choice of candidates, in fact there was, as in the past, only one candidate on their ballots.[48]

All this meant that when polling day came for ordinary people, quite a lot of them had at first had their hopes for a reasonably fair election raised, but by now, even if they knew nothing about the *neformaly*, they had good reason – from their purely individual knowledge – to feel that those hopes had been disappointed. This explains why, if there was any acceptable candidate who was in some way against the status quo, they may well have voted for him. Otherwise, they may have protested by crossing off all the names on the ballot paper. Thus Yeltsin got almost 90 percent of the ballots cast because, as an early biographer says, he had 'ridden the wave of popular protest against the apparat'.[49] In other words, while *neformaly* played an important role in mobilizing popular revolts in some big cities and leading a peaceful revolution in the Baltic republics, elsewhere in the USSR the jarring contradiction between Gorbachevian rhetoric and its subversion by local realities visible to the average citizen explained quite a lot about the far from triumphant performance of the Establishment in the election. Although, for example, 87.6 percent of the new deputies were communists, many of them were not from the party apparatus and showed at least some signs of independence, while one of them was the fully independent Yeltsin. Of the 191 first party secretaries from the republican and regional levels who ran, 153 were elected, but 38 of them were defeated, including all 32 who dared to square off against opponents.[50] The others went down because, although they ran unopposed, they failed to get the minimum number of 50 percent of all the votes cast. This meant that over half of those who voted had crossed out the only name on the ballot. In Russia as a whole, one sixth of those who voted crossed out the name or names on the ballot, and in Ukraine almost one quarter did so.

In a political system in which, theretofore, no electoral candidate had either been opposed or had received less than some 90 per cent of the vote, the outcome of the 1989 election was a major trauma for the party apparatus. This can be documented at length from the public records of the main party meetings over the next few months.[51] One regional leader said, for example, that not a single party official in his region was prepared to run in the forthcoming elections to the regional soviet, because defeat seemed certain.[52] No one rose to paint a happier picture of the situation in any other area. The elections were soon postponed. Perhaps the most fundamental cause of the pessimism of the party apparatus was the fact that its members clearly realized that Gorbachev no longer had much faith in them as his main political base. This was why he had created a new base for himself in the revamped Soviet structures, which would be more important than the party and might foreshadow their own total eclipse.

In his memoirs, Yegor Ligachev, then the party's second ranking figure, presents this perspective more frankly than he did at the time. On the pre-election period, for example, he writes:

> The Central Committee was sending directives to the localities one after another: don't interfere, don't interfere! Keep your distance! In many party committees a feeling of helplessness reigned: they saw that among the candidates for parliament there were many unworthy people, even ex-criminals who had been sentenced for crimes as serious as murder. And as for the loudmouths and demagogues who had built their election programs exclusively on anti-Sovietism and anti-communism, there was simply an incalculable number of them... But the Central Committee refrained from providing political guidance, and the party organs in the localities found themselves disarmed.[53]

On the other side of the fence, what the campaign workers of successful outsider candidates discovered was that it was quite possible, with good organization, strong leadership, and hard work, to mobilize – on behalf of certain candidates – popular disaffection with orthodox communism, with Soviet imperialism, or, perhaps most often, just with the undefined Establishment, or 'them'. If the candidates had previously been imprisoned or disgraced for their beliefs, and if in their campaigns they attacked the above mentioned objects of popular hatred with sufficient boldness, they had, in the more politicized cities and throughout the Baltic, a good chance of being elected. Most of them, of course, spoke strongly if generally in support of democracy or nationalism, or both. But this moved the voters less than attacks on many of the institutions and symbols, and much of the ideology, of a regime which had mistreated them with little respite for decades.

In the wake of this profound shock for the Establishment came ano-ther event of great significance for understanding the role of popular disaffection in the USSR's collapse. In April 1989 Soviet troops killed nineteen Georgians, many of them women, when dispersing a long-running demonstration by non-violent nationalists in Tbilisi. In the post-election atmosphere of anti-Establishment euphoria[54] this action – clearly planned to be the trigger for a countrywide crackdown on opposition, a crackdown that Gorbachev managed to abort at the last moment[55] – in fact provoked exactly the opposite effect, a new, more militant offensive by the democratic and nationalist forces. Nationalist groups in the Baltic and the Transcaucasus grew bolder in opposing Moscow's diktat and in coordinating their activities with each other, even openly. And other *neformaly* became more anti-communist, or at least more hostile to the anti-democratic forces in the party. In addition, several commissions were set up to investigate the massacre, while the top politicians, including Gorbachev and Ligachev, tried to disclaim responsibility for it, and numerous military commanders and officials around the country declared that the army must never again be used for internal police work.[56] As a result, the resolve of party officials and commanders of MVD and KGB troops, as well as army troops, over perhaps killing people in future policing actions of this sort was severely weakened. It was further weakened in January 1990, when a somewhat similar action in Baku, the capital of Azerbaidzhan, killed at least 130 people and ignited still more outrage. And it was constantly sapped, as month after month the media carried detailed attacks on a wide variety of officials and institutions. Among these were many delivered in parliamentary forums like the first CPDU, the whole proceedings of which were shown live on television. The reaction to all this of an embattled member of the communist party was to lament that the media had successfully created a public image of 'a party of mistakes and crimes'.[57]

As suggested earlier, one outcome of these events and trends was that in an increasing number of non-Russian republics (where conditions varied widely from one to another in many respects) nationalism made rapid strides and became more separatist in its tenor. Key factors were the union-wide revulsion at the killings in Georgia and Azerbaidzhan, the resulting statements by troop commanders about future restraint or non-participation in such situations, the Kremlin's minimal punishment of Lithuania, Latvia, and Estonia for moving steadily towards independence in the face of all Gorbachev's persuasion and bullying to the contrary, the Kremlin's inaction and virtual silence at the fall of communism throughout most of Eastern Europe in late 1989, and the decision by leading communists in the republics to, in many cases, defy Moscow and, in an opportunistic bid to retain their power, engage the local nationalists in political combat by suddenly claiming to be as nationalist as they were.[58]

January 1990 saw the formation of the first countrywide coalition of democratically-oriented groups, known as Democratic Russia. These voter groups and clubs had mostly come into being to campaign before the elections of 1989 and 1990. This trend toward consolidation of the opposition helped it to use popular disaffection to press its cause. First, in January and February, it organized demonstrations of several hundred thousand people in Moscow. Covertly helped by Gorbachev's group, these demonstrations forced the Central Committee of the party, much against the will of many members, to support the opposition's demand that the communists' legally-based monopoly on political power be ended through the amendment of Article 6 of the Constitution. The amendment was quickly passed in March by the third CPDU, which thus, in effect, sanctioned the formation of alternative parties. The opposition and the party liberals had used 'the street' against the party conservatives and the elected legislature. The latter could be successfully intimidated not only because it had just seen communist governments summarily voted out of power in Eastern Europe, but also because elections to the new, revamped legislatures of the fifteen republics were imminent. Both the party and individual deputies feared that they would suffer in those elections if they did not accede to the demands of the demonstrations. These could also have led to serious violence, had they not been appeased.

Interestingly, as indicated above, Gorbachev, after initially resisting strongly the amendment of Article 6 on the grounds that the party was not yet ready for such a radical change, had eventually, under pressure from Sakharov and others in the CPDU, capitulated and joined in the process of 'using the street'.[59] As the Mayor of Leningrad Anatolii Sobchak recounted, on February 3 Gorbachev's lieutenant Anatolii Luk'ianov met the organizers of the demonstration planned for February 4, the eve of the crucial plenum of the Central Committee. He gave them permission to hold an open-air meeting right under the windows of the Moskva Hotel, where the delegates to the plenum would have just arrived. As a result, the delegates witnessed the unprecedented and intimidating spectacle of a demonstration against Article 6 by no less than 'half a million Muscovites'.[60]

For assessing public opinion, broad-based and carefully conducted surveys can often be more illuminating than election results. By late 1989, when the All-Union Center for the Study of Public Opinion (VTsIOM), headed by Tat'iana Zaslavskaia, carried out a survey in seven republics, the quality of such surveys had become broadly acceptable to Western sociologists. So an analysis of this VTsIOM survey by two such scholars is of interest. One of their conclusions was that popular support for political reform was strong, but not for a 'wholesale abandonment of socialist principles'. These had to be guaranteed by the state. 'The communist party, as the engine of that obligated state, was rejected, but not the obligation itself; the institution failed, but not the norm. Indeed, the institution's failure may have been due largely to its unwillingness or inability to service the norm.' The authors also found that 40 per cent of respondents regarded public order as more important than free speech, and that the survey showed: 'Overall, party people are as divided about political reform as is the rest of the population.'[61]

These findings sum up the evidence of a number of polls of 1989 which record massive loss of public confidence in the communist party. (This was followed in 1990 by a similarly large loss of confidence in the leadership of Gorbachev.) But the findings do not explain why the communists did not do much worse in the republican and regional elections of February–March 1990 than in the all-union ones of March 1989. True, the 1990 elections saw the sweeping away by the opposition of the old political leaders in Georgia and the Baltic, and the opposition took some key seats in Ukraine, Belorussia, and Russia. But 86 percent of the deputies to the new Russian (RSFSR) Congress were still communists, thanks to careful preparation by the party, the candidates' focus on local issues of direct concern to voters, and their advocacy of republican sovereignty. True, some of the elected communists were communist only in name, but nonetheless anti-communism as such was not a widespread feature of the campaign, even though the *neformaly* had multiplied rapidly in the wake of the 1989 election, with anti-communism becoming more widespread among them.

There are, I believe, two main explanations for why simple, overt anti-communism was not much on display, except in a few big cities. First, shrewd electoral tactics suggested in 1990, as also in 1989, that to be strongly anti-communist would push many voters who were only fairly nominal communists away from supporting a candidate. It would also increase the danger that communist party conservatives might feel so threatened that they would remove Gorbachev and reestablish the party's dictatorship.

Second, 1990 was the year in which candidates could gain the most mileage both out of championing the sovereignty of their republic and its right to self-determination, and also – the other side of the coin – out of denouncing the rapacious, wasteful, dictatorial, and incompetent federal government in Moscow. Since this powerful rhetoric clashed, for communist voters, with their duty to obey the centralized party structures in Moscow, it was more sensible for candidates not to sharpen this dilemma, but, rather, to emphasize republican patriotism (a form of nationalism) and downplay explicit anti-communism. In this way they could create a wide base of supporters, as Yeltsin did brilliantly in both 1989 and 1990, and eventhough he eventually resigned from the party in July 1990 – in the presidential election of 1991. None of this precluded his appealing to the latent or conscious anti-communism of many voters, using a relatively soft-sell, anti-Moscow, and anti-Establishment approach. Candidates could and did, for example, denounce Stalin's crimes, the monopoly on power held by a single party, the central government's refusal to grant the republics the sovereignty proclaimed by their Constitutions, and so on. But candidates did not adopt such broad-brush slogans (displayed in demonstrations by some of the *neformaly*) as 'Down with the Communists!', let alone spell out some new, militantly anti-communist philosophy or programme. All in all, voters were more swayed by the cleavage between the upper crust of society and the lower orders than by the cleavage between left and right. Thus they would happily vote for a communist, for example, if they believed, or half-believed, in his populist promises to increase wages or do away with the party's privileges. In short, it was a time for populism.

This was sensed instinctively by Yeltsin and his advisors. Hence his skilful political handling, from 1988 on, of the *neformaly* and of Democratic Russia. He discerned their moral standing, he courted them, he used their support and their organizational abilities, he relied on them, he thanked them, he was friendly and consulted with their leaders, he was a co-leader of the liberal Inter-Regional Group in the CPDU, and Democratic Russia was a central part of his coalition and his campaigns. But he never made implied or explicit promises to them or their leaders. This was shrewd, because, as he progressed from one triumph to another, he was not obliged to reward them or remain loyal to them, except to the extent that doing so seemed desirable at the time.

Here we should note that Sakharov and other democrats had realized from the start that Yeltsin was more of an authoritarian than a liberal. But they supported him for tactical reasons, as the only candidate who seemed capable of bringing about substantial change. Later, after he won the Russian presidency in 1991, democrats, like the public at large, took varying lengths of time to become disappointed in him. They did so, of course, in varying degrees and not necessarily to the point of voting against him. In sum, though, for the purposes of this chapter, we can say that Yeltsin won power in the RSFSR thanks to the support of democrats, discontented citizens, and newly minted Russian nationalists, and that his victory was a major factor in the collapse of the Soviet Union.

To return to chronology, the elections of 1990 took place in freer conditions than those of a year earlier. Though scholars differ on how to characterize the outcome, the opposition can be said to have scored further, though not spectacular gains.[62] Soon, however, thanks in part to persistent, counter-productive opposition to Yeltsin from the increasingly unpopular Gorbachev, Yeltsin was elected speaker of the Russian parliament – by a margin of four votes. Later, in June 1991, he won popular election to Russia's newly created executive presidency with 57 percent of the vote, and the government he formed proceeded to quietly appropriate from the federal government some of its powers, thus weakening it and causing confusion.[63] These developments, which simply would not have happened without the mobilization of popular discontent behind them, created almost overnight a politicized Russian nationalism that could be compared in part to the nationalism of several other republics. It was not in most cases an ethnic nationalism, nor was it a separatist nationalism of the Baltic type, but – partly in order to have some defences against the Kremlin's economic incompetence – it insisted on republican 'sovereignty' and a new union treaty that would be much looser than what Gorbachev wanted, and would, in reality, be no more than confederative in nature. Like the Baltic and Georgian nationalist movements before them, the Russian movement exploited the existing non-party Soviet institutions to press its case against the federal government. As Rigby has put it, 'the constant democratic rhetoric of Soviet political life' and the pseudo-democratic political structures were taken at face value by these movements and filled with genuine democratic content. The federal authorities had no basis on which to denounce such activity as illegitimate.[64]

Thus 1990 saw the steady loss by Gorbachev and the federal government of popular support and legitimacy, as the disaffection of parts of society was channeled into the powerful movements for republican sovereignty or even separatism, and also into voting for individual candidates who were simply seen as standing up against the Establishment. In the fall, this threat to the millions of officials who worked for the federal government at last produced serious action from the hardliners whom Gorbachev had so brilliantly blocked and out-manoeuvered for three and a half years. They accused him publicly of having unleashed revolutionary anti-Union and anti-communist forces which were now making an alliance to overthrow communism and dismember the country.[65] In October they forced him to drop his support for Academician Shatalin's radical economic reform plans. In November and December they induced him to start replacing the more liberal members of his government with hardliners and to take a more authoritarian line on freedom of expression.[66] And in January 1991 they got him to sanction – if not in writing – military action to suppress the secessionist Baltic governments by force.

At this point a crucial test of both the hardliners' resolve and the strength of popular opposition in the Baltic region took place. When the first military actions caused 18 deaths in Vilnius and Riga, Gorbachev called a halt, in order to appraise the situation. He found that there were heavy costs, no benefits, and no prospects of any benefits unless he was prepared to kill hundreds of people. The 18 deaths had not caused the thousands of defenders of the Baltic parliaments to run away; many of them, it turned out, were ready to die. Moreover, within 48 hours the deaths had provoked large-scale demonstrations against the regime in many cities around the USSR. Yeltsin had strongly denounced the killings and called on Russian troops not to shoot. Several military commanders in the Baltic said or indicated publicly that they would not give such orders. Foreign leaders and international organizations were threatening and even adopting economic and other sanctions against the Soviet Union.

If, then, Gorbachev were now to carry through with the full-scale military plan, these serious consequences of the actions in Vilnius and Riga would be multiplied a hundred times. His own cherished international reputation as a humane man of peace would be destroyed,[67] non-Baltic republics like Georgia would secede in protest, there would not be enough willing troops to prevent them from seceding, and even holding down a seething Baltic for the indefinite future would be problematic. In short, it was easy for Gorbachev to show the hardliners that their policy of suppression could not work. From their point of view, even if they were to oust him in a coup, the instruments at their disposal were too unreliable for them to be able to hold the union together by force. Officers and men would mutiny in large numbers – and probably in the MVD and KGB, as well as in the military.

January 1991 was thus the decisive moment which showed that the USSR could no longer be preserved, except perhaps, for a short time, as a loose confederation of nine or ten of the 15 republics. Over the next few months the reformist opposition in Russia maintained the momentum generated by its protests against the Baltic killings, focusing now on trying to reverse Gorbachev's swing of late 1990 towards hard-line positions. Demonstrations by hundreds of thousands of citizens were organized in various cities. That of 28 March in Moscow constituted a landmark victory, because it took place in face of an outright ban by the federal government. The ban had been reinforced by 50,000 troops who had been brought into the centre of the city. At the last minute Gorbachev decided not to unleash these troops, evidently using a calculus similar to the one he had applied two months earlier when he suddenly halted the already launched suppression of Baltic independence. On top of all this, in March–April the coal-miners resumed on a large scale their strikes of summer 1989.[68]

Not surprisingly, then, in April Gorbachev felt constrained to swing reluctantly in the direction of curbing his hard-line policies. On 23 April he moved to appease the nationalism of the republics by getting serious, two years too late, about a new Union Treaty in talks at Novo-Ogarevo. But soon the hardliners' brief coup of 18–21 August – brought to an end with important assistance from sections of the general public, if only in a few big cities[69] – precipitated the final collapse of the federal government's and Gorbachev's authority, and, in December, the end of the USSR.

The mafia and the end of communism

Few scholars from the non-communist world can have read Arkady Vaksberg's book *The Soviet Mafia*, without then rethinking some of their assumptions about the Soviet system. Vaksberg showed how the long latent symbiosis between political bosses and underworld bosses at all levels made steady strides during the increasingly corrupt Brezhnev era. The underworld – the economic component of the symbiosis – provided the officials with goods, cash, and other services. And the political component, the officials, provided the underworld kings with freedom of activity and immunity from arrest. While most officials did not formally belong to a mafia, any official who took decisions inimical either to overall mafia interests, or to the vital interests of a particular mafia, was likely to find himself subject to strong pressures to reverse them. The mafias were at, or close to, the core of the system. Overall, Vaksberg concluded, writing in 1990, 'any leader who supports the system is inescapably upholding the mafia as well, even if he is bursting with a sincere desire to finish it off. This is an objective and inescapable fact of political reality. In *this* sense, as long as Gorbachev remains a defender of the present political system, he will *ipso facto* remain a defender of the mafia.'[70]

The central interests of these loose associations of politicians and underworld figures were political stability and monopoly prices for their goods and services. Also important, but perhaps less continuously, were the opportunities that might occur to increase their geographical turf or the range of goods and services they could provide. And when the chance came in 1987 – thanks to the lifting of an unprecedented number of controls on the economy and foreign travel – to increase dramatically their turnover and their networks of foreign business partners, mafia groups naturally took it. This chance compensated for the accompanying decrease in political and economic stability. However, this decrease soon became worrying, and officials began to respond to mafia pressures both to crack down on political opposition, and to provoke inter-ethnic clashes, the most bloody being those of 1988 that led to the Armenia-Azerbaidzhan war. The clashes provided good pretexts for clampdowns, some of which are discussed earlier in this chapter. They were intended to shore up the political and economic status quo.[71]

Thus prolonged political instability presented the mafias with both challenges and opportunities. Apparently most of them (at least in Moscow) did not support, but, rather, opposed the attempted hardline coup of August 1991. They presumably saw that the Union's collapse was inevitable, and that their interests lay in promoting a smooth transition to post-Union conditions, with political power remaining as far as possible in the hands of their existing partners in the communist party.

Conclusion

In conclusion, then, we see from this condensed analysis of complex processes that popular disaffection with Soviet imperialism, orthodox communism, or just 'the Establishment', played indispensable roles in the disintegration of the Soviet Union. In Russia it provided essential electoral votes for the Yeltsinite coalition of democrats and variegated nationalists that led the opposition. It provided many of the bodies needed at key physical demonstrations of popular will. In some industries, especially mining, it supported strike actions which seriously weakened the resolve of the government at key moments in summer 1989 and March–April 1991. It subverted the will and reliability of the 'organs of coercion', without which the USSR could not survive. Increasingly, it drove events, putting the party and its mafia allies on the defensive, forcing them to react and make hard individual choices, and thus dividing them. In short, the opposition alliance became increasingly the subject of policy, and less the object.

None of this is to say that popular disaffection was a 'bigger' factor in the collapse than other indispensable factors mentioned at the beginning of this article. Nor is it to say that there was some inevitability about the

USSR disintegrating six years after Gorbachev took over. The country would probably have survived longer if Gorbachev had died or been ousted early on, or if he had conducted political liberalization more gradually, or if he had taken Sakharov's and Iuri Afanas'ev's advice in 1988 and started negotiating a new union treaty two years earlier than he did. As it was, ethnic and republic-based nationalisms, unleashed by glasnost and perestroika and greatly strengthened by the republican elections of early 1990, quickly posed the most acute threat to the USSR's survival. More broadly, Gorbachev's mix of political and economic policies enabled the various nationalist and anti-federation movements, including Yeltsin's in Russia, to break up the country more rapidly, I suggest, than any other conceivable set of Kremlin policies would have done. Unintentionally, Gorbachev was a destroyer of world class.

In the short run, the loss of life was relatively small. However, over the next two decades the rapid and almost uncontrolled collapse of the Soviet 'internal empire' produced or exacerbated in Russia, along with some benefits in the sphere of human rights, a larger number of exceptionally baneful results: all-pervasive corruption, massive social injustice, aborted democratic beginnings, an unchecked executive branch, censored media, a perverted capitalism, and a noxious, money-based class system that allowed for little social mobility.

From the perspective of this chapter, the nascent civil society of 1987–91 needed more than four years in which to develop and grow, to be energized and broadened by emerging waves of diverse types of popular discontent. With more time, it could have matured, put down roots, and prepared the soil in which democracy might have been able to grow. In this way, too, it would have had a better chance, as communism evolved and eventually collapsed, of thwarting, at least in part, the inevitable manipulations and depredations of the groups that have in fact triumphed, the robber barons and the secret police.

Notes

1 I am grateful to Catherine Dale for her valuable help on the research for an earlier version of this article. Her diligence is reflected especially in the analysis of the elections of 1989–91. I am likewise grateful to Dmitri Glinski for his insightful comments on the same version, and also for his enormous input into his and my book, input that has helped me in writing this chapter. The book is *The Tragedy of Russia's Reforms: Market Bolshevism Against Democracy* (Washington, DC: US Institute of Peace Press, 2001).

2 See, for example, Stephen Cohen, 'Gorbachev and the Soviet reformation', in Stephen Cohen and Katrina vanden Heuvel (1989), *Voices of Glasnost:*

Interviews with Gorbachev's Reformers (New York and London: Norton), pp.13–32.

3   Martin Malia, 'The August revolution', *The New York Review of Books*, 26 September 1991, pp.22–8; 'The Yeltsin revolution', *The New Republic*, 10 February 1992, pp.21–5.

4   Robert Byrnes (1983), *After Brezhnev* (Bloomington: Indiana University Press). The authors were Robert Byrnes, Seweryn Bialer, Robert Campbell, Coit Blacker, Gail Lapidus, Maurice Friedberg, Andrzej Korbonski, and Adam Ulam.

5   Byrnes, *After Brezhnev*, p.xvii.

6   Ibid., p.65. See also Lapidus's conclusions on p.245 and Friedberg's on p.288.

7   For a survey of some of the work of scholars who had drawn attention to vulnerabilities and signs of decline in the Soviet regime's defenses, see my article 'Research on Soviet decline', *Post-Soviet Affairs*, IX, 2, 1993, 176–81. For an historically informed analysis of the decline, see Reddaway and Glinski, *Tragedy of Russia's Reforms*, chapter 3.

8   For an exceptionally stimulating and wide-ranging discussion of this question, which used as a springboard a symposium on the reasons for the Soviet collapse in *The National Interest*, no. 31, Spring 1993, see Dominic Lieven (1994), 'Western scholarship on the rise and fall of the Soviet regime: The view from 1993', *The Journal of Contemporary History*, XXIX, 195–227.

9   Hence Gorbachev's numerous references, first to Lenin's statement that communist parties which had perished in the past had done so because they had not had the resolve to face up to and correct their weaknesses, and second to the fact that the USSR would not enter the 21st century 'in a manner worthy of a great power' unless it seriously reformed itself.

10 In the view of Gaddy and Ickes, the USSR 'had become dependent on loans from first Western banks and then Western governments simply in order to import enough food to prevent hunger'. Thus 'it collapsed because it lost political sovereignty as a result of losing all financial autonomy'. See Clifford Gaddy and Barry Ickes (2009), 'Putin's third way', *The National Interest*, no. 99, 47.

11 Alexander Yakovlev (1983), *The Fate of Marxism in Russia* (New Haven: Yale University Press), pp.228, 211.

12 Nearly 80 issues of this voluminous privately circulated journal were compiled between 1964 and 1971. Many of them were published in Russian by the Alexander Herzen Foundation in Amsterdam, in two volumes, *Politicheskii dnevnik*, 1972 and 1975. Selected articles make up Stephen F. Cohen (ed.) (1982), *An End To Silence* (New York: Random House).

13 Reprinted in *Sakharov Speaks* (London: Collins & Harvill, London, 1974), pp.55–114.

14 See P. Reddaway, 'Soviet policies towards the early dissent of Andrei Sakharov (up to 1973)', October 2008, Andrei Sakharov Foundation website, http//asf.prime-task.com/asfconf2008/asfconf_pan1.pdf, pp.16–24. For a valuable collection of 203 annotated archival documents from the years 1968–89 on the Soviet leadership's policy towards Sakharov, see Joshua Rubenstein and Alexander Gribanov (eds) (2005), *The KGB File of Andrei Sakharov* (Yale: Yale University Press). Rubenstein's lengthy introduction is also valuable.

15 See, for example, the tributes of Yuri Afanasiev and Len Karpinsky in Cohen and vanden Heuvel, *Voices of Glasnost*, pp.100, 300.

16 Cohen and vanden Heuvel, *Voices of Glasnost*, p.122.

17 Ibid., *Voices of Glasnost*, pp.118–21.

18 T.H. Rigby, 'Reconceptualizing the Soviet system', in Stephen White, Alex Pravda, Zvi Gitelman (eds) (1992), *Developments in Soviet and Post-Soviet Politics* (Durham: Duke University Press, 2nd edition), pp.312–13.

19 Robert Horvath has performed a service by focusing on the political and ideological influence in late communist and early post-communist Russia of the ideas and to some extent activities of four key dissidents of various stripes: Andrei Sakharov, Sergei Kovalev, Aleksandr Solzhenitsyn, and Igor Shafarevich. While conceding that only a little such influence can be directly documented, he argues that the impact of these men on events was in fact – in diffused and largely unacknowledged ways – extensive. Regrettably, there is no space in this chapter to pursue this fascinating and elusive topic at the length it deserves. See Robert Horvath (2005), *The Legacy of Dissent: Dissidents, Democratization, and Radical Nationalism in Russia* (London and New York: RoutledgeCurzon).

20 See the description by the chief editor of *Ogonek*, Vitaly Korotich, of some of the mechanisms used in 'Press freedoms: New dangers', his chapter in Uri Ra'anan, Keith Armes, Kate Martin (eds) (1992), *Russian Pluralism: Now Irreversible?* (New York: St. Martin's Press), pp.141–2. When I took part in a round-table on *perestroika* at *Ogonek* in November 1988, editors of the journal explained in private that continuing party-run censorship meant that the published transcript of the proceedings would have to omit certain points, for example, any criticism of party leaders. Some idea of the amount of censorship involved can be seen by comparing the transcripts published in *Ogonek*, 50, December 1988, 10–14, with those in the American journal *Soviet Economy*, IV, 4, 1988, 275–318.

21 On how the first political groups and parties were formed, see Michael McFaul and Sergei Markov (1993), *The Troubled Birth of Russian Democracy: Parties, Personalities, and Programs* (Stanford, CA: Hoover Institution Press); Geoffrey Hosking, Jonathan Aves, Peter Duncan (1992), *The Road to Post-Communism: Independent Political Movements in the Soviet Union, 1985–1991* (London and New York: Pinter).

22 See Donna Bahry (1993), 'Society transformed? Rethinking the social roots of Perestroika', *Slavic Review*, LII, 3, 513. Bahry used primarily the results of the Harvard Project of the 1950s, the Soviet Interview Project of the 1980s, and the *Times-Mirror* surveys of the early 1990s.

23 See, for example, the following books by dissidents and defectors: Valery Chalidze (1974), *To Defend These Rights* (New York: Random House); Arkady Shevchenko (1985), *Breaking With Moscow* (London: Cape); Petro Grigorenko (1983), *Memoirs* (London: Harvill); Ilya Dzhirkvelov (1987), *Secret Servant: My Life with the KGB and the Soviet Elite* (New York: Harper & Row); Michael Voslensky (1984), *Nomenklatura* (New York: Doubleday). Let me note that Voslensky's book was badly translated into English and poorly edited (see my review-article 'Nomenklatura: The Soviet ruling class', *L.S.E. Quarterly*, I, 1, Spring 1987, 115–26), and that it was later published in a longer and amended Russian edition as *Nomenklatura – Gospodstvuiushchii klass Sovetskogo Soiuza* (London: Overseas Publications Interchange, 1990).

24   The dissident Ludmila Alexeyeva describes well this evolution in herself and
her friends. See her and Paul Goldberg's book, *The Thaw Generation* (Boston-
Toronto-London: Little, Brown, 1990), esp. chapters 3 and 4. For guidance
on the thousands of *samizdat* documents and books and their authors see
S.P. de Boer, E.J. Driessen, H.L. Verhaar (eds) (1982), *Biographical Dictionary
of Dissidents in the Soviet Union, 1956–1975* (The Hague-Boston-London:
Nijhoff), which has entries on 3,400 individuals; Ludmila Alexeyeva (1987),
Soviet Dissent (Middletown, CT: Wesleyan University Press); Peter Reddaway
(1972), *Uncensored Russia: The Human Rights Movement in the USSR* (London:
Cape); and the full translations of the samizdat journal of 1968–82, *A
Chronicle of Current Events*, published by Amnesty International Publications, London, and distributed by Routledge. The full Russian texts are
available on the website of Memorial, the independent historical research
organization in Moscow, at www.memo.ru/history/diss/chr.index.htm. This
organization has also published books and compiled extensive files on
many aspects of dissent and opposition in the Soviet period.
25   This complex and under-researched topic has been the main research focus
for some years of the historian Benjamin Nathans of the University of
Pennsylvania.
26   P. Reddaway, 'Patterns in Soviet Policies Towards Dissent: 1953–1987', to
appear in an upcoming book edited by Wolfgang Eichwede of Bremen University; and Rubenstein and Gribanov, *The KGB File*. For the first wide-ranging
and painstakingly edited collection of archival documents on dissent policy
issued in the years 1970–85 by the party's Politburo and Secretariat and
the KGB, see A.A. Makarov, N.V. Kostenko, and G.V. Kuzovkin (eds) (2006),
Vlast' i dissidenty: Iz dokumentov KGB i TsK KPSS (Moscow: Moskovskaia
khel'sinkskaia gruppa).
27   This has been my view since the late 1960s. See, for example, the articles
'Dialectic is backfiring', *The Times*, 21 June 1968, and 'The resistance in
Russia', *The New York Review of Books*, 12 December 1974, as well as the
introduction to Reddaway, *Uncensored Russia*.
28   1958 saw the prosecution of 1,416 citizens on the one charge alone of
anti-Soviet agitation and propaganda. P. Reddaway (1993), 'Sovietology
and dissent', *RFE/RL Research Report*, II, 5, 14. The stimulus given to Soviet dissenters by the 'Prague Spring' of 1968 is documented in Natalya Gorbanevs-
kaya (1972), *Red Square at Noon* (London: Andre Deutsch, London); Reddaway,
Uncensored Russia, chapters 4–6. In response to the Polish upheavals of 1980–1
the Kremlin intensified a crackdown on dissent at home that it had begun
for other reasons in 1979. Going further, it was so disturbed by the Polish
developments that it launched a high-level, semi-public debate on how, in
certain circumstances, contradictions under socialism might lead to a revolutionary situation in the USSR. See Ernst Kux's analysis of this debate, in
which various euphemisms and veiled references do not conceal the essence
of the concern, 'Contradictions in Soviet socialism', *Problems of Communism*,
XXXIII, 6, 1984, 20 ff.
29   This is one of the points made by several authors in Michael Ellman and
Vladimir Kontorovich (eds) (1998), *The Destruction of the Soviet Economic
System: An Insiders' History* (Armonk: M.E. Sharpe).
30   See Archie Brown's summing up of this issue in his book *The Gorbachev
Factor* (Oxford: Oxford University Press, 1996) pp.193–4.

31 *Pravda*, 26 February 1987.
32 *Pravda*, 29 January 1987. One can interpret the communist doctrine of 'democratic centralism' in a similar way, except that in the communist party the hold-out sometimes had to be actually ejected from the relevant body, for example, Yeltsin from the party leadership in 1987.
33 Glinski, personal communication.
34 See the official transcript of the relevant Politburo meeting in Rubenstein and Gribanov, *The KGB File*, pp.326–8, and, on the intra-Politburo politics behind this move, Brown, *Gorbachev Factor*, pp.164–6. Later, in 1991, Gorbachev's more conservative colleague Yegor Ligachev claimed that the Politburo had taken into account Sakharov's ideas about democracy, including 'a lot of his ideas about democratization and elections and so forth, about freeing people who had been oppressed, or who were in prison. They were all let go, they were all freed ....'. He admitted, though, that 'maybe we didn't take all his ideas into account'. *Speeches of Egor Kuz'mich Ligachev at the Kennan Institute*, Occasional Paper no. 247 (Washington DC: Kennan Institute for Advanced Russian Studies, 1991), meeting of 14 November, p.12.
35 Valery Boldin (1994), *Ten Years That Shook the World* (New York: Basic Books), pp.238, 272. Although Boldin turned against Gorbachev in the 1991 coup, and his book reflects his disenchantment, these quotations ring to me.
36 For example, Eduard Shevardnadze said flatly in a speech in Moscow to the Foreign Correspondents' Association that, as regards the possible use of force to preserve communist rule in Eastern Europe: 'At the highest level the question was not raised.' *The Guardian*, 1 May 1991. Shevardnadze's statement was later confirmed by Yegor Ligachev at a lunch I attended at Johns Hopkins University's School for Advanced International Studies on 14 November 1991.
37 See Michael Dobbs, 'Politics on the front line of Perestroika', *The Washington Post*, 26 March 1989, p. A1. See also Vladimir Brovkin (1990), 'Revolution from below: Informal political associations in Russia 1988–1989', *Soviet Studies*, XLII, 2, 235–6; Hosking, *Road to Post-Communism*, p.75. According to Blair Ruble (personal communication), who has studied the politics of Yaroslavl since the late 1980s, the KGB in Yaroslavl had a strong grudge against Loshchenkov, evidently because of his Mafia ties. This may have facilitated the actions taken against him by the KGB's local boss, Major-General Alexander Razhivin, who gave a long interview to Dobbs. Thus it appears that a corrupt party boss and the local mafia were defeated by a coalition of the KGB, Gorbachev's group, and some activist Yaroslavl citizens.
38 On Yeltsin's populism, his humiliation, and his triumphant resurrection in the CPDU elections, see Timothy Colton (2008), *Yeltsin: A Life* (New York: Basic Books), pp.118–67.
39 A.V. Berezkin, V.A. Kolosov, M.E. Pavlovskaya, N.V. Petrov, L.V. Smirnyagin (1989), 'The geography of the 1989 elections of people's deputies of the USSR (preliminary results)', *Soviet Geography*, XXX, 8, 624. This article is a forerunner to a book on the 1989 elections from which I have taken some facts, V.A. Kolosov, N.V. Petrov, L.V. Smirniagin (eds) (1990), *Vesna '89: Geografiia i anatomiia parlamentskikh vyborov* (Moscow: Progress).

40   See, for example, Brovkin, 'Revolution from below'; V. Brovkin (1990), 'The making of elections to the congress of people's deputies in March 1989', *The Russian Review*, XLIX, 417–42.

41   See, for example, Thomas Remington, 'Towards a participatory politics?', in White, *Developments*, pp.147–73; Tolz (1990), *The USSR's Emerging Multiparty System* (New York and London: Praeger).

42   For an overview of these elections see Reddaway and Glinski, *Tragedy*, pp.142–6.

43   Some of these press materials, especially those in *Pravda*, were helpfully analysed in Max Mote (1989), 'Electing the USSR congress of people's deputies', *Problems of Communism*, XXXVIII, 6, 51–6.

44   The impact was somewhat amplified by foreign radio broadcasts in Russian and other languages by Radio Liberty, the BBC, Voice of America, etc. But these stations were listened to mainly by the well-educated minority of the population, and anyway had a reduced listenership in the late 1980s, since glasnost had made the Soviet media exciting for the first time.

45   *Moskovskaia Pravda*, 25 March 1989.

46   Stephen White and Gordon Wightman (1989), 'Gorbachev's reforms: The Soviet elections of 1989', *Parliamentary Affairs* (London), XLII, 566.

47   *Pravda*, 16 March 1989.

48   Brendan Kiernan (1993), *The End of Soviet Politics. Elections, Legislatures, and the Demise of the Communist Party* (Boulder: Westview), p.67.

49   John Morrison (1991), *Boris Yeltsin: From Bolshevik to Democrat* (New York: Dutton), p.93. This point was made for me anecdotally when, just before the election, I was in Tarusa in the Russian provinces and met the director of a large government rest home. Although he was not a party member, he had just been summoned and told by the local communist authorities to throw a party for all his employees. When enough alcohol had been consumed, he was to give a short speech instructing them to vote for Yeltsin's main rival, Nikolai Ryzhkov. If he refused to do this, the party would have him prosecuted for one of the many violations of the law that any Soviet manager was compelled to commit, if he were to operate effectively. The director had not yet decided whether to comply. He speculated, though, that if he did comply, his speech would probably be counter-productive from Ryzhkov's point of view: he would in fact increase Yeltsin's vote, because most of his employees now resented official manipulation of this sort.

50   Jeffrey Hahn (1990), 'Boss Gorbachev confronts his new congress', *Orbis*, XXXIV, 2, 169.

51   See a partial analysis of these meetings in P. Reddaway (1989), 'Is the Soviet Union drifting towards anarchy?', *Report on the USSR*, I, 34, 2–3.

52   Speech by Vladimir Melnikov, *Pravda*, 27 April 1989.

53   E.K. Ligachev (1992), *Zagadka Gorbacheva* (Novosibirsk: Sibirskii tsentr SP 'Interbuk'), pp.76–7, 94. Ligachev may not be exaggerating greatly about the Central Committee's directives, but, as we have seen, local party organizations nonetheless showed an instinct for survival and were far from completely paralysed.

54   On the continuation of large public rallies after the election, aimed at influencing the agenda of the approaching first CPDU, see McFaul and Markov, *Troubled Birth*, pp.7–8.

55 See the evidence of the legislative preparations in Peter Reddaway, 'The threat to Gorbachev', *The New York Review of Books*, 17 August 1989, pp.19–24. For evidence of the crackdown planned for the provincial cities of Ryazan and also, apparently, Novokuznetsk, see Pilar Bonet (1992), *Figures in a Red Landscape* (Washington DC: Woodrow Wilson Center Press, and Baltimore MD:Johns Hopkins University Press), pp.86, 115.
56 For a penetrating insider's account of the whole episode, and of the Establishment's success in preventing anyone being held accountable for the deaths, see Anatoly Sobchak (1991), *Khozhdenie vo vlast'* (Moscow: Novosti, 2nd edition), pp.77–104. Sobchak was the chairman of the Congress's commission of enquiry.
57 *Pravda*, 21 July 1989.
58 Nadia Diuk and Adrian Karatnycky (1990), *The Hidden Nations: The People Challenge the Soviet Union* (New York: William Morrow); Diuk and Karatnycky (1993), *New Nations Rising: The Fall of the Soviets and the Challenge of Independence* (New York: John Wiley).
59 For details see Brown, *Gorbachev Factor*, pp.193–4.
60 Sobchak, *Khozhdenie vo vlast'*, p.134.
61 Ada Finifter and Ellen Mickiewicz (1992), 'Redefining the political system of the USSR: Mass support for political change', *American Political Science Review*, LXXXVI, 4, 860, 861, 866.
62 On the 1990 elections see Remington, 'Towards a participatory politics'; Kiernan, *End of Soviet Politics*; Timothy Colton (1990), 'The politics of democratization: The Moscow election of 1990', *Soviet Economy*, VI, 4, 285–344; on Yeltsin's election in Ekaterinburg, see Colton, *Boris Yeltsin*, pp.177–9; Reddaway and Glinski, *Tragedy*, pp.150–5; Gavin Helf and Jeffrey Hahn (1992), 'Old dogs and new tricks: Party elites in the Russian regional elections of 1990', *Slavic Review*, LI, 3, 511–30.
63 On this election see Reddaway and Glinski, *Tragedy*, pp.188–94; Colton, *Boris Yeltsin*, pp.191–4; Morrison, *Boris Yeltsin*, chapter 20.
64 Rigby, 'Reconceptualising', p.314.
65 Evidently to try to appease them, in September 1990 Gorbachev apparently sanctioned some military manoeuvers that were designed at least to be a rehearsal for dealing with the opposition. See Bonet, *Figures*, p.117; P. Reddaway (1990), 'The quality of Gorbachev's leadership', *Soviet Economy*, VI, 2, 132, note 13.
66 Reddaway, 'Quality', pp.131–9.
67 Boldin notes Gorbachev's 'fondness for reading flattering reports about himself'. He also received piles of flattering letters from admirers at home and abroad, and 'was so fond of them that he would sit for hours rereading passages that he liked and quoting excerpts from foreign individuals'. See Boldin, *Ten Years*, p.78.
68 John Dunlop (1993), *The Rise of Russia and the Fall of the Soviet Empire* (Princeton: Princeton University Press), pp.32–3, 51, 107.
69 Dunlop, *Rise of Russia*, chapter 5; Reddaway and Glinski, *Tragedy*, pp.194–227.
70 Arkady Vaksberg (1991), *The Soviet Mafia* (New York: St Martin's Press), p.255. Other notable books which shed light on the subject and include various amounts of theoretical analysis are Maria Los (ed.) (1990), *The Second Economy in Marxist States* (London: Macmillan); William A. Clark (1993), *Crime*

and Punishment in Soviet Officialdom: Combating Corruption in the Political Elite, 1965–1990 (Armonk: M.E. Sharpe); Federico Varese (2001), *The Russian Mafia: Private Protection in a New Market Economy* (Oxford: Oxford University Press); Reddaway and Glinski, *Tragedy*, pp.109–18, 303–7; Vadim Volkov (2002), *Violent Entrepreneurs: The Use of Force in the Making of Russian Capitalism* (Cornell: Cornell University Press). The last three books trace the Mafia through to the late 1990s.

71 Vaksberg, *Soviet Mafia*, chapter 10.

8
Pantouflage à la russe: The Recruitment of Russian Political and Business Elites

Eugene Huskey

The elimination of the Communist Party at the beginning of the 1990s foreshadowed a new path to power in post-communist Russia.[1] In the first years after the Soviet collapse, it appeared that patterns of political elite recruitment in Russia might parallel those found in many democratic countries, where parliament and private business serve as training grounds for those assuming leading executive posts. By the beginning of the Putin era, however, it was clear that careers in state administration – rather than elective politics or private industry – had become both the dominant path to political power and an important training ground for business elites.[2] This is not, of course, just a Russian pattern. As Aberbach, Putnam, and Rockman observed, 'although most countries of the Third World today have organizations labeled "legislatures", "parties", and "bureaucracies", in few of these systems is power actually divided between elected politicians and career administrators'.[3]

Such phenomena are not unknown in Western democracies. Although bureaucratic careers in many European states still respect the spirit of the Weberian model, in which specialization discourages lateral moves beyond one's ministry or administrative sector, in France *pantouflage* describes the phenomenon of civil servants using their state careers as a launching pad to prominent positions in business and politics.[4] In the United States a revolving door has also operated, where elites circulate regularly between federal agencies and the business community.

As C. Wright Mills observed over a half-century ago, drawing political, social, and economic leaders from a narrow pool of candidates risks creating an incestuous power elite that is insufficiently responsive to popular demands.[5] To measure political accountability, therefore, one must consider not only the competitiveness of elections but also patterns of elite recruitment. A revolving door between high-ranking public and private posts can undermine public trust in government and contribute to patterns of influence that marginalize large segments of society, and in this sense there are parallels between the American, French, and Russian experiences.[6]

This is not to say, however, that technocratic rather than political motivations should govern all hiring decisions in executive institutions. As Fred Riggs argued long ago, a limited spoils system is essential for a democracy, not only because it assures the responsiveness of the state bureaucracy to the political leadership but also because it allows opposition parties to attract strong supporters by holding out the promise of government posts. 'Otherwise,' Riggs wrote, 'they will only attract intellectuals and dreamers.'[7]

In the Russian case the heavy recruitment of officials with technocratic careers into the political elite was a logical result of a political transition that dismantled the Communist Party but imposed serious constraints on democratic and market institutions. Where the weakness of political parties helps to explain the reliance on the ministries as reservoirs of political talent, it was the interruption and distortion of marketization that allowed officials with careers in state administration to assume key posts in private and state-controlled industry. By the second half of the 1990s, as Peter Rutland noted, it 'became common for officials to be hired in senior positions in the oligarchs' organization after leaving state service'. Although it is tempting to see this as an example of state capture, even in the Yeltsin period 'lobbying in Russia [was]', as Rutland observes, 'a two-way process – and more top-down than bottom-up, since the state creates and sustains most business groups'.[8] By the Putin era, and especially after the assault on Yukos, the relationship began to approximate what Peregudov, Lapina, and Semenenko called state 'patronage' of industry.[9] In this pattern, 'family' circles continue to operate across the public/private divide, but the source of control shifts from private wealth to state power. In the words of Easter, 'the corporate elite remained concessionaires instead of proprietors'.[10] Moreover, the share of economic elites drawn from state administration grew significantly under the Putin presidency. According to Kryshtanovskaya and White, '...while the main business elite of 1993 were typically of Komsomol origin, now [2003] the main source of recruitment of the business elite is government ministries'.[11] As I argued in an earlier work on the nexus between politics and administration in Russia:

[i]f a primary feature of an open and democratic society is a plurality of elites, then post-communist Russia, and especially Putin's Russia,

has witnessed a kind of re-integration of the ruling class that will complicate efforts to move Russia in a liberal and democratic direction. By drawing heavily on administrative personnel – whether from the military or civilian sectors – for leaders in political and economic institutions, Putin used cadres policy as part of his broader campaign to centralize power and eliminate, or at least marginalize, elite groups that could serve as sources of political opposition or provide leadership alternatives in public and private institutions.[12]

Senior state administrators as a recruitment source for the Russian political leadership

There is now a significant literature on elite recruitment in post-communist Russia, associated most notably with the works of Olga Kryshtanovskaya, Stephen White, David Lane, and Cameron Ross. Although the concern of much of this research has been the degree of continuity between the late Soviet and early post-Soviet elite,[13] in recent years Kryshtanovskaya and White have explored one dimension of *pantouflage*, that related to the movement of military, secret police, and law enforcement personnel – the so-called *siloviki* – into prominent posts in politics and business.[14] This chapter seeks to extend that work by focusing on the full range of officials who use careers in state administration as a springboard to membership in the political and economic elite.

In most advanced countries, civil service careers do not serve as preparation for party politics or elective office. However, in post-communist Russia, as in France, it is not unusual for civil servants to pursue a career in politics following their work in the state bureaucracy. The difference appears to be the age at which this shift is made: in France, it is among early to mid-career state officials, whereas in Russia it is among those in mid- to late career. Among the 217 deputy ministers seeking work outside federal executive institutions in the period from 1995 to 2004, more than 10 percent (27) found positions in the Federal Assembly or party politics, with 12 serving as Duma deputies, eight as members of the Federation Council, and the remainder as leaders of new political parties or members of the parliamentary staff.[15] Facilitating this career shift in Russia is the existence of parties of power, such as United Russia, which are ideologically flexible organizations that are 'in the pocket' of the core executive and use the state bureaucracy as their major base of support.

Another destination for members of the administrative elite moving into a political career is a high-ranking post in the Russian government.

As the careers of both Putin and Medvedev illustrate, it is not usually elective office which is a springboard to political power, but rather a life devoted largely to administrative service. At Dmitrii Medvedev's election as president in March 2008, of the six top members of the current Russian government (*Pravitel'stvo*) – the prime ministers and the deputy prime ministers – only Alexandr Zhukov came to office with experience in elective office, in his case lengthy service in the Duma, including a period as chair of its budget committee.[16] This pattern continues at lower levels of the government hierarchy. Only one of 16 ministers had been an elected official in his career: Iurii Trutnev served as mayor of the city of Perm' and then governor of the Perm' region before coming to Moscow to work as minister of natural resources. If one considers the 65 deputy ministers in the government in early 2008, only ten had held elective office earlier in their careers, with half having served in the Duma and the other half in regional assemblies or in mayor's or governor's posts.

An examination of the 86 ranking members of the government at the beginning of the Medvedev presidency reveals that almost half, or 47 percent, had spent their entire careers in state service. A full 20 percent of the total had reached their positions after a career devoted exclusively to a single ministry. This latter tendency was especially pronounced in the ministries of agriculture, defense, health, and transport. Those who came to prominent posts in the government with some experience outside of state service or elective office had held academic posts (14 percent) or positions in business (20 percent) at an earlier point in their careers, at times in academic or business institutions with close ties to particular ministries. More importantly, there are few Russian leaders whom we or others code as having business backgrounds that are representatives of society in the way that one understands that concept in countries as diverse as Brazil, South Korea, and the United States. These findings confirm T.H. Rigby's conclusions in 1999 that only in the Government [*pravitel'stvo*], the sole surviving institution from the old regime, does one find 'natural heirs' to take the place of those in the upper reaches of this sector of Russia's ruling class.[17]

Senior state administrators as a recruitment source for Russia's business elite

The partial marketization of the post-communist Russian economy created new career opportunities for state officials in the private economic sector.[18] To assess the nexus between careers in business and state administration, we constructed two extensive datasets that offer evidence on the circulation of administrative, political, and economic elites. The first database tracked career changes of senior state administrators from early 1995 through the end of 2004;[19] the second consists of the biographies of the members of the boards of directors and management teams of the top 20 Russian companies by market capitalization, as of January 2009. The first database shows that, between 1995 and 2004, 608 persons working just beneath the level of minister – in the posts of deputy minister, first deputy minister, or state-secretary – left their positions, whether because of promotion within their ministry, retirement, a lateral move within state administration, or the assumption of a post in business, industry, party politics, or the non-profit sector.[20] At least 217, or approximately 36 percent, took up positions outside of the federal executive.[21] If one excludes the 58 persons who went into retirement immediately, with no evidence of further employment, then almost 40 percent of this group of senior state administrators went on to gain experience outside the traditional confines of Russian officialdom.[22]

Almost a third of the group moved into positions in what might be termed the non-profit sector, whether in traditional NGOs, such as the Russian Regional Ecological Center; trade associations, such as Association of Oil and Fat Producers; or academic and cultural institutions, such as the Center for Research in Statistics. The range of organizations within the non-profit category is admittedly vast, and the title 'non-profit' is in some cases misleading, given that many of these bodies were tied closely to industry or were known for their ancillary business activities (for example, sporting associations). In five of the 22 instances of transfers to NGOs or trade associations, former deputy ministers assumed positions in sporting organizations, including in two cases the national Olympic committee.

The large number of former state administrators finding late-career positions in academic and cultural institutions represents one of the many legacies of the Soviet era. In the Soviet period, high-ranking civil servants often pursued graduate degrees to enhance their prestige, to receive the 'advanced-degree' supplement to their income, and to prepare for themselves a comfortable 'emergency landing strip' in case they lost their ministerial post. Given the tradition of hiring others to write one's dissertation, it is likely that many of the new workers in the academy lack the requisite knowledge for their positions. It should be noted, however, that those moving into the academy were almost always assuming administrative posts, such as department chair or institute director, rather than teaching and research positions. And while some took up positions in leading national institutions, such as the Academy of Medical Sciences or Moscow State University, others found employment in higher educational institutions affiliated with their ministry. For example, Valerii Ivanovich Kovalev, a former deputy minister in the Ministry of Railways, became the rector of the St Petersburg Railway University.

Almost half of the deputy ministers in our first database (95) found work in business or industry following their ministerial careers. In a few cases, former ministerial officials founded their own businesses, such as Iurii Nikolaevich Korsun, who started his own construction firm. Another former deputy minister, Boris Petrovich Maslii, was described simply as an 'entrepreneur' in his biography. However, the vast majority of these former high-ranking state administrators moved to companies at the commanding heights of the Russian economy, where the state's presence increased in the Putin era. Among the most common destinations in business and industry were banks (14) and the state electrical monopoly, RAO EES (7).[23] In about half of the cases, the deputy ministers who moved into banks or RAO EES had served in ministries related to the sector, such as the Finance Ministry for bankers or the Fuel and Energy Committee or the Energy Ministry for those in the electric monopoly. Especially with regard to the banks, even those coming from seemingly unrelated ministries often had some background in the sector. For example, Andrei Korotkov took up a position at Vneshtorgbank after having served previously as a department head in the government apparatus and deputy minister of communications, but he had a graduate degree in economics and expertise in the computerization of the banking business. Among transfers from the ministries to RAO EES, those without a background in the Fuel and Energy Ministry or similar agency[24] were drawn from the Government's bloc of economic ministries.

The largest group of transfers from senior state service, representing more than a quarter (23) of the total of new entrants into business and industry, went to work in the oil and gas complex, with six in Gazprom alone. Although many of the former deputy ministers moving into the energy sector had served previously in the ministries of energy or natural resources, a significant number had had careers in ministries with no direct ties to the oil and gas industry. And even many of those with a background in the energy branch ministry had spent only a short period in that agency before circulating into the oil or gas industry. In contrast to most ministries and state committees in post-communist Russia, the Ministry of Natural Resources recruits a significant share of its senior personnel from other ministries or organizations, which suggests that these outsiders were granted positions not for their technical expertise or even management skills but because of their links to important patronage networks.[25] Given its ability to grant licenses and to shape the regulatory environment of the energy sector, senior posts in the Ministry of Natural Resources have the potential to enrich their occupants on a scale that is unimaginable in most other federal agencies.[26]

One might hypothesize that the late-career transfer of deputy ministers into business and industry was little more than a reward for services rendered to firms under their supervision. If this were the case, one would expect deputy ministers to move into honorific positions or into low-visibility and, in some cases, low-responsibility posts, such as *sovetniki* (advisors) to corporate leaders. The evidence illustrates, however, that most former deputy ministers who moved to Russian business and industry became key players there. Of the 95 former deputy ministers who moved into business and industry, 22 occupied positions as CEOs, presidents, or general directors; 30 became vice-presidents; 18 were chairs of corporate boards; 11 were regular members or deputy chairs of boards; and 14 assumed other posts in businesses, including two who worked as *sovetniki.*

Evidence from our second database confirms the importance of Russian officialdom as a source of leading personnel for Russian industry under the Medvedev presidency. Examining the biographies of the boards of directors and management teams of the top 20 Russian companies by market capitalization, one finds that in January 2009, 83, or 30 percent, of the 275 board members or senior managers of these companies had worked in state service at some point after the collapse of the Soviet Union in 1991. The bond between state and corporate careers is even tighter than these figures might initially suggest because 30 of the 83 individuals were still working as high-ranking state officials while serving on corporate boards. Put another way, 30 board members of the largest Russian companies were seconded from the state to oversee the operation of the commanding heights of the Russian economy. Where four board chairs of the top 20 Russian companies had worked previously in state service in the post-communist era, three board chairs were sitting state officials, including a first deputy prime minister, Victor Zubkov (Gazprom), and a deputy prime minister, Igor Sechin (Rosneft'), whose portfolio includes the energy sector.

If we examine the biographies of those who left Russian officialdom behind for positions in the top 20 Russian companies, we find that they had served in state posts in the post-communist era for an average of

5.4 years.[27] Although a few moved from public administration to the corporate world in the initial transition from communist rule, most had some experience in officialdom in the second Yeltsin administration and beyond. Indeed, almost half of the group made the shift from government to corporate posts during the Putin presidency. In some cases, of course, the circulation of elites at mid- or late-career is from the private sector to the state. For example, Victor Savel'ev, who was affiliated with prominent companies such as Sistema, Menatep, and Gazprom, left the private sector for a two-year tour as deputy minister of economic development in Putin's first term before returning to Sistema as first vice-president; Sergei Ushakov left his post as head of security at Gazprom to join the Federal Security Agency in 1996; and in June 2008 Viacheslav Siniugin, a young businessman with a background in investment banking and the electric industry, plus a year in 1997 in the Omsk branch of the Federal Securities Commission (FKTsB), left his post at RAO EES to become deputy minister of energy. Despite such instances of recruiting state officials from the business world, the dominant direction of elite movement appears to be from state to industry and not the reverse.

Which state institutions serve as the most prominent launching pads for positions at the apex of Russian industry? As Table 8.1 illustrates, *pantouflage* is associated most frequently with careers that pass through the core executive and through ministries associated with finance and economics, national security, and the industrial branches linked to leading Russian companies. An almost equal number of persons who

Table 8.1   Earlier State Service of Leading Russian Corporate Directors and Managers (By Sector of Russian Officialdom, post-1991 only*)

Presidential Bureaucracy	14
Government (including Apparatus)	14
Ministry of Finance	13
Power ministries (KGB, MVD, etc.)	10
Ministry of Economic Development	8
State Committee on Property	8
Ministry of Energy or Natural Resources	5
Ministry of Foreign Affairs	4
Anti-Monopoly Committee	2

*Directors or managers may have served in more than one institution.
Source: Company websites and online biographical materials.

moved from the state to the top 20 Russian companies had spent part of their careers in the presidential bureaucracy, the government or its apparatus, or the Ministry of Finance (14, 14, and 13, respectively). For example, Andrei Reus was one of several officials from Cheliabinsk who were promoted to key government positions in Moscow by their patron, Viktor Khristenko. Several years as Khristenko's chief of staff earned Reus a seat on the board of directors of Rosneft' and the post of CEO of the state-dominated military-industrial concern, OAO Oboronprom.

The revolving door between state agencies and the corporate world was clearly evident in the energy sector, where five members of boards or senior management teams of leading energy-related companies had worked earlier in state organizations responsible for energy regulation and oversight. More intriguing is the significant number of officials, 18 in all, who had worked for a time in state institutions – the State Property Committee (*Goskomimushchestva*), the Anti-Monopoly Committee, and the Ministry of Economic Development – that have been associated with liberalizing economic reforms. The benign explanation of this phenomenon is that these institutions attracted some of the most impressive minds in economics and finance, who would naturally be sought after by leading Russian companies. A more cynical – and perhaps more realistic – view would claim that many persons in key positions in these 'liberalizing' institutions, such as Anatolii Chubais, used the levers of the state to provide lucrative sinecures for themselves and their allies at the apex of Russia's new corporate structure.[28]

Although our databases do not allow us to reach firm conclusions about the prominence of the *siloviki* in the peak organizations of Russian industry, the evidence we have does not support claims of a pervasive presence of former security personnel in the country's corporate leadership. To be sure, there were several cases in which former KGB officials of Putin's generation changed careers as the Soviet Union was collapsing and entered directly into the business world. One of the most prominent of these was Vladimir Strzhalkovskii, who opened a travel firm in St. Petersburg in 1991 and then left the private sector to become deputy minister and then minister of tourism before being appointed to head Norilsk Nickel, a company whose location and profile have little in common with the tourism industry.[29] At least two vice-presidents of Gazprom in 2009 were KGB veterans who assumed posts in civilian state administration before receiving a position on the management team of the country's largest company. Aleksandr Kozlov moved to Gazprom in 2005 from his post as deputy head of the presidential business office (*upravliaiushchii delami*), and Valerii Golubev joined Gazprom in 2004, having worked in St. Petersburg local government and then as a member of the Federation Council. As Table 8.1 points out, however, individuals from other branches of Russian officialdom far outnumbered business elite members with security or law enforcement backgrounds. Moreover, the corporate positions occupied by some of the former *siloviki* raise questions about their impact on strategic and even key operational decisions of Russia's top companies. At least three of the ten *siloviki* were vice-presidents for security or the head of human resources, positions that would seem to lie at the periphery of a company's leadership team.[30]

Both of our databases illustrate that the geographical circulation of the Russian elite is limited. Although 25 leaders of the 20 largest Russian companies gained experience in state administration at the regional or local level, very few in this group worked outside of city governments in St. Petersburg and Moscow, which accounted for 11 and 8 persons, respectively. Most of the remaining six individuals with experience in state administration below the federal level had worked in the city government of Norilsk or the regional government in Tatarstan, which were the headquarters of two of Russia's largest corporations, Norilsk Nickel and Tatneft. One also finds a pronounced geographical imbalance in the birthplaces of directors and managers of the largest Russian enterprises. Among the 203 persons whose place of birth we can identify, 80 (39.4 percent) came from Moscow[31] or Leningrad/St. Petersburg. Given that these two cities have a combined population of 15 million, or just over ten percent of the country's total population, those born in Russia's official and 'second' capital are almost four times more likely to enter the country's economic elite than their provincial peers.

Even more significant is the increasing geographical concentration of business leaders in the post-communist era, a finding which parallels that reached by T.H. Rigby in the late 1990s with regard to the country's top political elites.[32] Of the 185 corporate leaders for whom we have precise information on both age and place of birth, only one-third of those aged 50 and above were born in Moscow or Leningrad, whereas the figures for the cohort aged 49 and under was 47 percent. This pattern of elite distribution creates the potential for the delegitimation of the ruling elite on representational and distributional grounds. Especially in a crisis-ridden country with a yawning gap between living standards in the centre and periphery, a capital-centric elite invites a provincial revolt.

As in Britain, France, and many other capital-centric countries, the pull of life in the big city also discourages the geographical mobility of civil servants after they begin their careers in the federal government in Moscow. Information from our first database illustrates that deputy ministers who left their positions in the period from 1995 to 2004 rarely returned to their native regions. Of the ten deputy ministers who did find work in regional government or politics after leaving federal service, four assumed positions in the Moscow city government. Only two returned to their home regions to pursue a career in politics, one as governor of Tver *oblast'* and the other as speaker of the regional duma in Volgograd. A similar capital-centric bias is evident in the careers of deputy ministers who found positions in academic or cultural work following state service. Of the 42 officials in this group, only three left Moscow for late-career posts in the academy. Two of those went to St. Petersburg and the other returned to Moscow after a stint in Tver'.

The transition from communist to post-communist rule has also brought a change in the educational backgrounds of Russia's economic elite. Our second database, on directors and managers of the top 20 Russian companies, reveals that the Soviet-era focus on engineering training has given way to an emphasis on economics and business degrees. Whereas well over half of board members and company leaders aged 50 and over received their first degree in engineering or other technical specialties, just over a quarter of the persons aged 49 and under had a similar educational background (see Table 8.2). Within this younger cohort, almost half had trained in economics and business or the law. Although only 11 percent of those aged 49 and under had their first degree in law, this figure rose to 21 percent for the youngest cohort, those aged 29 to 35.[33]

Finally, the educational data also challenge claims of the widespread representation of *siloviki* on leading corporate boards and management teams, though the evidence on this point is far from conclusive. Whereas personnel in the armed forces and the Ministry of Internal Affairs (MVD) usually train in special academies for the uniformed services, and would therefore be reflected in the numbers in Table 8.2, recruits to the KGB may be drawn from graduates with any educational

Table 8.2   Education Backgrounds of the Russian Business Elite (First Degree of Directors and Senior Managers of the Top 20 Russian Companies, By Market Capitalization)

Age	Engineer	Econ/Business	Law	Military
49 and under	47 (28%)	58 (35%)	18 (11%)	7 (4%)
50 and over	91 (56%)	37 (23%)	7 (4%)	3 (2%)

Source: Company websites and online biographical materials.

background, witness Putin's training in law. It is also possible that the *siloviki* represent a disproportionate share of those in our database for whom educational background is unknown, though this appears unlikely because persons whose educational background is not known are typically less senior members of the management team working in the smaller companies of our dataset.

As one might expect, there were significant differences by age in the frequency of overseas education among the leaders of top Russian companies. If only three persons aged 50 and over had attended a lengthy educational programme in the West, 28 of the younger cohort had done so. Similarly, when compared to their older counterparts, almost twice as many directors or senior managers under 50 had work experience in the West (17 vs. 9). In addition to the dozens of corporate leaders from Russia or other post-Soviet countries who had work or educational experience in the West, 39 members of the boards of the top 20 Russian companies were businessmen from Western Europe or North America. There are numerous indicators that measure the degree of integration of Russia into the world economy, but surely one of the more revealing of these is the presence of Western or Western-educated personnel on boards and management teams. One could conclude, therefore, that the post-communist era has witnessed an impressive internationalization of the upper reaches of Russian business.

Russia's economic elite continues to be a male bastion, and there is little indication – at least with regard to the commanding heights of the economy – that the post-communist era has witnessed an increase in the proportion of women in the boardroom or the executive suite. In the top 20 Russian companies, women accounted for less than ten percent of positions on boards of directors and on senior management teams (11 and 23, respectively, with three women serving both as directors and managers).[34] Although there was no significant difference in the average age of men and women in this slice of the economic elite (49 vs. 47.5 years), women did tend to be concentrated in what have for decades been considered 'female-appropriate' posts in Russia. Thus, 11 of the 23 women on the management teams of the 20 largest Russian companies, or almost 50 percent of the total, held positions related to finance, bookkeeping, or auditing.[35]

Conclusions

Where much of the research on contemporary Russian elites has focused on the background of elites or the degree of turnover of cadres, whether from the Soviet to the post-Soviet eras or within the post-communist era itself,[36] this study has illustrated the changes in career patterns since the collapse of communism. In the USSR, the few state administrative officials who rose to the senior political leadership did so either through a lateral move into the party apparatus, usually made at mid-career, or through vertical promotion to the post of minister, which in a small number of cases led to membership in the Politburo. Given the disappearance of the Communist Party as a recruiting institution, and the immaturity of the alternative sources for government leaders, such as the parliament and market-oriented institutions, it was reasonable to hypothesize that an increasing share of the country's ruling elite would come from the senior ranks of state administration.

What is unclear is the extent to which the *pantouflage* described here results from a conscious policy by state leaders to dominate industry or is instead a natural by-product of social networks that cut across the traditional agencies of state administration and private and state-controlled industry. Because high-ranking officials in the presidential administration – in addition to those in the government and its ministries – have assumed key posts in strategic industries in recent years, it is likely that more than social networking and individual ambition are involved in the Russian practice of *pantouflage*. Kryshtanovskaya and White point out that in the Putin era 'the state has taken back the role of principal decision-maker' on state personnel matters, implying that it has virtually eliminated society's role in selecting the country's political class. One could go further and assert that the state has reclaimed that role in important sectors of the economy as well.[37]

In those countries in the West where the movement between state posts and private industry is common, governments tend to establish ethics requirements to prevent state officials from using information or contacts to lobby their previous employers during a set period after their departure from government service. In the United States, it is generally two years in matters in which the former employee had a 'direct and substantial interest', and one year for all other issues where the employee is lobbying his former agency.[38] Reacting to what many regarded as excessively tight restrictions on lobbying by former *hautes fonctionnaires* who moved from government to the private sector, the French government has recently reduced the waiting period for lobbying one's former associates from five years to three years.[39] Although Russia has a formal prohibition against lobbying one's former agency within two years after leaving state service, there is little indication that this law is enforced. Indeed, whereas the law establishing the waiting period was adopted in 2004, it was only in March 2007 that Putin created by decree the necessary ethics commissions to review such violations. Given the lack of maturity of Russia's legal culture and the difficulty of enforcing such restrictions in even the most fastidious legal environments, it is likely that communications and influence will continue to flow relatively freely between current policymakers and erstwhile government officials operating in the private sector.[40]

In comparison with post-communist countries to Russia's west, such as Poland and Hungary, the 'self-reproducing of a bureaucratic caste' is far more pronounced in Russia, which means that those in key political and administrative positions are highly unrepresentative of the social backgrounds of the population as a whole.[41] As we pointed out earlier, this narrowing of the geographical and class bases of a country's ruling elite will at some point pose serious challenges for regime legitimacy and efficiency, never mind the efficiency of the largest private firms.[42] According to the comparative research of Rauch and Evans, the 'three key ingredients in effective state bureaucracies [are]...competitive salaries, internal promotion and career stability, and meritocratic recruitment', with the last being the most important of the three – and, in our view, the most likely to be compromised by the interlocking elite system that we have described in Russia.[43]

The reliance on senior state officials rather than parliamentary or business leaders for Russia's political elite also discourages defection or dissent within the ruling elite because of the high level of insecurity among state officials. This insecurity, which enhances elite cohesion at the expense of openness and political competition, is based in part on the financial vulnerability of many administrative elites. It also reflects, however, their lack of a natural political support base, whether in a region or a segment of society, and of course the absence of a mature legal system. Increasingly in the post-communist era, Russian politicians, as creatures of the bureaucracy, do not represent a portion of the society but, at best, a small slice of officialdom. Without links to society, such political elites are atomized actors in a vast bureaucracy where the only protection comes from membership in an informal network or, increasingly, loyalty to the president. Clan politics and personalism are the products of such an environment.

As students of the Latin American experience remind us, this lack of security raises the stakes of politics to an unusually high level and complicates elite cooperation. According to Burton, Gunther, and Higley, in order for the elite ideological unity of the communist era to develop into a new consensual unity necessary for democratic development,

> ...recognized elites must feel relatively secure in their leadership positions at the head of coherent and organized social groups....elite insecurity can impede the concessions necessary for compromise resolution of divisive issues; and unless elites are acknowledged as valid interlocutors for their respective groups, any agreements they reach with their opponents will not hold.[44]

Unfortunately, as they observe, many post-communist countries 'have retarded or prevented the emergence of stable, secure elites at the head of institutionalized and competitive secondary groups'.[45] There is little in the current practice of *pantouflage a la russe* to suggest that Russia is on its way to producing such elites.

Notes

1   On political recruitment in the Soviet era, see T.H. Rigby (1968), *Communist Party Membership in the USSR, 1917–1967* (Princeton: Princeton University Press); Grey Hodnett (1978), *Leadership in the Soviet National Republics: A Quantitative Study of Recruitment Policy* (Oakville, Ontario: Mosaic Press); Bohdan Harasymiw (1984), *Political Elite Recruitment in the Soviet Union* (New York: St. Martin's); and T.H. Rigby and Bohdan Harasymiw (eds) (1983), *Leadership Selection and Patron-Client Relations in the USSR and Yugoslavia* (London: Allen & Unwin).
2   On the decline of party competition and the rise of 'dominant power politics' in Russia, see Vladimir Gel'man (2006), 'From "feckless pluralism" to "dominant power politics"? The transformation of Russia's party system', *Democratization*, no.4, 545–61. Despite the rise of a single 'dominant' party, United Russia, the country's political leadership is hesitant to associate itself formally with this party. The unofficial head of the party, Vladimir Putin, is not a member, and only three government ministers have been willing to join, while a fourth member of the Government in 2008, Igor' Shuvalov, was said to be 'close' to the party. The head of the analytical section of the Kremlin's website rejected the idea that Russia was moving toward the European model of party government, describing the system instead as 'a typically Russian variant'. 'Ministry poluchat partbilety', *Gudok*, 28 May 2008, http:/edinros.er.ru/er/prtext.shtml?42597.
3   Joel D. Aberbach, Robert D. Putnam, and Bert A. Rockman (1981), *Bureaucrats and Politicians in Western Democracies* (Cambridge: Harvard University Press), p.3. Unlike Russia, in several East European countries 'the introduction of multi-party competition after the change of regime inevitably destroyed this cosy relationship between politicians and bureaucrats'. Jan-Hinrik Meyer-Sahling (2004), 'Civil service reform in post-communist

Europe: The bumpy road to depoliticisation', *West European Politics*, XXVII, 1, 79.

4   On *pantouflage* in France, see Pierre Birnbaum (1982), *The Heights of Power* (Chicago: University of Chicago Press); Jeanne Siwek-Pouydesseau (1969), *Le Personnel de Direction des Ministeres* (Paris: Armand Colin); Philippe Bezes (2001), 'Defensive versus offensive approaches to administrative reform in France (1988–1997): The leadership dilemmas of French prime ministers', *Governance*, XXIV, 1, 99–132; Luc Rouban, 'The senior civil service in France', in Edward C. Page and Vincent Wright (1999), *Bureaucratic Elites in Western Europe: A Comparative Analysis of Top Officials* (Oxford: Oxford University Press), pp.66–87.

5   C. Wright Mills (1956), *The Power Elite* (New York: Oxford University Press). The risks of a revolving door between the public and private sectors became apparent in the recent global financial crisis. According to two critics of *pantouflage* in the US Securities and Exchange Commission (SEC): '[i]f you work for the enforcement division of the S.E.C. you probably know in the back of your mind, and in the front too, that if you maintain good relations with Wall Street you might soon be paid huge sums of money to be employed by it'. Michael Lewis and David Einhorn, 'The end of the financial world as we know it', *New York Times*, 3 January 2009.

6   On the revolving door phenomenon in the United States, see the figures provided in http://www.opensecrets.org/revolving/. On state capture generally, see Oleksei Omelyanchuk (2001), 'Explaining state capture and state capture modes: The cases of Russia and Ukraine', PhD Dissertation defended in the Department of International Relations and European Studies, Central European University Budapest.

7   Fred Riggs, 'Bureaucrats and political development: A paradoxical view', in Joseph LaPalombara (1963), *Bureaucracy and Political Development* (Princeton: Princeton University Press), p.130.

8   Peter Rutland, 'Introduction: Business and the state in Russia', in Peter Rutland (ed.) (2001), *Business and the State in Contemporary Russia* (Boulder: Westview), p.25.

9   S. Peregudov, N. Lapina, and I. Semenenko (1999), *Gruppa interesov i rossiiskoe gosudarstvo* (Moscow: Editorial URSS), cited in Andrew Yorke (2003), 'Business and politics in Krasnoyarsk Krai', *Europe-Asia Studies*, LV, 2, 259.

10   Gerald Easter, 'Building fiscal capacity', in Timothy J. Colton and Stephen Holmes (2006), *The State after Communism: Governance in the New Russia* (Lanham, MD: Rowman & Littlefield), p.40. See also Stefan Hedlund (2005), *Russian Path Dependence* (London: Routledge).

11   Olga Kryshtanovskaya and Stephen White (2005), 'The rise of the Russian business elite', *Communist and Post-Communist Studies*, XXXVIII, 3, 300. On the perception of state-business relations among leaders of Russian firms, see Timothy Frye (2002), 'Capture or exchange? Business lobbying in Russia', *Europe-Asia Studies*, LIV, 7, 1017–36. Although it is true, as Frye argues, that the relationship between state officials and businessmen is closer to that of elite exchange than state capture, the term exchange suggests a rough parity of partners that is fading in the Putin era. For a view that emphasizes the pre-eminence of state officials in this relationship, see Andrei Yakovlev

(2006), 'The evolution of business-state interaction in Russia: From state capture to business capture?', *Europe-Asia Studies*, LVIII, 7, 1033–56.

12 Eugene Huskey, 'The politics-administration nexus in postcommunist Russia', in Don K. Rowney and Eugene Huskey (2009), *Russian Bureaucracy and the State. Officialdom from Alexander III to Vladimir Putin* (London: Palgrave Macmillan). In his annual address to parliament in 2008, President Medvedev himself recognized, at least implicitly, the dangers of rule by the *apparatchiki* when he noted that 'our state apparatus is the largest employer, the most active publisher, the best producer, its own judge, its own party, and, in the end, its own public [*...sam sebe sud, sam sebe partii i sam sebe v konechnom schete narod*]. Such a system is absolutely ineffective and creates only one thing – corruption. It produces legal nihilism in the public...[and] it impedes the development of institutions of an innovative economy and democracy.' http://kremlin.ru/appears/2008/ 11/05/1349_type63372type63374type63381 type82634_208749.shtml.

13 See, for example, Olga Kryshtanovskaya and Stephen White (2006), 'From Soviet nomenklatura to Russian elite', *Europe-Asia Studies*, LVIII, 5, 711–33; David Lane and Cameron Ross (1999), *The Transition from Communism to Capitalism: Ruling Elites from Gorbachev to Yeltsin* (New York: St. Martin's).

14 Olga Kryshtanovskaya and Stephen White (2003), 'Putin's militocracy', *Post-Soviet Affairs*, XIX, 4, 289–306. For a critique of the some of the methods and conclusions in Kryshtanovskaya and White's work, see Bettina Renz (2006), 'Putin's militocracy? An alternative interpretation of *Siloviki* in contemporary Russian politics', *Europe-Asia Studies*, LVIII, 6, 903–24, and Sharon Werning Rivera and David Rivera (2006), 'The Russian elite under Putin: Militocratic or bourgeois', *Post-Soviet Affairs*, XXII, 2, 125–44.

15 Data from database described in footnote 19.

16 The information in this and succeeding paragraphs is drawn from biographies compiled from the websites of the Russian Government and its ministries on 31 March 2008.

17 T.H. Rigby (1999), 'New top elites for old in Russian politics', *British Journal of Political Science*, XXIX, 2, 337. By natural heirs Rigby meant those persons who could have been expected to have been promoted from below under the logic of the old regime.

18 For earlier assessments of the intersection between the state and business, see Kryshtanovskaya and White, 'Rise of Russian business elite', 293–307; Peter Rutland (2001), *Business and the State in Contemporary Russia* (Boulder: Westview); Gerald Easter, 'Building fiscal capacity'; Juliet Johnson (2000), *A Fistful of Rubles: The Rise and Fall of the Russian Banking System* (Ithaca, NY: Cornell University Press).

19 The information was compiled from the *naznachenie* section of *Sobranie zakonodatel'stva* from issue no. 4 of 1995 through issue no. 52 of 2004. The fields in the database are: name, sex, ministry (or presidency or government apparatus), position, action taken, official taking action (president or prime minister), date of appointment or dismissal, and reason for action. Further biographical information, notably that on post-civil service careers, was obtained from Labyrinth and other Russian web-based sources.

20   Although the database contains officials at comparable positions in the presidential and government apparatus, this analysis includes only personnel working in senior ministerial posts.

21   The pace of departure of deputy ministers varied considerably over the decade under study. Whereas 51 deputy ministers left office in the year following Yeltsin's re-election to office, whether for promotion within the ranks, retirement, or transfer to other work, the figures were 47 for the year after Putin's election in 2000 and 163 after Putin's re-election in 2004.

22   Ninety-eight of the 608 job changes resulted from retirement from the state service but not from the workforce altogether. For the 60 percent of the 98 for whom we have data, the average age at retirement from state service was 61.23 years. The largest number of persons went into retirement in 1996, 2001, and 2002.

23   Many others moved into firms created by state officials in the 1990s. Based on their interviews with former party and state officials, Kryshtanovskaya and White report that 'only "our own people" were given appointments in forms of this kind'. Kryshtanovskaya and White, 'Rise of Russian business elite', 301.

24   Although several high-profile ministries maintained their name and jurisdictional reach during the post-communist era, such as Finance, Justice, and the MVD, many less visible agencies underwent frequent name changes and reorganizations, including the agency responsible for conventional (non-nuclear) energy. For part of the post-communist era it was known as the State Committee for Energetics.

25   The turnover rate of deputy ministries was slightly higher than average in the Ministry of Natural Resources. During the decade between 1995 and 2005, 37 new appointments were made to the average eight deputy ministerial positions maintained in the ministry, which gives a ratio of 4.63, whereas the average turnover ratio in this period for all ministries was 3.79. Turnover ranged from 0.75 in the Ministry of Emergency Situations to 7.0 in the State Committee on Energetics.

26   For several years running, the minister of natural resources, Iurii Trutnev, had the reputation as the wealthiest Russian official, though some of the wealth was acquired through the sale of shares in his former company. 'Samyi bogatyi rossiiskii chinovnik – Iurii Trutnev', *Novaia gazeta*, 2 August 2007. The bureaucratic politics inside the ministry, in this case with respect to cadres policy relating to an inspection of Norilsk Nickel, is discussed in Galina Shakirova, 'Oleg Neuvol,'' Gazeta.ru, 1 September 2008, http://www. gazeta.ru/business/ 2008/09/01/2827783.shtml. For an account of the enrichment of the former deputy minister of agriculture, who became head of the state economic enterprise, Soiuzplodoimiport, see Roman Porozhenko, 'Biznes i gossluzhba: kto kogo?', *Tribuna*, 14 April 2006, p.7.

27   The 30 sitting state officials had an average tenure of 14.5 years in state service after 1991, which confirms that most had spent their entire careers in government and were not briefly circulated through a ministry between positions in the private sector.

28   On the abuse of office by Chubais and other 'liberal reformers', see Peter Reddaway and Dmitri Glinski (2001), *The Tragedy of Russia's Reforms: Market Bolshevism against Democracy* (Washington, DC: United States Institute of Peace).

29 Between stints in the state's tourist agency, Strzhalkovskii worked for four years as deputy minister of economic development overseeing questions relating to tourism.

30 The use of *siloviki* in human resource offices builds on a Soviet-era tradition, in which the *otdely kadrov* of enterprises served as information-gathering points on the career tracks and behaviour of Soviet workers.

31 This excludes Moscow *oblast'*, where six members in our database were born.

32 Rigby, 'New Top Elites', pp.338–40.

33 Compare these figures with those in Rigby, 'New top elites for old in Russian politics', p.341, which provides a table outlining the educational backgrounds of the top political elite in 1996, divided by those in Duma, presidential, and Government posts.

34 The 9.3 percent of women in our database compares favourably, however, with the 5 percent of senior state administrators who are women. See Huskey, 'The politics-administration nexus'.

35 The current research of Joel Moses confirms this financial orientation among women administrators working in Russian republican, regional, and city government.

36 An example of the latter may be found in Iulia Shevchenko (2004), *The Central Government of Russia: From Gorbachev to Putin* (Aldershot: Ashgate).

37 Kryshtanovskaya and White, 'Rise of Russian business elite', 306. On the expanding role of the state in personnel matters in the private sector, see Eugene Huskey (2004), 'Nomenklatura lite? The cadres reserve in Russian public administration', *Problems of Post-Communism*, LI, 2, 30–9.

38 18 U.S. Code 207. It is important to recognize, however, that many states in the United States do not impose such restrictions on personnel involved in the revolving door between government and private business, which, given the nature of American federalism, allows an unusually wide scope for influence peddling on important policy matters. For data on the movement of officials between the federal government and big business in the US, see the Revolving Door database at www.opensecrets.org.

39 Loi no. 2007–148 du 2 fevrier 2007 de modernisation de la fonction publique; Decret no. 2007–611 du 26 avril 2007 relatif a l'exercise d'activites privees par les fonctionnaires ou agents non titulaires ayant cesse temporairement ou definitivement leurs fonctions et a la commission de deontologie.

40 'Zakon o gosudarstvennoi grazhdanskoi sluzhbe ot 7 iiulia 2004, st. 17, no. 3: O komissiiakh po sobliudeniiu trebovanii k sluzhebnomu povedeniiu gosudarstvennykh grazhdanskikh sluzhashchikh Rossiiskoi Federatsii i rueg-ulirovaniiu konflikta interesov', *Rossiiskaia gazeta*, 7 March 2007, p.19.

41 Ivan Szelenyi and Szonja Szelenyi (1995), 'Circulation or reproduction of elites during the postcommunist transformation of eastern Europe: Introduction', *Theory and Society*, XXIV, 5, 631, 663.

42 On this latter issue, see Andreas Heinrich (2008), 'Under the Kremlin's thumb: Does increased state control in the Russian gas sector endanger European energy security?', *Europe-Asia Studies*, LX, 9, 1539–55.

43 James E. Rauch and Peter B. Evans (2000), 'Bureaucratic structure and bureaucratic performance in less developed countries', *Journal of Public*

Economics, LXXV, 1, 49–71. On the role of merit in the hiring and pro-motion of contemporary Russian officials, see Vladimir Magun, Vladimir Gimpelson, and Robert Brym, 'Hiring and promoting young civil servants: Weberian ideals and Russian realities', in Rowney and Huskey, *Russian Bureaucracy and the State.*

44 Michael Burton, Richard Gunther, John Higley, 'Elites and democratic con-solidation in Latin America and Southern Europe: An Overview', in John Higley and Richard Gunther (eds) (1992), *Elites and Democratic Consolidation in Latin America and Southern Europe* (Cambridge: Cambridge University Press), pp.346–7.

45 Ibid.

9
Conclusion

Stephen Fortescue

In the Introduction to this volume I listed four things that T.H. Rigby knew about the Soviet Union which drove his theoretical ideas and empirical research: that legitimacy issues were important and particularly complex, that there had been great debate within the discipline of Soviet studies over the nature of political and social control, that the system was heavily bureaucratic in its structures and behaviours, and that despite that personalist politics and relationships played a major role.

These four pieces of knowledge have resolved themselves into two themes in this volume: issues of legitimacy (dealt with in the chapters by Gill, Holmes, and less directly Brown and Reddaway), and the relationship between institutionalization and personalist rule (dealt with in the chapters by Fortescue, Fitzpatrick, Huskey, and less directly Brown). Most of the volume has been, like Rigby's work, devoted to the Soviet Union. Perestroika and the collapse of Soviet communism – something that inevitably attracted Rigby's attention as it was happening – has been the particular focus of the chapters by Brown and Reddaway. Post-Soviet Russia has been by no means ignored, being the sole focus of the chapter by Huskey and receiving attention in those by Fortescue and Holmes.

In this Conclusion I will discuss the findings of the various chapters in the light of Rigby's consideration of these matters, in the expectation not just of reinforcing the contribution to our knowledge of Soviet and post-Soviet Russian politics of the chapters in the volume, but also of the continuing relevance to the discipline of the writings of Harry Rigby.

Legitimacy

One of Rigby's major contributions to our understanding of Soviet politics was his concept of goal-rationality. Adapted from Weber's category of legal-rational authority, it holds that the leaderships of the Soviet Union drew their legitimacy from claims to be pursuing an ultimate goal, the construction of communism. The achievement of that goal required the fulfilment of tasks, tasks that were set by the leadership but implemented – not without a degree of practical initiative and discretion – by those granting legitimacy to the leadership.

At the time Rigby put forward such an interpretation of the nature of authority relationships in the Soviet Union it usefully challenged the totalitarian view that the political leadership maintained its hold on society purely through coercion and terror. A particularly interesting aspect of his approach was the stress on task fulfilment as the practical realisation of the goal. Task fulfilment involved operating within a complex and rule-heavy bureaucracy. But while the bureaucracy was rule-heavy, it was not rule-bound. Indeed a capacity for well-judged flexibility and initiative was expected of its staff.

Rigby's is a view of the Soviet Union which no doubt remains controversial, but should encourage historians to continue to examine closely what the members of Soviet society – particularly those working within the bureaucracy – believed and how they behaved in fulfilling the tasks set for them by the political leadership.

In the end the greatest test not just of the legitimacy of a system but also of commentators' models of legitimation is survivability. Clearly that is a test which the Soviet system failed. Did Rigby's view of Soviet legitimation also fail the test?

In the Introduction I was somewhat critical of the concept of goal-rationality, at least as applied by Rigby, for overconcentrating on the authority relationship between the leadership and the bureaucracy, in a way that could have led to the neglect of the leadership-mass relationship, which could in turn could have led to a failure to notice major changes in Soviet society.

In the light of the contributions to this volume it is worth returning to that point and to the general issue of Rigby's contribution to our understanding of the decline and collapse of Soviet communism. Firstly, an observation which arises from Gill's chapter. Rigby on occasion noted the potential for a combination of charismatic and goal-rational legitimacy claims to produce a powerfully authoritarian regime. In his chapter Gill describes the shift, as reflected in official policy on urban planning and architecture, from goal-rational legitimacy claims under Stalin to eudaemonic claims under Khrushchev and Brezhnev. It might be suggested that the goal-rational element of Stalin's urban planning and architectural policies had precisely the dose of the charismatic

– in its grandiose scale of design and decoration – to which Rigby referred. The charismatic and eudaemonic, however, cannot be easily combined, making the task of Stalin's successors to legitimize authoritarian rule very difficult (despite their somewhat pathetic attempts to maintain the charismatic element through cults of personality).

To return more directly to the collapse of communism, let us begin by rather crudely setting up two alternative interpretations of what happened: the 'revolution from above' view, and the 'civil society' view. The first, in its most extreme version, suggests that it was Gorbachev and those in the elite around him who destroyed communism, quite deliberately and quite possibly against the will of the people; the second suggests that it was in fact the people's will that communism collapse, and that they achieved that goal against the best efforts of the 'reformer' Gorbachev to save it.

It appeared that we might have had a head-to-head confrontation of the two views in this volume, in the chapters by Brown and Reddaway. The former presents a chapter containing 'revolution from above' in the title; the latter stresses the role of long-standing popular dissatisfaction. Of course, our two contributors are far too wise and experienced to fall into extremes, and so for those who like a lot of body contact in their intellectual debates this head-to-head fizzled. Brown devotes considerable attention to pressure from below and admits that as of the First Congress of People's Deputies, held from 25 May to 9 June 1989, movement from below became more important than change directed from above. Reddaway recognizes the importance of changes in attitudes and behaviour within the elite which allowed popular dissatisfaction to take on coherent political form. I do not believe that it is doing violence to Brown's account to suggest that both contributors agree that there was a strong 'civil society' element in the collapse of Soviet communism, albeit one that was able to acquire political potency only when allowed and even encouraged to do so by the General Secretary.

That is a view to which Rigby adhered. Given his emphasis throughout his career on intra-elite bureaucratic 'crypto-politics' this might appear as a forced repudiation of his long-held views of the nature of the Soviet system. No doubt Rigby was as surprised as the rest of us by the speed and extent of change from the mid-1980s. But he was in fact better equipped, in two ways, to deal with the changes than might appear at first glance.

Firstly, his concept of goal-rationality was applicable not just to the bureaucracy, but also to the general population. As he made clear in his early analyses of the consequences of the absence of a significant level of market relations in the Soviet Union, it was not only the Soviet apparatus that had its tasks set for it by the state, and therefore it was not only the apparatus that was being asked by the state to grant it the authority to do so. The entire population was, and for those tasks to be taken on with the required degree of commitment required acceptance of the goal.

A strong argument could be made that it was the ever increasing failure of both the bureaucrats and the general population to fulfil the tasks required of them – presumably because of a collapse in their acceptance of the ultimate goal – that rendered the Soviet economy unviable (and therefore incapable of maintaining eudaemonic legitimation, if the legitimacy claims shifted in that direction).

The second way in which Rigby was well-equipped to deal with the decline and collapse of Soviet communism was his long-standing awareness, despite his commitment to the concept of mono-organizational socialism, of elements of Soviet society that were not totally controlled by the central leadership. He was never an adherent of the totalitarian view. In a 1964 paper he discussed remnant 'market' elements (with in the context of that paper 'market' having both political, that is, democratic, and economic components).[1] As noted in the Introduction, he was wary of but did not totally reject even the participatory version of Hough's pluralism. He often noted the potential significance of the lipservice which was constantly paid to democracy in the Soviet ideology.

These elements of Rigby's knowledge of the Soviet Union easily came to the fore as events unfolded in the second half of the 1980s, and enabled him to propose a typically clear and sensible explanation of those events, essentially of a 'civil society' nature.

I will conclude this discussion of the collapse of Soviet communism with something of an aside which reflects the fascination with issues of institutionalization that I gained as a graduate student under T.H. Rigby. It is a commonplace – and an accurate one – to note that Gorbachev had enormous confidence in his own personal powers of persuasion. His was a very 'personalist' regime in that sense. But he was also very aware of the importance of institutions. The party apparatus which came to oppose him was not just a collection of individuals. They were individuals occupying positions within an elaborate bureaucracy. Both the positions and the bureaucracy gave them more political potency than they had as individuals. Gorbachev demonstrated his awareness of this by his commitment to administrative reorganization as a way to overcome opposition. He did not rely purely on his powers of persuasion. But it was at the next step that he fell down badly. Like Khrushchev he was better at removing old institutions than putting new ones in their place. One suspects that this was a matter of temperament and prioritization rather than simply the difficulties of institution-building in the circumstances of the time. The contrast between Gorbachev and Lenin is striking in this regard. As Rigby described so well, Lenin was obsessively dedicated to creating business-like executive structures. Although he was often frustrated in his efforts, he undoubtedly enjoyed greater success than Gorbachev.

Gorbachev was unable, either through personalist or institutional means, to save the Soviet Union. What, then, of the post-Soviet period? The first point that Rigby would almost certainly make is that in the post-Soviet period the market – with all its weaknesses and vulnerabilities – deals with a considerable part of the task fulfilment that in Soviet circumstances came within the domain of the state. Although the existence of the state is necessarily part of the legitimacy claims of the new system, the state is not burdened with the day-to-day process of task setting, performance measurement, and consequently rewarding or sanctioning the entire population.

Beyond that, is there anything in Rigby's treatment of legitimacy, in particular his concept of goal-rationality, that is applicable to the post-Soviet period? Holmes, in his contribution, sees the post-Soviet leadership as using a complex mix of legitimacy claims, with shifts in focus from some to others according to circumstances. This is taking place in a time of transition, in which there is considerable stress on relatively short-term regime legitimation, as distinct from longer-term system legitimation. That is a plausible view, and fits well with the sense of a regime with no great purpose beyond its survival and, for the more cynically minded, self-enrichment.

But can we find something more parsimonious, particularly as we move from regime to system legitimation? Holmes offers two more parsimonious possibilities, based on the three types most used by Rigby – Weber's charismatic and legal-rational and his own goal-rational. The first sees Putin as combining the charismatic and legal-rational, in something close to what Weber tentatively saw towards the end of his life as the most desirable form of rule: a charismatic leader pulling staff and population into a world of legal-rational rule. The second is Putin and then Medvedev combining legal-rational and goal-rational claims to legitimacy, with the goal being 'to make Russia great again'. (Presumably Holmes finds it too hard to find any charisma in Medvedev to retain the charisma-legal-rational combination in a Medvedev presidency.) Both these possibilities require putting a great deal of faith in the two presidents' commitment to the rule of law. To be blunt, this author finds it difficult to have that faith. That is not only because he finds it hard to believe that they have such a commitment, but also because he finds it hard to believe that they would believe that an appeal to the rule of law is a credible legitimacy claim in contemporary Russia. Neither population nor bureaucracy is committed to the rule of law, and neither believes in the leadership's commitment. In the author's cynical view, the rule of law, including anti-corruption law, exists to provide the means to discipline uppity oligarchs and bureaucrats, and for little other purpose.

That excludes any legitimacy based on legal-rational claims. But is there another possibility: the same charisma-goal-rational combination that Rigby applied to the Soviet, essentially Stalinist, period? The goal is, as suggested by Holmes, 'to make Russia strong again', a goal which in itself has a charismatic element. That element, with a charismatic leadership promoting it, reinforces both staff and popular commitment to the tasks needed to bring it about, and obedience to the regime in the meantime. The great popularity, as revealed in opinion polls, of the leaders compared to the institutions and other personalities of the regime might support such a view. The authoritarian tendencies that many identify with the regime – if not the system – confirm the prediction made by Rigby as to the power-concentrating capabilities of such a combination.

But if the persistent popularity of the regime is based on such charisma-goal-rational legitimacy claims, it is hard to see them being sustainable, particularly at systemic level. Charisma, which in this case is not in abundance to begin with, is difficult to institutionalize in order to extend its effect from one individual to the next. Already the record of the regime in generating effective task fulfilment in those areas for which it has responsibility is not reassuring. At present there is a clear case of popularity not producing performance-generating commitment.

Institutionalization and personalism

I will admit to finishing this project with a more pro-personalist view than when I started it. Like T.H. Rigby I continue to be impressed by the constant pressure throughout the Soviet period towards the institutionalization of political affairs, but also like him, and many others, have to admit to the equally constant reversion to type of personalist rule. Rigby and I essentially agree on the reason for this reversion: the lack of external constraint on the leadership in his case; the lack of external pressure to perform in mine.

The persistence of the reversion to personalist type should not lead us to neglect the pressure for institutionalization and indeed its extensive presence – with both positive and negative consequences – throughout the Soviet period. Nor should we fail to examine the nature of personalist relations closely.

The close connection between institutionalization and personalist rule is very evident in Fitzpatrick's chapter in this book. She describes Stalin's 'team', with its very close personal connections, strong sense of being in or out, and a particularly strong sense of loyalty to its captain. But it is a team which, as Fitzpatrick regularly stresses, has to do more than to be loyal to the captain; it also has to govern. To do that the members of the team are not just, to use Rigby's private terminology, 'chaps', but also the wearers of 'hats'. They have institutionalized jobs and to the extent that they are allowed to by Stalin they use institutionalized means to do those jobs. As Rigby so persistently stressed, it had to be that way because a consequence of the system's goal-rational legitimacy was a commitment to the fulfilment of tasks, tasks that were complex and technically demanding. Although Stalin's team was formed early enough in the Soviet Union's existence – if not actually before – for its 'hats' component to come chronologically after its 'chaps' component, that was not to reduce in any way the relevance of the former once the team settled down seriously to the business of governing. With time 'teams' came to be formed on the basis of shared work experience, providing thereby not just a sense of a potential team member's capacity for loyalty, but also capacity for getting the job done.

Fitzpatrick and I disagree on whether the hats vs. chaps element of Stalin's team produced tensions that made team arrangements unviable. Fitzpatrick believes that Stalin was relaxed about and even welcoming of team members defending agency interests, and that, for example, Stalin drove Ordzhonikidze to suicide not because of his vigorous promotion of his agency's policy interests but because he failed the Stalinist loyalty test of accepting the repression of relatives without demur. That is a matter on which I will defer to the infinitely better qualified historian, although it is interesting to note that the change in Stalin's approach to the agency-promoting activities of his lieutenants came in the mid-1930s, a time when, as Fitzpatrick points out, he also became a lot less involved in economic policy-making and devoted much of his time to foreign affairs. Could it have been that as he became less interested in being the referee in inter-agency competition he decided that brutal new rules of the game should be introduced, that would not require the same degree of refereeing commitment? The tension between the institutional and the personal at this time and indeed throughout Soviet history deserves further attention.

In my view that attention requires close attention to the purposes of patron-client relationships. Three broad categories of purpose offer themselves: to ensure personal political survival, to facilitate policy-making outcomes to the liking of the team captain, and to facilitate implementation of policy once made. There are few who would argue with the supreme relevance of the first to Soviet politics. One had to ensure that one had the numbers on the increasingly rare occasions that the numbers would be counted. That aspect of patron-client relations is well covered in the literature. The role of such relationships in policy implementation is also well-established, although perhaps more consideration is required of the use made of personal contacts at different levels of policy implementation. Many of the examples that are presented in the literature relate to day-to-day assistance in operational plan fulfilment: using a contact to source a scarce input, to schedule transport delivery arrangements, etc. But were personal contacts as important in the implementation of large-scale policy initiatives, for example, organizing the implementation of the Virgin Lands scheme? Khrushchev certainly sent a then loyal ally, Leonid Brezhnev, to Kazakhstan to facilitate implementation of his new policy. But I would suggest that Khrushchev's confidence in his administrative competence was as important as his personal loyalty. Are implementation processes such as the Virgin Lands scheme of a scale that more institutionalized structures and procedures became unavoidable?

It is the same consideration that leads me to question, as I did in the conclusion to my chapter in this volume, the role of patron-client relationships in policy-making. Certainly the team captain would be ensured party loyalty for what might be called system-defining policies. Stalin's personal political security required the loyalty of team members regarding industrialization in the early 1930s; it was what could be called a 'vote of confidence' measure. But beyond that the complexities of governing required that policy-making, one way or another, took account of institutional policy positions, regardless of personal relationships. As argued in my chapter, the system was not well set up to take those positions into account effectively, but my own feeling is that the failures were structural, rather than resulting from an excessive reliance on patron-client relations within the policy process.

There is plenty of room for further empirical investigation and analysis of the role of patron-client relations in the Soviet political process. Rigby's categories and arguments still serve very well as guides for that further work. What of the post-Soviet period? As pointed out in the Introduction, Rigby saw such relations in the post-Soviet period as different from those of the Soviet period. He suggested that the greater market and democratic elements of the new system meant that patron-client relations were less important in the rise of a leader to full power, were less stable, and were characterized by less 'loyalty' on the part of the team captain. That seemed a reasonably accurate portrayal of things at the time Rigby was writing, during the Yeltsin presidency. But what now, in the post-Yeltsin era of Putin and Medvedev?

It is presumably a reflection of the nature of the post-Yeltsin regime – less market and less democratic – that Rigby's differences seem less relevant. Having a series of patrons was more important for Putin than it was for Yeltsin; for Medvedev it was all-important. A strong potential or actual client base was important for Putin. It will be a major test of the continued importance of the patron-client relationship in post-Yeltsin politics if Medvedev is able – if indeed he tries – to claim supreme power by abandoning his patron without an obvious client base. It is certainly the grounds on which many commentators question Medvedev's capacity to abandon the tandem.

It would require more serious analysis than is possible here to be sure, but one's sense is that turnover has not been great within Putin's team, whether narrowly or broadly defined. One feels that, despite turnover in positions, Putin has been loyal to his clients, as they move from one position to another, in a way that reminds one of Brezhnev and his nomenklatura carousel.

The market and democratic elements that remain in the system mean that patron-client relations have to be established in slightly different ways. The oligarchs are hardly traditional Soviet-style clients, but there is surely something of the client about their relationship to state power nevertheless. It has been extraordinarily difficult to come up with an effective format for a 'team' which includes the Duma and United Russia, but it is not for want of trying.

As one would expect if patron-client relationships in post-Yeltsin Russia do not differ so much from those of the Soviet period after all, the main issue in Rigby's analyses – the hats vs. chaps issue – remains. This is very evident in Huskey's contribution to this volume. Like Rigby's work on the same period, it is not actually a Kremlinological study of patron-client relations, but a more 'sociological' analysis of the origins and career backgrounds of members of the elite and particular elite categories and institutions. Huskey makes it clear that his findings do not support the existence of a legal-rational bureaucracy in post-Soviet Russia. There is certainly something about the career movements – in and out of particular business sectors, bureaucratic agencies and political posts – that, given what else we know of the post-Soviet regimes, smacks very strongly of 'teams' (to use Fitzpatrick's word). But, as always, the phenomena of the 'hat' and the representation of sectoral interests are here as well. While the career links between, for example, the staff of energy firms and energy-related bureaucratic agencies and political posts might be far too close for ethical and socially responsible policy comfort, they are not necessarily incompatible with 'getting the job done'. The job has to be done perhaps because, as very tentatively suggested earlier in this Conclusion, the system is indeed goal-rational in its legitimacy claims. Appointments are not to sinecures and recruitment is job-based. (This has tended to produce as a byproduct – as it did in the Soviet period – a strong regional bias in the origins of team members). And, as I suggested in my chapter in this volume, the issue of the competition between sectoral interests within the team is very much present, with policy inaction often being the consequence.

It is to be hoped that my more discursive remarks in this Conclusion, when combined with the more focused work from the other contributors, demonstrates not just the importance of T.H. Rigby's contribution to Soviet studies at the time that he was active in the field, but also its continuing relevance, as we continue to try to understand the Soviet past and – perhaps to a degree that he himself did not suspect – the post-Soviet present and future.

Note

1 T.H. Rigby (1964), 'Traditional, market, and organizational societies and the USSR', *World Politics*, XVI, 4, 547.

Index

All-Union Centre for the Study of
    Public Opinion (VTsIOM), 118,
    140–1, 170
Almond, Gabriel, 2, 115
Andropov, Iurii, 93, 161
architecture
    constructivist, 81, 91, 97
    de-urbanist, 81, 83
    garden city movement, 82
    and legitimation, 76–95
    monumentalist, 82, 85–6, 88, 90,
        91, 93, 94, 98
    neo-classical, 81, 84
    Soviet classicism, 90
    triumphalist, 87, 91, 93, 94, 98
    urbanist, 81, 83
authority, see legitimation

Balcerowicz, Leszek, 111, 124
behaviouralism, 2, 3, 6, 7, 159
Beria, Lavrentii, 68
Boldin, Valerii, 38, 162–3, 181
Brezhnev, Leonid
    approach to policy making, 35–7,
        40, 45
    and architecture, 88, 94
    and corruption, 175
    cult of personality, 11, 35, 207
    and 'developed socialism', 95
    and eudaemonism, 89, 206
    funeral of, 93
    and institutionalization, 13, 35
    and patronage, 13, 35, 212, 213
    personality of, 37
Bukharin, Nikolai, 53, 55, 58, 69, 70,
    129, 136
bureaucracy
    and crypto-politics, 9, 17
    and institutionalization, 12–13
    and legal-rational legitimation, 4, 5,
        18, 103, 110, 214
    and personalism, 14
    and political leadership, 6, 198

revolving door, 185–6, 193, 200
Rigby on, 4, 8, 11, 18, 103, 205, 206
vedomstvennost', 12, 63, 64, 211
see also officials
business elites
    backgrounds, 188–9, 196
    gender, 196, 203
    oligarchs, 42, 213
    under Putin, 41, 42, 43, 186, 192,
        200
    recruitment to, 186
    reproduction of, 198
    and the state, 186, 191

charismatic legitimation
    and cult of the leader, 77
    and goal-rationality, 5, 206, 210
    longevity of, 105–6, 108, 120
    Rigby on, 4, 5, 10, 206–7, 210
    and Stalin, 4, 5, 10
    and tyranny, 4, 5, 10, 26, 206–7
    and Yeltsin, 109
Chernenko, Konstantin, 49, 93, 134
Cherniaev, Anatolii, 36, 37, 38, 49,
    139
China, 116–17, 125, 133
Chubais, Anatolii, 193, 202
civil society
    and collapse of USSR, 16, 207, 208
    in late Soviet period, 16, 177
    Rigby on, xiv, 9–10, 16, 208
    'shadow culture', 16
Cold War, 130, 142
collapse of USSR
    August 1991, 154, 175
    causes of, 16, 37, 152–84, 206
    and Gorbachev, 39, 163, 177
    and mafia, 154, 175–6
    predictions of, 153, 159
    'revolution from above', xiv, 127,
        141, 147, 151, 154, 207
    Rigby on, 15–16, 205, 206
collectivization, 65–6, 74

communism
  collapse of, *see* collapse of USSR
  as goal, 4, 5, 6, 76, 77, 86, 88–9,
    103, 206, 208
  symbols of, 79
Communist Party of the Soviet
    Union
  apparatus, 12, 14, 15, 29, 143, 145,
    147
  Central Committee, 14, 47, 58, 59,
    64
  Central Committee secretariat, 30,
    33, 36, 133, 145
  democratic centralism, 146, 158,
    181
  General Secretary of, 127, 133, 134,
    139
  leading role of, 10, 15, 142, 143,
    170
  opposition to, 128–9, 171
  Programme of, 89
  16th Congress, 57
  18th Congress, 67
  19th Conference, 139, 141–4, 163,
    166
  see also Politburo
'conditional tolerance', 104
Congress of People's Deputies, 144,
    145–6, 147, 164, 207
consultation
  under Brezhnev, 36, 49
  forms of, 23, 26, 28
  under Gorbachev, 38
  under Khrushchev, 33–4
  under Putin, 42–3, 44–5
  under Stalin, 32
  under Yeltsin, 41, 49
corruption, 114, 118, 201, 210
crypto-politics, 8–9, 11, 15–16, 17,
    207

democracy
  and Gorbachev, 144, 161
  and legitimacy, 121
  and logic of specialization, 25–6
  and the policy process, 25–6, 46
  popular attitudes towards, 170–1
  in post-Soviet Russia, 15, 50, 111,
    126, 213

  and Putin, 50
  in USSR, 9, 16, 46, 173, 208
Democratic Russia, 169–70, 172
dissidents, 148, 152, 155–7, 159, 180
  among intellectuals, 155–6
  passive, 156
  prosecution of, 160
  release of, 163, 164
  semi-, 156
Duma, *see* parliament
Dzerzhinskii, Feliks, 93, 137

Easter, Gerald, 22, 40, 47
Eastern Europe
  collapse of communism in, 141–2,
    169, 170
  disaffection in, 160
  military intervention in, 163, 181
elections
  to Congress of People's Deputies,
    144, 145–6, 164–5, 166–8
  and legitimacy, 76
  during perestroika, 143, 144, 154,
    164, 166, 170, 171, 173
  of Russian president, 164, 172, 173,
    182
  in USSR, 76
elites
  accountability of, 185
  circulation of, 185–6, 194–5, 214
  governmental, xiv, 15, 85, 185,
    198
  and legitimation, 104, 117, 185–6
  recruitment to, 185–99
  and revolution, 104
  post-Soviet, xiv, 185–99
  provincial, 15, 194
  revolving door, 185–6, 193, 200
  Soviet, xiv, 197
  see also business elites
Enukidze, Avel, 57, 67, 74–5
eudaemonic legitimation
  under Brezhnev, 89, 206–7
  definition of, 77, 106
  under Khrushchev, 89, 206–7
  and Moscow, 77, 94
  under Putin, 112, 120–1
  under Stalin, 89
  in USSR, 76, 77, 94, 208

Exhibition of Economic
  Achievements (VDNKh), 89–90
Ezhov, Nikolai, 67

Five-year plans, 31, 82, 83

Gaidar, Yegor, 111, 148
Gazprom, 190, 191, 192, 193
Georgia
  and nationalist movement, 173,
    174
  and Stalin, 66
  1989 incident, 168–9
  2008 crisis, 113
glasnost, 131, 137, 139, 156, 157
goal-rational legitimation
  and architecture, 94, 95
  and bureaucracy, 103, 206, 214
  and charismatic legitimation, 5,
    206, 210
  and communism, 4, 94, 95
  longevity of, 106
  in post-Soviet Russia, 122, 209, 214
  Rigby on, xiv, 4, 101, 103, 106, 122
  and task fulfilment, 22
  in USSR, 4, 89, 94, 95
Gorbachev, Mikhail
  appointment as General Secretary,
    37, 127
  approach to policy making, 38–9,
    40, 41, 49
  career background, 133, 162
  as chairman of Supreme Soviet, 143
  characterizations of, 49, 129, 141,
    208
  cultural interests of, 130, 132–3
  and democracy, 144, 161
  and economic reform, 129–30, 154,
    161, 173
  and the environment, 130–1
  and foreign policy, 163
  and Iakovlev, 130–3, 135, 162
  on Lenin, 108, 128
  and markets, 129, 161
  and the media, 157
  and perestroika, 127–47, 154
  and Politburo, 134–5
  and political reform, 148, 154, 161
  as president, 144

and Presidential Council, 130, 148
  relations with intellectuals, 155,
    162
  as social democrat, 128, 143
  on Stalin, 150
Gordon Skilling, Harold, 8, 34
Gosplan, 47, 59, 62
Great Patriotic War, 86, 88, 93
Great Terror, 67, 86, 138
Gromyko, Andrei, 49, 134–5, 138, 142

Heller, Agnes, 104
Hough, Jerry F.
  and institutional pluralism, 8, 12,
    19, 35, 208
  on political participation, 9

Iakovlev, Aleksandr
  as architect of perestroika, 132,
    137–8, 147, 154, 162
  and conservatives, 131, 137–8
  and glasnost, 139
  and Gorbachev, 130–3, 135, 162
ideology
  failure of, 16, 159
  and goal rationality, 103
  Marxist-Leninist, 122
  Rigby on, 3, 6
industrialization, 29, 34, 61, 62, 83
institutionalization
  and Brezhnev, 35
  and Lenin, 12
  pressure for, xiii–iv, 21–2, 40, 46,
    49, 210–11
  and Putin, 42, 44
  Rigby on, xiii–iv, 21–2, 46, 205
  of Sovnarkom, 12
  and Stalin, 211
  in USSR, xiv, 12–13, 15, 21–2, 208
  and Yeltsin, 41

Kaganovich, Lazar
  career of, 30, 62, 63–4, 67, 68
  correspondence with Stalin, 52, 62,
    66
  and Moscow, 82, 83, 84, 93
  relations with Stalin, 53
Kalinin, Mikhail, 55, 57, 58, 62, 67,
    137

Khodorkovskii, Mikhail, 43, 114
Khrushchev, Nikita
  and architecture, 88, 89, 91, 94
  approach to policy making, 33–4,
    38, 39, 45, 212
  and communism, 89, 94
  effectiveness of, 35, 37, 45, 209
  and eudaemonism, 89, 206
  in Stalin's team, 67, 68
Kirov, Sergei, 62, 79, 80
Koba, 53, 67, 70, 74
  see Stalin
Kremlinology, 7, 8, 9, 14, 34
Kuibyshev, Valerian, 53, 56, 58, 72,
    73

legal-rational legitimation
  and bureaucracy, 4, 5, 11, 18, 103,
    110, 214
  definition of, 102
  and Putin, 110, 111, 112, 209–10
  Rigby on, 4, 11
  in the USSR, 4, 77
  and Yeltsin, 109
legitimacy, *see* legitimation
legitimation
  and architecture, 76–95
  and coercion, 109–10, 115, 118,
    120, 121
  and collapse of USSR, 16, 206
  and corruption, 114, 119
  crisis of, 121–2
  and distribution of wealth, 112
  external, 108–9
  measurement of, 115–20, 123
  and nationalism, 108, 112–13, 120,
    121–2
  popular, 76, 104, 107, 121
  regime, 104, 105, 118, 209
  Rigby on, xiii, xiv, 1, 2–6, 16,
    102–3, 104, 115, 120, 205–10
  and rule of law, 4, 105
  self-, 104, 108–9, 121
  staff, 104
  system, 104, 118, 209
  and urban development, 76–95
  see also charismatic legitimation,
    eudaemonic legitimation,
    goal-rational legitimation,

legal-rational legitimation,
    traditional legitimation, Weber
Lenin, Vladimir
  approach to policy making, 27–9,
    39, 45
  and institutionalization, 3, 12, 47,
    209
  mausoleum, 79, 80, 88
  memorials to, 80, 88, 93, 96
  and monumental propaganda, 78,
    82
  on Moscow, 93
  and Sovnarkom, 58–9, 60
Ligachev, Yegor
  and Andreeva affair, 138
  as conservative, 134, 136, 139, 168
  demotion, 145
  as reformer, 134
  relations with Yeltsin, 135
  on Sakharov, 181
  on use of force, 169, 181
Lipset, Seymour Martin, 106, 115
logic of specialization
  and Brezhnev, 35–7
  consequences of, 25, 37, 45
  and democracy, 25–6
  and Gorbachev, 38
  and Khrushchev, 33–4, 35
  and Lenin, 28
  meaning, 23
  and patron-client relations, 26–7,
    40, 44, 45
  and political leadership, 24–5, 26
  and Putin, 43–4
  and Stalin, 29, 31–2
  and Yeltsin, 41
  see also specialization

mafia
  and collapse of USSR, 154, 175–6
  links with political leaders, 158,
    181
market
  elements of in USSR, 3, 4, 7, 9, 10,
    208
  post-Soviet, 15, 209, 213
  Rigby on, 7, 9, 10, 208, 209
Marx, Karl
  influence on Rigby, 1, 15, 18

Matlock, Jack, 143, 145
Medvedev, Dmitrii
  career background, 188
  and corruption, 114, 122, 201
  and Khodorkovskii, 114
  election as president, 109, 188
  and legitimation, 113, 209
  and patron, 213
  and personalism, 45
  popularity of, 118
  on rule of law, 113, 114, 120, 122,
    210
  on state apparatus, 201
  and tandem, 45, 114, 213
Medvedev, Roi, 35, 155
Medvedev, Vadim, 134, 135, 139
Mikoian, Anastas
  membership of Politburo, 67, 68
  relations with Stalin, 53, 55, 60, 64
Military Revolutionary Council, 28
Minagawa, Shugo, 19
Ministry of Natural Resources, 190–1,
  202
Molotov, Viacheslav
  correspondence with Stalin, 52, 55,
    56, 62, 66, 69, 70
  as head of Sovnarkom, 30, 60, 62,
    64, 72
  relations with Stalin, 53–4, 58,
    68
mono-organizational socialism
  features of, 10–11, 19
  and institutional pluralism, 8, 12
  and leading role of party, 10
  and Stalinism, 10
  and totalitarianism, 8, 10, 208
mono-organizational society, *see*
  mono-organizational socialism
Moscow
  as capital, 77, 83
  Cathedral of Christ the Saviour, 80
  churches, 92
  constructivist buildings, 81
  General Plan for Development,
    84–5, 88, 91–2
  Gorky Street, 85, 86
  housing, 85, 88, 91–2
  and Kaganovich, 82, 83, 84, 93
  Kremlin, 78, 79, 87, 91, 93

Lenin on, 93
Lubianka, 93
mausoleum, 79, 80, 88, 93
Metro, 82, 83–4, 86, 88, 90, 93,
  98
monasteries, 80
officials from, 194
Palace of Congresses, 91
Palace of Soviets, 80, 83, 85, 87,
  91
reconstruction of, 82
as socialist city, 77, 81, 85, 92
street names, 78, 92
Red Square, 79, 85, 93
and urban development, 76–101
verticals, 86–7, 94
vysotnie zdaniia, 86–7
Moscow-Volga Canal, 82, 83

Narkomtiazhprom (People's
  Commissariat for Heavy
  Industry), 62, 63, 64, 85
nationalism
  in Baltics, 164, 169, 171, 173
  and collapse of USSR, 154, 168,
    169, 177
  in Georgia, 168, 173, 174
  and Gorbachev, 130–1, 132, 163
  and legitimation, 107–8, 112–13,
    120
  and Putin, 112
  republican, 171–2, 173, 175, 177
nomenklatura, 140, 150, 158, 213
Norilsk Nickel, 193, 194, 202

officials
  and academic posts, 189–90, 195
  as class, 5, 18, 198
  corruption of, 122
  educational background, 195–6
  and KGB, 193, 195–6
  and legitimation, 104, 115–17
  and patron-client relations, 5
  and *pantouflage*, 185, 187, 192, 197,
    199, 200
  and political leadership, 6
  performance, 14, 122
  place of residence, 85, 88
  from private sector, 192

officials – *continued*
to private sector, 188–9, 196, 198
promotion, 13, 197
and rules, 5, 103
see also bureaucracy
oligarchy, 10–11, 13
see also business elites
Ordzhonikidze, Sergo
death of, 64–5, 211
as head of Vesenkha, 61, 62, 63, 64, 72
personality, 53, 55
relations with Stalin, 52, 54, 55, 56, 63, 64–5

pantouflage, 185, 187, 192, 197–8, 199, 200
parliament
and business, 42
members of, 187–8
and Putin, 50, 213
role of, 41, 50
and Yeltsin, 50
patronage, *see* patron-client relations
patron-client relations
and business, 186, 191, 193, 200
origins of, 13, 14, 22, 26–7, 47, 212
and policy making, 22, 33, 40–1, 45, 212
and Putin, 44, 186, 191, 213
Rigby on, 5, 13, 21, 213–14
and Stalin, 33, 40
see also personalism
perestroika
and Congress of People's Deputies, 144, 145–6, 147, 164–5, 170, 207
conservative attitude to, 127, 130, 131, 136, 142, 147, 149, 158, 170, 171, 173–4
and Gorbachev, 127–47
and Iakovlev, 132, 154–5
and the media, 131 132, 137, 149, 165, 179
meaning of, 127–8
and *neformaly*, 165, 166, 169, 171
'Nina Andreeva' affair, 137–9, 163

and Soviet history, 135–6
support for, 158
violence during, 169, 174–5
and 19th Party Conference, 139, 141–4
personalism
and accidents of personality, 13, 22
and Brezhnev, 37
and bureaucracy, 14
and factionalism, 27, 44
'family circles', 186
and Gorbachev, 39, 208
and Khrushchev, 34–5
origins of, 26, 37, 43, 45, 198
post-Soviet, 15
Rigby on, xiv, 2, 11–15, 13, 21, 46, 51, 133, 150, 205, 211, 213
social networks, 197
in USSR, xiv, 2, 11, 21–2, 46, 211
and Yeltsin, 41
see also patron-client relations
pluralism
institutional, 8, 12, 14–15, 19, 35, 208
and Khrushchev, 34
post-Soviet, 16, 199
and Rigby, 7–8, 9, 14, 16–17, 208
socialist, 128, 136
Poland, 111–12, 155, 160
Politburo
and Brezhnev, 35
commissions, 31, 36
conflict within, 30–1, 54, 61
decline of, 32, 35, 36
effectiveness of, 31, 49, 59
institutional representation in, 61–2, 63–4, 73
membership, 30, 40, 61–2, 73, 75, 134–5
revival of, 33
role of, 29, 30, 59, 148
and Stalin, 59, 60, 61, 62
policy process
dacha teams, 41, 49
and personalism, 22
stagnation of, 32, 49
see also consultation
political culture, 3–4

political leadership
  change in, 133, 138
  and policy process, 24–5, 26, 29, 37, 43
political regime
  and legitimation, 104, 105, 118, 209
political system
  and legitimation, 105
Prague Spring, 127, 132, 160
presidential system
  Russia as, 41, 42, 109
  super-, 109
  Teflon, 113, 125
Putin, Vladimir
  approach to policy making, 41–5
  and business, 41, 43, 186, 190, 192, 200
  career background, 188, 196, 213
  and charismatic legitimation, 112, 209–10
  and clients, 44, 213
  and constitution, 114
  and corruption, 114
  and democracy, 50, 187
  and dictatorship of laws, 110
  effectiveness of, 41, 44
  and elite recruitment, 186–7, 197, 213
  and eudaemonic legitimation, 112, 120–1
  and Khodorkovskii, 43
  and legal-rational legitimation, 110, 111, 112, 113, 209–10
  and the media, 113, 126
  and nationalism, 112
  and oligarchs, 41, 43, 210
  popularity of, 118
  as prime minister, 44
  and rule of law, 110, 114, 210
  and tandem, 45, 114, 213
  and traditional legitimation, 110, 112, 113
  and United Russia, 199

rational-legal legitimation, *see* legal-rational legitimation
rationality, 4, 22

'revolution from above', xiv, 127, 141, 147, 151, 154, 207
Rigby, Thomas Henry Richard (Harry)
  on behaviouralism, 2, 3, 6, 7, 159
  biography, xii–xiii, 1
  on bureaucracy, 4, 5, 6, 8, 18, 103, 205, 206
  on charismatic legitimation, 4, 5, 10, 109, 206, 207, 209, 210
  on civil society, xiv, 9–10, 16, 208
  on collapse of USSR, 15–16, 17, 206, 207–8
  and crypto-politics, 8–9, 11, 15–16, 17, 207
  on democracy in USSR, 9, 46, 156, 173, 208
  on elites, 9, 15, 194
  on eudaemonic legitimation, 106–7, 120
  on goal-rational legitimation, xiv, 4, 5, 6, 14, 76–7, 101, 103, 106, 205–7, 209, 210, 211
  hats and chaps, 11–15, 30, 211, 213
  intellectual influences on, 1, 115
  on institionalization, xiii–xiv, 21–2, 46, 205, 208, 209
  on Khrushchev, 11
  and Kremlinology, 7, 8, 9, 14
  on legal-rational legitimation, 4, 6, 11, 103, 209
  on legitimation, xiii, xiv, 2–6, 16, 102–3, 104, 115, 120, 205–10
  on the market, 7, 9, 10, 208, 209
  and Marx, 1, 15, 18
  and mono-organizational socialism, 8, 10–11, 12, 16, 17, 19, 156, 208
  on personalism, xiv, 2, 11–15, 21, 46, 51, 133, 150, 205, 211, 213
  PhD, xii, 1
  on pluralism, 7–8, 9, 14, 16–17, 208
  and policy, 14–15, 17, 46
  on political culture, 3, 4
  on post-Soviet period, 15–17, 188, 209
  on Stalin, 67
  on totalitarianism, 7–8, 10, 15, 206, 208
  on traditional legitimation, 4, 7, 10

Rigby, Thomas Henry Richard
   (Harry) – *continued*
   use of theory, 2, 15
   and Weber, 1, 2–6, 11, 15, 101–2,
      110
Rudzutak, Ian, 54, 55, 57, 62
rule of law
   and democracy, 110
   and Gorbachev, 145, 156
   and institutionalization, 13
   and legitimation, 4, 105
   and the market, 112
   and Medvedev, 113, 114, 120, 122,
      210
   and Putin, 110, 114, 210
   Weber on, 110
Rykov, Aleksei
   as head of Sovnarkom, 53, 59, 60
   relations with Stalin, 54, 55, 58,
      69
Ryzhkov, Nikolai, 130, 134, 136, 146,
   182

Sakharov, Andrei
   attitude to Yeltsin, 172
   in Congress of People's Deputies,
      144, 170
   end of exile, 162, 163
   influence of, 179, 181
   on perestroika, 128
   political development, 155
samizdat, 155, 156, 159
Schroeder, Gerhard, 113, 125
Shevardnadze, Eduard, 134–5, 162,
   181
shock therapy, 41, 124
siloviki, 50, 187, 193–4, 195–6, 203
Siberian rivers scheme, 131, 148
Sobchak, Anatolii, 170, 183
Solomontsev, Mikhail, 136, 138, 142
Solzhenitsyn, Aleksandr, 162, 179
Soso, 53, 67, 70
   see Stalin
Sovnarkom (Council of People's
   Commissars)
   consultation processes, 28–9
   effectiveness of, 29, 30, 31, 47
   and Lenin, 58–9, 60
   under Molotov, 60, 62, 64

   and Stalin, 58, 59, 60, 61
   structure of, 28
   under Rykov, 53, 59, 60
specialization
   of function, 23, 24, 29, 30, 35, 44
   of knowledge, 23, 29, 32, 34–5
   see also logic of specialization
Stalin, Iosif
   and anti-specialist campaign, 57–8
   approach to policy making, 29–33,
      35, 39
   and architecture, 91, 206
   biographies of, 68
   and bureaucracy, 65
   and charismatic legitimation, 4, 10,
      210
   and client networks, 33, 40
   correspondence with Kaganovich,
      52, 62, 66
   correspondence with Molotov, 52,
      55, 56, 62, 66, 69, 70
   and eudaemonic legitimation, 89
   Gorbachev on, 140
   as head of Politburo, 62
   as head of Sovnarkom, 59, 61, 72,
      73
   as '*khoziain*', 51–2, 62
   and mausoleum, 93
   monuments to, 89–90
   and Moscow, 93
   rehabilitation of, 138
   status of, 89, 90, 93
   and his 'team', xiv, 51–68, 211, 212
   and tyranny, 4, 10, 15, 33, 44
   and urban development, 95, 206
   and *vedomstvennost'*, 31, 63–4. 65,
      211
   wife, 56–7
   see also Stalin's team
Stalin's team
   discipline within, 55, 56–8, 66, 67
   forms of address, 53, 67, 68, 69, 70,
      74
   and the Great Terror, 67–8
   and the Left, 55
   members of, 52–3, 54, 55, 62, 67
   and the Right, 55, 56, 57, 58, 59,
      61, 65, 67, 75
Strzhalkovskii, Vladimir, 193, 203

Supreme Soviet
  and Gorbachev, 143
  standing commissions of, 9, 19

Tikhonov, Nikolai, 130, 134
Tomskii, Mikhail, 55, 58
totalitarianism
  and atomization, 7, 9
  and charismatic legitimation, 5
  Gorbachev on, 148
  influence of, 6, 7, 51
  Rigby on, 7–8, 10, 15, 206, 208
traditional legitimation
  definition of, 102
  longevity of, 105
  new, 108, 120
  and Medvedev, 113
  and Putin, 110, 112, 113
  Rigby on, 3, 4
  in USSR, 4
Trotsky, Leon, 52, 54, 55, 70

USSR (Union of Soviet Socialist
    Republics)
  Constitution of, 77, 136, 144, 170
  and democracy, 9, 153
  legitimacy of, xiv, 1, 4, 6
  president of, 144
  see also collapse of USSR
United Russia, 187, 199, 213
urban development
  and legitimation, 77, 94–5
  of Moscow, 76–101

VDNKh, *see* Exhibition of Economic
    Achievements
VTsIOM, *see* All-Union Centre for the
    Study of Public Opinion
Vesenkha (All-Union Council for the
    National Economy), 57, 58, 59,
    61, 62, 64
vedomstvennost'
  and 'capture', 27, 33, 40
  definition of, 12, 73

and policy process, 12, 45
  in Politburo, 61
  Stalin's attitude towards, 31, 63–4,
      65, 211
Voroshilov, Klim, 52, 54, 60, 62, 63,
    67, 68
Vorotnikov, Vitalii, 134, 136, 138

Weber, Max
  and bureaucracy, 5, 103, 110–11,
      185
  and charismatic legitimation, 3, 4,
      26, 76, 102, 105–6, 109, 110,
      209
  and democracy, 110, 121
  influence on Rigby of, 1, 15, 101–2
  and legal-rational legitimation, 3, 4,
      5, 11, 76, 102, 105, 106, 110,
      120, 209
  and political leadership, 111
  and *Rechtsstaat*, 110
  and traditional legitimation, 3, 76,
      102, 105, 110

Yeltsin, Boris
  access to, 41, 42
  approach to policy making, 41
  and business, 186
  and charismatic legitimation, 109
  and democracy, 50
  effectiveness of, 42, 43
  under Gorbachev, 135, 136–7, 146,
      149, 164, 166, 172, 173, 174
  and October 1993, 109
  and legitimation, 109, 112
  and parliament, 111
  and personalism, 41, 213
  personality of, 135
  and populism, 172
  resignation of, 109
Yukos, 42, 43, 186

Zaslavskaia, Tat'iana, 140, 155, 163,
    170